GET LUCKY

A Rogue's Tale

GET LUCKY

A Rogue's Tale

PAUL EAGLES

Matador
9 Priory Business Park,
Wistow Road, Kibworth Beauchamp,
Leicestershire. LE8 0RX
Tel: 0116 279 2299
Email: books@troubador.co.uk
Web: www.troubador.co.uk/matador
Twitter: @matadorbooks

ISBN 978 1785892 400

British Library Cataloguing in Publication Data.
A catalogue record for this book is available from the British Library.

Printed and bound in the UK by TJ International, Padstow, Cornwall
Typeset by Troubador Publishing Ltd, Leicester, UK

Matador is an imprint of Troubador Publishing Ltd

My thanks to Geoff Bavin;
I lived the life, but you wrote the words.

CONTENTS

CHAPTER ONE

A Dog-Shaped Doorstop

What you don't need when you're a mature twenty-two-stone man is to be sitting on a bed in a busy hospital ward wearing a fetchingly short nightgown, especially when chained to two prison warders and the nightgown's flannel off-white with yellow flowers. Still, you reason, at least the flowers match your eyes.

It's tough coming down from your daily habits at such short notice but when fifteen coppers surround your home it's difficult to explain that you'd rather be in a pub. The tablets help though. They keep the shakes away, but do your head in. The last thing you want when you're feeling bitter is to dwell on the bad stuff. So you try to remember the good times.

Thirty-eight years earlier I'm in an Amsterdam art gallery staring at a voluptuous naked woman. A Rubens. Joke (sounds like poker) is standing slender by my side. "Paul, do you wish for me to be all plump and pink like is this woman?"

"No." If I'd said yes I might have had to buy her lunch. Paul Rubens wouldn't have glanced at her. Fashions change.

We wandered through the gallery, idly passing time, tanned by a Spanish summer. Not being art experts we feigned interest in that exaggerated way seen in galleries the world over: the step or two backwards, the cocked head, the over-close scrutiny, all that chin stroking. In my case the mime masks my examination of the gallery's alarm system, exits and guard deployment.

We toured Holland visiting a number of suitable galleries until I settled on the Singer Museum in Laren, at first sight an unlikely repository for St Francis Of Assisi, but here was a Ruben's exhibition on loan. Security was lax, the world a more forgiving place then. No laser alarms, CCTV or armed guards; just trust.

Strolling with me through the gallery, Joke was quiet, her natural ebullience stifled by fear. After all, she knew I was thinking of stealing a priceless painting by one of history's greatest artists. Surely you do not do such a thing? It is surely something you see only in movies? I didn't bother with such doubts. I wanted one so I'd have one. "You must not do this," whispered Joke, grabbing my hand as later we sat outside a café. "It is a bad thing you do." I just looked at her, grinning, saying nothing. "Paul, this is not so funny, you know." My grin turned to giggles. "Paul …!" Joke tried to look cross, but she too collapsed in giggles. "Trust Uncle Paul. Stick with me kid and I'll make you a star." Not so avuncular though, at only twenty-four, but my size seemed to confer on me an early air of authority beyond my years. At least it did with Joke.

Back to an unloved present and a lingering Indian Summer. It's almost November 2005 and Autumn is late this year. I watch through the window as the leaves at last begin to fall. This hospital number can't last much longer. Back to the cells soon, although they'd run tests and found plenty wrong. Blood pressure up, liver going down, brain going, going, gone. Heart broken. "Keep off the booze. The uppers. The downers. Eat. And Paul …"

"Doctor?"

"Special K."

"Eh?"

"Ketamine."

"Yes?"

"Do try to think of it as a breakfast food." Good advice. After all, when you're screwed-up it's easier to get screwed-over.

They get into your head to the point that you begin to believe in it all. They come at you from all directions so that even with a clear head it's as if they're right. There's no way out. The police, the judiciary, the sidelong glances in the hospital, the nurses' heads popping round the curtain to look at who – Hannibal Lecter? Even your friends. All pointing the finger, and it's not paranoia you can get with a hangover; no drink or drugs left in the system. But you can't take it personally. You've been in worse situations. So you think now. But remember, you were young then. A five-stretch in those days would've been a breeze. Now it'd be a life sentence. Life means life. Did I rape? Did I murder and maim? Did I blow up a train? This will kill me. It will. I don't even know when it's meant to end. What did I do? For this? What? I'd loved the wrong woman. And the rest of it.

Sitting on the hospital bed in this undersized nightgown I remembered a similarly brief outfit I'd worn a few years earlier in happier times. In a Tokyo hotel room I had used a tiny complimentary kimono designed for a Japanese frame. JP too, but hers fitted (I use her initials throughout to help obscure her identity). In spite of having borne three children, she was in remarkable shape for a fifty-five-year-old woman. It seemed to me that this was the relationship I'd needed all my life, for JP was everything I'd ever wished for – attractive, physical, clever, funny... but then again, who's perfect? A series of reflections came into my head, like they do when you've time on your hands –

I was pissed, living on wine, amphetamines and strong black coffee, with sugar for nourishment. On a healthy day it was KFC, the fat dribbling down my chin onto a shirt that had never seen an iron. Why iron it when it hadn't been washed in a month? Inside my raincoat I carried a heavy metal dog-shaped door-stop and inside my head thoughts of murder most foul. I'd played the scene in my mind like a familiar film; the kind where you can mouth along to the dialogue because you've seen it so many times. Lights, camera, action – I'm standing there in the shadows cast by her Fifteenth-Century farmhouse. I've been there for hours, waiting in the chill night, not knowing when she might return. Her BMW crunches the gravel drive. In the icy air I can see my breath in the glare of the halogen security lamps put up especially for me. Then it's the clack of her heels drowned out by the loud voice in my head – "JP." But she doesn't turn. My throat is so dry. No sound, like when you scream in a dream. Again – "JP!" Now she turns. She says nothing. Why would she? How could she, her brain stove in by twenty-stone plus wielding a heavy-metal dog-shaped door-stop. Claret seeps into the gravel and onto her camel cashmere coat. I'd always liked that coat. Used to like what was in it too. Still, she had it coming. "Bitch!"

I awaken, sweating and needing a drink, wearing a raincoat and carrying a heavy metal dog-shaped door-stop in the inside pocket. I get out of the house, into a pub. No idea what time or day it is. A friend comes over, counselling caution. "Think about it Paul, you cave her head in your own life's over too." "I don't care about me."

I tried to put myself into JP's head – She was terrified. She'd put in the halogen lamps. In a paranoid fantasy she'd convinced herself I was a master criminal. She knew she'd pushed too far this time, but felt she was right, or so ran her warped rationale, and her litany of imagined crimes was endless: this violent man had lied, robbed, murdered. He'd ran prostitutes, counterfeited money, robbed banks at gun-point. Then there were the drugs. Bad. Bad. Bad. And the fraud. Millions. £8-million! He'd beat her, defamed her. Those disgusting allegations about the kids. He deserves everything coming to him, and she'd deliver it. Cock your head sideways and flutter your eyelashes – "He's a very bad man officer. I …I don't feel safe. I … I really don't know what to do, who to turn to next." She smiles, eyes sad. "Now don't you worry your pretty little head, ma'am." At least, that's what she hears the nice young policeman say. After all, how could such a charming woman be a liar?

Back to the present reality; every time you're taken from the cells to court for another bail hearing there's a knock-back. You're harassing her. You phoned her. At least another month inside for being confused and pressing the wrong buttons. You love her so much you can't believe she has done this to you. Your friends and family can. So too can your lawyer. But not you. A phone call will fix everything – "I love you, JP. Let's get married." But you're in denial. You're just not getting it. She is though. She's making damn sure you're well and truly getting it. You're inside for intimidating a key prosecution witness for Christ's sake. So why are you phoning her? That call means no more phone privileges and another bail knock-back.

The old saying that you know you're getting old when policemen start to look young is put in the shade by when it happens with politicians. Jesus, I'm older than the Prime Minister. But to these kids I'm older than Methuselah, if they know who Methuselah was. Maybe it's the particular prison I'm in, but they're all so young. To this lot I'm an old man. I don't feel old, but then who does? Still, I have got a forty-year head-start on most of these guys. And what are they in for? Drugs, drugs and drugs. To them, prison is a home from home. It's hardly worth packing to leave. They're OK though. No trouble. Not in here at least. My relative age gives me a distance and I've been round a few more blocks than them. "Wha's 'appening, bro'?"

"I'm fine, Leroy, my SON." Elongated, that last word, at full volume. Like my other old favourite – "Right, my son!" Same intonation as before. It's not exactly street-speak, but at least it's mine. Got to hang on to some vestige of individuality in here because I sure as hell don't know when I'm getting out.

Still, it's not all doom and gloom. I've always been an on-off smoker. In here I'm off. That means my human rights allow me a single cell as most of the kids in here smoke. Then there are the little tricks. Soak muesli in milk heated over a light-bulb for long enough and you get porridge, which I love, but just can't get here in the slammer, of all places. Still, I have to admit that the muesli trick hardly makes me the Birdman of Alcatraz.

I get respect in here. The black kids are always banging on about respect, but at least everyone accords it to me. I like to think it's my menacing physical presence or that I was once an international art thief. Or perhaps they just think I'm old. But muttering darkly about the police looking into my missing millions certainly doesn't harm my standing. Someone calls me 'Big Daddy', like the late wrestler. I liked that.

I took stock; locked-up and with no smoking barrels. The woman I loved had betrayed me and run off with the man who was my chief prosecutor. I was facing charges both declared and unknown. I would be out in maybe five years, skint because they would have taken my money under The

Proceeds of Crime Act. Then I'd get a pension and eke out a retirement in Wetherspoons, drinking early morning pints of bitter along with those who look as if they cut their own hair. But no, I wouldn't get out. If I got five years I'd die inside, killed by a different kind of bitter. So there I was feeling sorry for myself and I didn't even know then that my lawyer aided by my business advisor and erstwhile friend had nicked most of my money.

I'd been passing London's Harvey Nick's with the aforesaid business advisor at the very moment when JP texted me about a shooting in the store's perfume department. It was a tragic story of love gone sour in that fragrant hall, but our own love story didn't smell too good either. JP's later statement to the police was twisted to make it look as if I had told her of the incident, couched in a way to suggest that a similar fate awaited her. Then there was the stuff about her being dead by Christmas. I'd said – 'If we go on like this we'll both be dead by Christmas', but she had taken the core truth and twisted it into a death threat. I was taken to holding cells in Slough, the UK prison system under such pressure that no available remand unit could be found in the Home Counties. I needed to stay close to home as there was business to be done, and stuffed away in York, which had arisen as an option, meant that people I needed to see probably wouldn't bother to make the trip to visit me. I was moved around a lot in that first week or so. Finally I was found space at HMP Bullingdon, near Oxford. Ah, the Bullingdon Club at last. Hello Boris, hello David. My blood pressure went up as soon as I saw that there was a need for it to do so. With me, it's somehow a self-regulatory process. At least that's how I like to pretend it to be.

So, that's how I came to be sitting on a hospital bed in the John Radcliffe in an off-white flannel nightgown chained to two prison warders. Still, I'd had a good run; I'd got to sixty and had never taken prisoners. That is not to say that I hadn't been taken prisoner from time to time, but I have to admit there have been happier days. Here's how it happened, and the rest.

CHAPTER TWO

Biggles Flies Undone

It was 1950, yet another year of post-war austerity. I was six. Southport was then a black and white Hovis ad, or that's how it now feels to me when remembering that far-off time. My mother, Sally, who passed away recently in her early nineties, was then an attractive thirty-five-year-old with a flair for business. Those thinking they had seen the end of me when I was incarcerated viewed with dismay her longevity, thinking it a genetic condition which I may possibly have inherited. In 1950, Mum was in the early stages of making a very comfortable living in the property market. Dad, on the other hand, the priest-like Fred, a lonely, introspective man who would today be labelled an under-achiever, went to live a solitary life in a bed-sit when the chalk and cheese relationship with my mother was finally over. The sole result of their union had been a well-behaved boy whose good behaviour gave lie to the dictum that the child is father to the man. We never discussed it, but I suspect my parents stayed together until I was seventeen or eighteen solely for my benefit. They sold the house then, and Dad's share enabled him to relocate to the bright lights and donkeys of Blackpool, in Coronation Street of all places.

He had been taught by Jesuits. Maybe this was a clue to the origin of his Spartan tastes. We used to chug around the countryside in our black Austin Seven in those 'it's-turned-

out-nice-again-let's-go-for-a-drive' days. I don't blame the
Jesuits for the car's blackness; they nearly all were then. Dad
wasn't an alcoholic, but he liked a drink. This resulted in
our car being left in odd places – 'where's it got to, lad?'; as
though the car was suffering from some sort of dementia and
had wandered off. It's funny, though, my clearer memories of
him come from later when he used to visit me in Kensington
right up until his death in his late sixties. With hindsight
I feel that my relative lack of childhood memories of him
comes from a gulf between us caused by his jealousy of the
attention I received from Mum.

Even as a child I had an eye for money and an innate
respect for those who made it, or at least those who strove
for it. My late father on the other hand, had not striven for
anything, save contentment. I never wished to be an engine-
driver or to run away to join a circus. Pop stardom never
beckoned nor suit-wearing activities at the local bank. Mum
thought the latter was the way forward, a nice, respectable job.
People would look up to me. So too would they if I achieved
my true ambition of becoming a wealthy entrepreneur;
including bank managers.

Of course, there is often a side to our parents of which
we are unaware at the time. It was only recently that I found
Dad's army discharge papers from 1923. They gave his then
height as five-feet-three, small to one day become the father of
little old six-two me. Then I spotted that he'd been discharged
because he'd faked his age, eager to get into the forces. He
grew after that, but not by so much that it prevented him
from serving as a rear-gunner, a Bomber Command 'tail-end
Charlie'. Many a smaller RAF man found himself exposed
in one of those cramped turrets, which for many became a
flying coffin. It makes the flak I've taken seem small beer by
comparison.

Mum and Dad, although she was the driving force, had a shop in Gorton, Manchester, the area already a template for what it has become. It was on a long road full of mum and dad shops, little family businesses eking out a living in those bleak post-war years. Mum's sold second-hand furniture, lots of heavy mahogany. My memory tells me it was retro pieces, but people kept stuff for years then and, with the Depression and the war having suspended the manufacture of luxury goods for awhile, I suppose most furniture was retro by default.

Like most of her generation then, Mum was hard-up, but this did not stop her from making a sacrifice by sending me to Heaton Moor College, a fee-paying prep school, wanting the best for her blue-eyed-boy. She would always take me to the school by bus from our house in nearby Heaton Moor, but for reasons that I do not know, probably because she had to run the shop, she would leave me to make the afternoon trip to Gorton alone, an independent six-year-old in his cap and blazer. I wasn't drinking in those days, so there really was no excuse for losing my bearings, but that's what I did. I got on the wrong bus and ended up God knows where.

It's strange really, given the sketchy memories of my short-trouser years, how this incident has always stuck with me. This lack of childhood memories is not because of, I should stress, any unhappy experiences. I was probably as happy as the next child, or as unhappy, as the case may be. It was, I suspect, to do with being an only child. I was certainly unhappy that day on the wrong bus. Then the world became a strange and fearsome place as the little blond boy I used to be sat on the back downstairs seat in his school uniform, clutching his satchel as he quietly sobbed, even more traumatised than when as a bigger boy I'd realised that my fence had lost my purloined Rubens.

I was eventually looked after by a bus inspector, one of my first brushes with a man in uniform, but thankfully a benign one. Everyone who passed me as they got off the bus felt sorry for me and gave me something. People didn't have much in those days, but that is when they are often at their most generous. Apples, sweets, even a toy, came my way, establishing a pattern that has continued throughout my life. When things are at their worst, I get lucky.

After this experience I did briefly nurture a career ambition of being a bus inspector. With no 'On The Buses' Blakey then to tarnish the dream, to me inspectors were impressive, authoritarian figures before whom mere clippies would visibly shrink. I used to clutch my ticket – sometimes I'd be given the bit at the end of the roll ready for tickets that would never be sold, except in my imagination – awaiting the moment when the godlike figure would join the bus. In those days inspectors often wore their war medals, and I'd imagine the bravery that had gone into their acquisition: thwarting fare-dodging old ladies and their sharp umbrellas and disciplining cheeky 'Spivs', whom Dad told me sewed razor blades into the brims of their hats. I once saw 'my inspector' ordering one to pick up his chips from the floor in front of his jeering mates and witnessed by his girlfriend. Even at that age I somehow knew she would be moving on after her beau's humiliation.

At eleven, North Cestrian Grammar beckoned, a school founded in 1951 by Mr Hamblin, formerly headmaster of Altrincham Grammar. Now even more of my life was spent on buses, up to two hours a day back and forth to school, breaking my journey to visit friends and even at weekends trudging off to Didsbury and the like just to hang out, only we didn't call it that back then. Still, the modern world had started. 'Pretty pretty pretty pretty Peggy Sue' filled our heads with a love so rare and true as a generation's brains turned to vinyl.

Mum had had a strict upbringing and she applied her own parents' attitudes to me. I was one of those children who grow up without any memory of having had friends home, hence my 'On The Buses' childhood. Perhaps Mum's strictness came from the military background of many of the men in my family. We're not talking colonels and captains here but sergeant-majors and colour-sergeants barking at the troops of the Empire on which the sun never set, in the Brennan's case on India's North-West Frontier. Many forget how much the Irish supported the British, including the Irish themselves.

I tell everybody these days that I was academically-accomplished, but whatever the truth, at least I tried. I do recall being the class clown, though. My affection for bus inspectors and a brief hero-worship of Flash Gordon nurtured from Saturday morning pictures at the Heaton Moor Savoy Cinema aside, my true hero was Sergeant Bilko. Here was a man so accomplished that even his alter ego Phil Silvers took to playing Bilko full-time in his dotage. That must have been quite a care home where he ended his days, although maybe he toned it down a bit and stuck to one-card tricks. My inner Bilko once ran a book on the school cross-country, and my friend, the favourite who carried on his shoulders the hopes and pocket money of our entire year, doubled back over a one-mile loop and finished mid-field. We were rumbled and I was suspended by Mr Hamblin, but of course I was honing a talent that was far more useful than knowing the intricacies of the Corn Law and all those other endless mind-numbing lessons that ate up our precious golden years.

I knew girls existed, but apart from a brace of cousins I don't think I'd ever met one. In those days the sexes were carefully segregated, certainly in education, and the girls in the convent school across the way from ours were as exotic as unicorns. I was about fifteen when I found a Saturday job riding one of those heavy, black delivery bikes with no gears and a metal basket front and rear. It being a Saturday I never thought that when I was asked to deliver vegetables to the girls' school there'd be any actual girls on the premises. I was wrong. To a tirade of 'hello little boy' and' isn't he sweet' coming from the windows of this St Trinians-like place of longing and dread I rode the ride of shame to the delivery door. At least they'd had a glimpse of my marrow.

Although I have little detailed recollection of day-to-day life as a child, this haziness of childhood memories seems to be not so unusual. I've spoken to friends about it and there seems to be a divide. You get people who continue to be on first-name terms with their teddy and still believe their toys come alive at night, while others awaken in their teens, rubbing their eyes, ready for battle. I think I was one of the latter camp, always an adult in waiting, serving out the time until I was ready to become a big bad bear. The change came when I learned to drive, when something came along and burst my bubble. I blame Biggles.

There was a time when I had a side-parting to satisfy my mother's aesthetic preference rather than my occasional latter-day professional needs. It was when I was about ten, a clean-living embodiment of an era, neat as a new pin with that scrubbed look you would find on any apple-cheeked kid in any Twentieth-Century decade right up to the Fifties. I was my mother's little golden prince. She doted on me in that way mothers do with an only child, inculcating in me that particular sense of place in society common to our breed. I mean, who are all these other people crashing the party? I read then, living in the imagination of the lonely only. Mum was busy, dad distracted, so James Bigglesworth became my role model. I was gimlet-eyed and firm of jaw. Bravery, honesty and fair play were the order of the day as I trained my gun-sights on Junkers and Messerschmitts, often prevailing against hopeless odds. I was also prone to odd utterances along the lines of 'steady on chaps'; that being the way I thought grown-ups talked outside of Gorton.

Apart from a bicycle, the preferred form of transport de nos jours was the home-made wooden soapbox car. For younger readers, this was a box with a four-foot wooden plank attached to its base and pointing forwards, two bike wheels at the rear, a pair of small wheels at the front end of the plank attached to a bolted axle, and rope for steering. You fitted a seat, but mine had wings too. I was Biggles. I could fly. I had a leather helmet and goggles and I must have put the fear of God up any surviving Nazi daft enough to goosestep up Gorton way. It was like that scene in Spartacus where trainee gladiators jump over revolving scythes as terrified shoppers leapt over my outstretched wings while I tally-hoed down Mount Road. In that postwar era people ate less and moved more, so most made it, but I took a few prangs. Still, nothing ventured, nothing gained, as my mum would say. Then one day I saw it, a real life Messerschmitt. A KR200 bubble car no less! Biggles trained his sites on the Hun-mobile. One day, one day.

Ginger Eric, or Eric the Red as he came to be known after one particular history lesson, was the first to spot it. I was sixteen, several years since my last sortie on Mount Road. Biggles had pulled it off and it was time to put away childish things. The soapbox car had long since become home to a silver tangle of spider webs, one broken wing evidence that not all post-war people were lithe and fit. "Paul, that Messerschmitt …"

"Where?" Looking up, listening for sirens remembered

from war films. "The bubble car. Remember? The one we used to see everywhere. Well, it's in Craigie's dad's garage." I'd forgotten. Too many missions over too many years. Too many Messerschmitts in my imagination to remember any one in particular. Then it clicked.

"That red one? What's it look like now?" "OK. Needs a bit of work. Let's go see it. Remember, it's got no reverse gear. Well, not really"

"So?"

"So you can drive it now you're sixteen." I had money. No idea where from. I'd given up on the vegetables, so it was probably from delivering Hovis or something. Whatever it was, then it would have come my way honestly. My reverse Road to Damascus was still a test drive away.

I took a couple of short runs; a bit faster than my soapbox and the cockpit like that of an aircraft, complete with joystick. I was pretty big and solid by then but it nudged sixty. A mile a minute! It was like breaking the sound barrier. I headed for open country, all winding lanes, vision-obscuring hedgerows and apparently one very large oak tree, or so I was told when I finally came to.

When St Paul saw his bright light he turned and became a good guy. I stopped dead and was never again likely to be canonised. Once the medics had stuffed my frontal lobes back in and closed the hole, it has to be said, and it has been, that the model boy became the rebellious youth; something about a damaged pre-frontal cortex resulting in an impairment of the ability to predict future outcomes from current activities, so trouble becomes your second name. For those who've wondered, those who've pondered the provenance of my errant ways, that was it. My epiphany. A personality change out of a life-threatening bursting of a bubble car. Biggles flies undone.

Maybe Craigie having rolled his yellow Isetta with me in

it should have been a warning. 'Craigie' was my mate then. Can't remember his first name, but that's what we all called him. Anyway, Craigie's dad, the one with the garage, was loaded. It was the Sevenways Service Station at Stretford, still there to this day. Craig senior taught me more than he ever knew, even though my contact with him had been minimal. He taught me that the key to a smooth passage in life is to get yourself a bread and butter business that would always tick over come good times, come bad times. Something that would give you the freedom to live life as your own man.

An awareness of those life-defining moments that change you forever, be it future events like DV's first rap on my door, Frankie's Rio leap, or my fingering St Francis, was fostered in me there. The one I'm about to tell of has reverberated throughout my life, a symbol of the freedom I had unwittingly craved. It was Friday afternoon. School's out.

I wasn't yet part of Craigie's set when I saw him pull up at the school gates in a brand new Daimler Dart, a car that still swivels necks today. I was transfixed as another of the slightly older boys tossed a bag in the back and the pair roared off into a weekend of unimaginable adventures, probably involving girls. Live fast, die young and the Devil take the hindmost was how I later came to articulate this brief cameo of privilege. Apart from the car, it was a mundane act in itself, yet for me it was a revelation. These boys had access to money, freedom, an insouciance way beyond their years. Other boys rode bikes.

My initiation into Craigie's world was when he invited me for a spin in that yellow Isetta, along with the Heinkel and Messerschmitt the third of that era's trio of bubble cars. We couldn't have been doing more than thirty-five on the Didsbury Road to Heaton Moor. Craigie was driving and I was an eager passenger, right up until we took a sharp bend and the inherent instability of the three-wheel bubble car design was demonstrated when we went into what seemed like an endless slo-mo roll. My face was contorted against the window and it seemed like we'd roll all the way home. Finally we stopped, upright. The anti-roll bar kept us both in one piece as we came to a stop. Craigie calmly switched on the engine and we tootled off as though nothing had happened. We were even pointing in the right direction.

Months later, when I'd recovered after being pulled from the wreckage of the Messerschmitt, I told mum that Craigie and me and the boys were off to Cornwall for a couple of weeks. I was still sixteen. Instead, we'd gone to Menton in the south of France, near the Italian border, where Mr. Craig kept a yacht. I was up, up and away. I didn't tell Mum because I didn't want her to worry, but as I was now an embryonic bad boy, perhaps I didn't care, showing the scant regard for the feelings of others that has dogged my relationships over the years. Anyway, I'd covered my ruse in a way that I thought ever so clever. I had a postcard of Newquay in my room and this I posted to Mum, from Menton. My talent for duplicity was then in its infancy. It took me awhile to click just how she'd sussed that I'd been in France.

Two years later the boy who'd tossed the bag into the Daimler Dart wrapped one of the first-ever E-Types around a tree. He'd lived fast, died young, all privilege revoked forever.

CHAPTER THREE

Snowdrops Bring Teardrops

Just before my final term at Cestrian Grammar I found a holiday job at a sticky-rock factory near Blackpool. The owner, one Albert Barrett, was a stereotypically cloth-capped northerner, a man of principle and few words. He'd been having a bit of difficulty with one of his workers, his foreman. The two men had once been friends, but had fallen out when circumstances dictated that one would work for the other; a situation that tests any friendship.

Albert, or Bert as he was of course known, decided to fire his mate. This he did early in the week, with the man's final day at the factory being on the Friday. All week neither of them exchanged a word and the air at the factory was heavy with expectation. But nothing untoward happened, and Friday came along as Fridays do. The latest consignment of sticky rock had been dispatched to local clients and the foreman was handed his brown pay envelope for the last time. Bert relaxed, his testing week over. But come Monday morning, the phone never stopped ringing. Now usually, the words inside Bert's rocks were along the lines of 'Welcome to Blackpool' and variations on that theme. But this latest batch of ten thousand rocks carried a different message. Inside each one were the words – 'Fuck Bert Barrett'.

A year later and school was out for the summer and forever. I was ready and eager to explore the big, wide world, but like so many of us my first foray was close to home. I was eighteen and applied as a management trainee at the Midland Hotel in Manchester.

It was part of the old British Railways group, and in those days the railway-owned hotels were a reflection of the pride that the English once had in giving good service. I was a trainee under the autocratic Mr Turpey, a name that no doubt still strikes fear in those who've had the experience of working under him. He was a highly-professional, frock-coated martinet who demanded utter respect in return for utter contempt, a never to be seen again product of another age.

Mr Turpey's rival in the martinet stakes, one Adolf Hitler, so local legend has it, visited the Midland in his younger days. So enamoured was he of this monument to Victorian pride that he later vowed to make it his UK northern HQ when the Nazis invaded Britain and gave the Luftwaffe orders not to bomb the hotel or the surrounding area. Herr Shicklgruber, as Churchill insisted on calling Hitler after his father's original name and because it sounded comical, had had a narrow escape though. Had the Nazis won the war their occupation would have coincided with Turpey's arrival at the Midland. Hitler, Göering and the boys would have sat down to breakfast on what for them would have been a joyous morn, anticipating the Midland's finest Full English silver service, less the bacon and sausages for the caring vegetarian Führer if you please. Enter Turpey. Who do you think you were kidding, Mister Hitler?

It was at The Midland that a fellow trainee suggested that I consider a life on the ocean waves. At first, my fertile imagination baulked at the idea. I didn't fancy experiencing rum, sodomy and the lash; well, maybe the first bit would have been OK. "It's Easy Street," I was assured by a young lad who hadn't even sailed on the Manchester Ship Canal. "Go for the Merchant Navy. You'll travel the world for free and get loads of booze and birds."

"Is it hard work?"

"Well, the birds might be. But the work? No. Anyway, a quick lad like you'll get a cushy number in no time."

I made enquiries. I knew enough to know that whatever trade you enter you do better if you've got a skill. An uncle told me that Signals Officer on cruise ships was a good number. That and Purser and Ship's Doctor. I didn't fancy my chances at the latter, both in qualifying and for the future well-being of my patients, although I did consider it on the grounds that Brigitte Bardot look-alikes might enter my surgery.

It was 1962. Born in '44 I had missed National Service by a whisker. Most of my contemporaries breathed a collective sigh of relief that they would not be called upon to defend a fading empire, but weren't the bolshie Bolshie's camped on the Polish plains, their missiles pointing our way? So I did what I had to do. I joined the RAF. I was walking down a high street in Manchester and saw a recruiting office. Since compulsory conscription had ended the joint services must have expected a dearth of recruits in the short-term, but as stated, I was ready to do my bit for Queen and country. Outside the shop stood a ramrod-stiff uniformed type with a 'now you look a likely lad' expression on his face. In I went.

So there I was, with instant respectability conferred by the blue-grey uniform of the RAF, World War Two still a relatively recent memory for most at that time. I was sent to RAF Bridgnorth for eight-weeks basic training. At the end of those few weeks I was the fittest I'd ever be, having learned training routines that I would ignore for the rest of my life. Our 'you 'orrible little scum-bags' instructor was a Flight Sergeant Orange. Luckily, he was given a public dressing-down by a Flight-Lieutenant early on in our training period, which taught me that was how it went in the services. I now knew it wasn't personal, so managed to keep a straight face. A good lesson that, to always let them think they're winning.

I'm not sure whether I've since made my parents proud, but when they got back together to attend my passing-out parade it was almost as though they were a couple once more as my father passed my mother his handkerchief. I was an Airman. After training I was sent to Compton Bassett on a signalling course. I learnt Morse Code, which was already on its way out, soon to give way to VHF radio. Still, it gave me a thrill, being redolent of all those black and white war films I'd grown up on. I passed the course in the required time. Then boredom took over. I was in for three years and I didn't think I could last that long. "Hello Mum."

The pride she'd felt at my passing-out parade must have quickly evaporated when the police rapped at the door. I was hoping that Mum would think AWOL was some title of honour, promotion perhaps, or a medal. It was only when I saw her silent tears that I realised she wasn't that daft. Quite the opposite, but we all underestimate our parents, don't we? The police handed me over to the 'Snowdrops' who came to collect me. They are the RAF's equivalent of the Army's Redcaps, and were no more keen on deserters than every soldier's least favourite adversary. Back at barracks I was put in a cell. I decided that the best place for me would be hospital. I was sent to the HQ Bomber Command's hospital at RAF Lyneham. Of all the prison wings I've ended up in, this ranked as one of the finest, with state-of-the-art facilities which would put the modern NHS to shame. They'd thought that I was at risk, given that I'd tried to hang myself. Not really, but my performance with a belt had been convincing enough for the authorities to decide that they didn't need a suicidal teenager on their hands.

Despite this, they did try to persuade me to stay. Perhaps, after all, they'd realised I'd been faking it, but when you're a nineteen-year-old boy you know more than everyone else, don't you? They sent me over to Germany on a Pembroke. It was an Indulgence Flight to RAF Wildenwrath, near Dusseldorf. This was shortly after my hospitalisation and I was near the end of my service. Once again I went AWOL, travelling around Germany seeking the company of compliant fräuleins. Not a Snowdrop in sight this time, though. Back to Compton Bassett and my brief flirtation with respectability was over.

During my time in the Air Force I met Peter Myers, son of a Keswick butcher, and a keen rock-climber. For extra money we had acted as stewards in the Officer's Mess. In between courses we got thoroughly pissed and did not impress our superiors by the wearing of our uniform tops and civvie bottoms, especially when Peter tripped and threw the contents of a drinks tray over the entire table. In spite of this he became an Air Signaller and was transferred to Air-Sea Rescue at RAF Kinloss. He now runs 'Myers of Keswick' in Greenwich Village, NYC, a world-famous emporium of sausages, pies and all the home-produced food craved by British expats in New York. I sent him a message from Montevideo, Uruguay, when I was in the Merchant Navy. This to his RAF unit – "Thank you for the coded information. This has been passed to the relevant authorities."

Good thing he's a smooth talker.

CHAPTER FOUR

All the Not So Nice Girls Love a Sailor

Equipped with my signalling qualification I somehow was accepted into the then all-powerful National Union of Seamen and the next thing I knew I was sailing out of London's King George V Docks on a Blue Star Line cargo ship en-route to South America. Bloody 'eck!

I have travelled extensively since that day, but the world will never seem bigger or more exciting to me than when we slipped into the English Channel and said farewell to the White Cliffs of Dover. Far ahead of me, over the edge of the known world, were dusky maidens the like of which had never trod the lino of our local chippie. Our first port of call was to be Las Palmas in the Canary Islands.

One of my fellow crew-members was Bruce Wells, the Golden Gloves and one-time Welterweight, later Light-Middle British and Commonwealth boxing champion. He won three-hundred and eighty-five bouts, including against Joe Erskine, losing only three. Outside the ring he maintained an unbeaten record. It was in Las Palmas that Bruce encouraged me as I nervously took my first steps in becoming a true sailor. He took me to my first brothel. That set me up nicely for the delights of South America, a destination then almost too impossibly exotic for a simple northern lad to even contemplate.

Very few boxers in those days quit the game while they

were financially ahead, and most of the top American names of the Forties and Fifties were in the pockets of the Mob. At least Bruce, as an English fighter in the Fifties, didn't have that problem. There was no money around to nick. So he fetched up in the Merchant Navy. Although this particular career path had been inspired by money and a desire to see the world, the fact that the Met were hot on his heels on account of his activities as an enforcer for Peter Rachman was an added inducement for him to sail the seven seas.

For those unaware of Rachman's notoriety, his was the property empire which specialised in slum tenancies in Notting Hill. The grand houses built in the 1860s had faded from their former glory and Rachman used his hired muscle to force out sitting tenants on low rents and replaced them with poor Afro-Caribbeans, as if there were any other kind in those days. Only he didn't refer to them as Afro-Caribbeans. This was the London of 'No Blacks, No Irish' signs. Forced into this ghetto, the Empire Windrush generation had swapped their islands in the sun for the drab bleakness of austerity Britain.

Hugh Grant and his fellow luvvies did as much to damage the area as Rachman, that film encouraging an invasion of Trustafarians, rich kids who unwittingly destroyed the very thing they sought to find. But at least floppy fringes were more subtle than the methods Rachman's boys employed. Once the sitting tenants were out, whether encouraged by baseball bats, dogs, fists, or no utilities in winter, Rachman brought in black tenants, putting whole families into sub-divided rooms at as high a rent as he could squeeze out of them. He died young. Bruce? Well, he was muscle. Work was scarce. You do what you do when times are hard.

He went around with the Lightweight, Dan Gilfeather, a couple of likely lads who were first off and last on at every port of call. There were officers on board, of course, but Bruce and Dan discouraged anything even approaching discipline, and certainly nothing that looked like interfering with the lads' nocturnal proclivities. On one occasion, when we were on the South American run down to Buenos Aires, we were carrying cargo and our usual quota of fare-paying passengers, this time Greeks. Bruce and I were stewards in the restaurant. For some reason my ability to send a 'Mayday' signal had been overlooked. As we headed south, just before the Equator, we noticed that our passengers were not showing up at the restaurant in their usual numbers. Just one or two familiar faces went missing at first, then more and more until there were none. They'd sussed that, as the voyage was nearing its end, they were better off eating in their cabins, thereby only having to pay their cabin steward a tip and getting away scot-free with us, who'd served them for the bulk of the trip.

In those days, when people travelled they tended to dress for the occasion, and as we tied-up in Buenos Aires there were enough linen suits on display to have kept Gieves and Hawkes in business for a year. The bell in Bruce's head that signalled another round in life's battle was about to begin rang loud and clear. Only this time he wasn't throwing punches but well-aimed potatoes. The Greeks ran for cover as they were bombarded by Bruce and I with the contents of several sacks of King Edwards. But what was truly extraordinary about the scene was that the quayside was thronged by the passengers' relatives and friends, all dressed to the nines in South America's most sophisticated city. The waiting throng stared in horror at the humiliation of their European cousins. Well, it served them right. Tight bastards.

On another trip we were in Santos, the port of Rio de Janeiro. Brazilian women were friendly souls, and still are.

A Greek crewmate, Frankie, was especially partial to the
delights of Rio and almost overstayed his welcome. The ship's
siren had sounded warning that we were about to set sail.
But Frankie was almost as partial to Caipirinhas as he was
to beautiful Brazilian women, and it was only when we were
about thirty metres from the quayside that we spotted him
weaving his way towards us. The problem was, we knew he'd
have no money left and there were no handy HSBC cash-
points in those days. He was stranded. The next port of call
was hundreds of miles to the south. It looked like he'd have to
stagger off to the British consulate.

Bruce, me and the others were all shouting encouragement
as he stood swaying on the quayside, though how he'd get to
the ship was anybody's guess. Then, at that moment a flat-
topped tender passed between the quay and our ship. We
signalled to its crew and, being seamen, they soon realised
what the problem was. They went in close to the quayside,
the plan being that Frankie would jump aboard and then
they'd come in close so that we could winch him up. So far
so good. But from our high position on the ship's deck it was
hard to judge distances, notably that from the quay to the
surface of the metal-decked barge was some six metres, the
river at that point having a huge tidal range.

Frankie prepared to jump. At that decisive moment in his
life a watch seller was pestering him to buy his wares. Rio is
still a city where you can be pestered night and day, usually
with wares more tempting than a plastic Rolex. Frankie knew
it was time to leave. He closed his eyes and leaped, landing
as badly as you do when flesh and bone meet steel. He lay
there, writhing in agony. The officer on duty hadn't seen him
jump and simply thought he was pissed. He wanted nothing
to do with Frankie and was more concerned with sailing for
our next scheduled port of call, Montevideo. He'd seen it all

before. We screamed at him, and when he understood what had happened, even his heart went out to a fellow seaman, and Frankie was winched aboard. The pain had sobered him up and he was now screaming in such agony that the girls in Copacabana must have looked up from their work.

It took us nearly two days of coffee and slaps to get the ship's doctor sober enough to tend to Frankie's injuries. While sobering up the good doctor, we did a reverse operation on Frankie, anaesthetising him with whatever ship's rum we could find that the doctor hadn't imbibed. In Montevideo we put him in the care of a nunnery, where we knew he would be treated with kindness, if not with expert medical care. Months later I saw Frankie in some other South American port, hobbling like the Dreyfus character in Papillion, eking out some kind of living on the margins of society. He was with a woman carrying a baby, so presumably, although crippled for life, he'd found some quantum of solace from his blind leap of faith. A leap that had lasted little more than a second and had changed his life forever.

That wasn't the only shipmate who'd had an odd experience. Jimmy McBride, aka 'See You, Jimmy', loved the sea but had never learned to swim. We called him James, because when he was sober he spoke in dulcet RP tones, yet when drunk, his preferred state, his habitual form of address was the Glasgow Kiss. He wasn't even a Scot. James, and an even more belligerent stoker, whose name eludes me, went out on one of their epic bar crawls in Porto de Galinhas, a coastal town on Brazil's north-east coast about forty-miles south of the city of Recife. Galinhas is now a resort but then was little more than a fishing village. The boys were on good form by all accounts when, for no apparent reason the stoker swept their evening's supply of bottles and glasses off their table and onto the floor. The waiters had left them there as a record of how many drinks they'd had. The stoker disappeared leaving James to try to apologise to the enraged staff in Pigin English, the regional dialect of Brazilian Portuguese being so difficult that even the locals had difficulty in understanding each other. James had told the story in such awed detail that I almost felt as though I'd been there with him. He clearly remembered apologising, then nothing, until he found himself wading ashore onto an uninhabited island about five-hundred metres offshore. He could see the lights of an unfamiliar town on the mainland and he guessed, from the first light of dawn on the horizon behind him, that it was about four a.m. He'd lost five-hours. That he could rationalise this meant that he hadn't gone completely crazy. He told me that he'd thought for awhile that he was dead and had gone to an alternative universe where he would sit alone for all eternity with no bar and not a soul to head-butt.

He had to get off the island, go towards the light. Problem was, there was water between him and his destination. Five-hundred metres of even shallow Atlantic Ocean is a long way for a non-swimmer, so James decided to walk. There were two other problems: the water was, he was soon to find out, neck-high and, perhaps more worryingly, two German tourists had been taken by sharks a few days ago on this stretch of coast. He said that he started to walk but soon realised that the sea-bed was too soft to support his vertical weight and his head kept slipping beneath the surface, a terrifying prospect for a non-swimmer. He took drastic action; a deep breath and down on his hands and knees to crawl along the sea-bed until his breath gave out and up again for a rest before more of the same. He got about halfway and needed a rest. He'd been aiming for another uninhabited island, smaller than his first spell in eternity, and eventually stepped ashore. He said it was like one of those islands you see in cartoons where a bearded guy clings to the only tree and watches a deflated inflatable doll wash-up. No doll, but clinging to his tree, he rested. The tide was rising, though, and he couldn't risk getting out of his depth, so he soon set off crawling again, all the while aware of sharks.

He finally made shore about two-hours after setting off from the first island. Now he was able to take stock. He was a seaman and knew he had to head north to his hotel and belongings and maybe a lift back to the ship in Recife. He had lost his shoes and knew he was in for a long barefoot walk. He hoped he'd make it in ten to twelve miles. So he started walking. He tried following a road and was occasionally greeted by the horns of passing trucks, but no-one stopped. After awhile he sensed he was going too far inland so decided to head across open country. He could see a rolling landscape between him and where he knew the ocean should be. The hills he needed to cross were two-hundred metres high and from the top of the first one he knew that there were five more to come. He'd headed too far north so he adjusted his course towards where Galinhas should be.

He was close to the Equator and the sun was strong and right overhead. He'd been on a cartoon island and now he had another cartoon image; vultures circling above him and not a drop to drink. He was so preoccupied with these that he barely registered the snakes wriggling close to his bare feet. Whatever they'd Mickey-Finned him some sixteen hours earlier had left him feeling half-dead, so much so that he'd locked to one side and was walking like the undead. He remembered stepping into some blue mud and sinking up to his knees in it before he could pull himself out. In the hot sun the mud almost instantly baked hard, making it look as if he were wearing blue boots. That's maybe how he'd managed to stagger though a shanty-town where even a hardened seaman feared to tread. He had vague memories of horrified onlookers rushing their children inside and shutters going down. Maybe it was a Voodoo thing; they hated Zombies. He finally made it back to a bar in Galinhas where sat his mate the stoker – "Where you been?"

"No fucking idea."

He told me later that the dawning of consciousness when he'd waded ashore on that first island had been the strangest sensation of his life. He was convinced that he wasn't even that drunk when the stoker had swept the table; if he was he wouldn't have cared enough to attempt an apology. He was a lush, he knew how drink felt. He was convinced they'd slipped him something, maybe taken him for a ride on a boat as payback for the stoker's action. A dead foreigner would raise no ripples on a stretch of coast that was home to all kinds of miscreants who'd jumped ship on the run from the law in Europe. Anyway, sharks could well have eaten the evidence. It was some weeks before we saw him deliver a Glasgow Kiss.

After I'd been to South America a few times I fancied a change of scenery, restless youth that I was. So I joined the Union Castle Line. Their ships were all named after a place, followed by the word 'castle'. Mine was the 'Rhodesia Castle'. With their lavender hulls, vermilion black-topped funnels and white superstructure, the Union Castle vessels looked more like pleasure cruisers than cargo ships, which is what many became when their cargo carrying days were over. But even as cargo vessels they took paying passengers, the rich and famous often choosing Union Castle's Africa run rather than P&O's. At the very moment a Union Castle ship left Southampton another vessel left Durban, each passing the other at the precise midway point of their voyage. Although I've never been a slave to the clock, I've always had a passing fascination for those who are, that the trains in Japan run on time and you get fined in Switzerland if you allow a public clock to stop. A friend can tell the time to within a minute, without any recourse to a timepiece. That, it is said, is the mark of a psycho.

I was on the Southampton to Durban route. Discounting our port of origin, the place names on our itinerary once again filled me with wonder at the prospect of the adventures which lay ahead in darkest Africa – Naples, then Alexandria, Port Said, Mombasa, Zanzibar, Lourenco Marks and Durban.

Like my friend back at The Midland Hotel had said, the work was easy. I looked after the ship's officers on their twenty-four hour shifts. They enjoyed wonderful food and an all-day bar. So did I. It amazes me, looking back, how I used to keep my white uniform immaculate at all times. This spilling of food and wine that people complain of today; when did that all start?

In Mombasa I visited a brothel, by then an old hand in such matters. The act over, the girl demanded payment, so I offered her the pre-negotiated rate. "No. I want all your money." I looked around the basic room. It was the first time that I'd noticed the locked door and the bars on the windows. "All your money, or I scream for my brothers." At that moment another door opened and I saw several faces peering at me. One of them belonged to a young boy of no more than twelve. He came towards me. I thought as fast as I could in the circumstances."Your sister is very beautiful," I said. "I will tell all the sailors on my ship about her. Many will come. All the sailors who ever pass through Mombasa will come." The boy looked at his sister. She had a little smile on her face. The kid smiled broadly. We shook hands. I was out of there.

That evening I was in the local celebrating not having been dissected by machetes when I heard my name called, followed by a familiar laugh. It was Big Johnnie Marsden, whom I thought was in Manchester. But there he was, weaving across the bar with a girl on each arm, and one of them was the girl with the brothers. She was smiling broadly at me, so I think she thought my prediction that she'd pull all the sailors in port was coming true. But Johnnie Marsden! A girl should have some standards.

Johnnie got posted to the same vessel as me on one trip. Many of the passengers on the cargo ships in those days seemed to be straight out of a Somerset Maugham novel. It was the 'White Mischief' set, colonial types more Edwardian than new Elizabethan. Pickled as they were in privilege and gin it came as no surprise when 'man overboard' echoed around the ship. We never knew whether it was the impending loss of privilege which had caused them to jump the ship's rail or whether the gin had pushed them, but it began to seem almost a rarity when it didn't happen.

On one such occasion Johnnie and I went to the cabin of one such ex-colonial, a dapper, drooping moustache-wearing character on whom the Empire sun had well and truly set. His packed wardrobe beckoned we two likely lads, even though neither of us were of a similar length nor girth as the dear departed. We knew there was likely to have been no inventory of his possessions at this stage, so the girls in the next port were in for a treat. We must have looked like an oversized Laurel and Hardy as we stepped ashore. In beautiful lightweight alpaca, I will have you know.

It was in the Mombasa local that I met the Shoe Man. He'd go up to sailors in bars and offer to cobble together a pair of handmade shoes. Payment was half up-front and the rest on delivery. His method would dismay the shoemakers at Lobbs, but it was quick and simple, and to my beer-goggled eyes it made sense. He made a rough outline of your foot on a piece of paper and that was it. The following morning I watched anxiously over the ship's rail as I awaited the arrival of my first pair of handmade shoes. True to his word the man arrived on time. There were a few quiet smirks from the old hands as I took delivery. I tried them on. Now I don't have small feet, but these made me look like 'Coco the Clown'. Still, they were hand-made and the leather was the softest I had ever felt. I polished them lovingly and then decided to give them a test run before our next port of call. I would cut a dash in Zanzibar. My young mind was convinced that I wouldn't be needing to pay the girls next time, not with these shoes, although I hadn't yet heard the old adage that you can laugh a woman into bed. As I did my rounds I felt as though I was walking on air. It's stating the obvious to say that Equatorial Africa is hot, but with an overhead sun beating down on metal decks I was effectively walking on a hot-plate. At first I thought I'd trodden on chewing gum. Then, step by step, I realised that the glue the Shoe Man had used was melting. I was virtually stuck to the deck. As I tried to walk away, the shoe's uppers came away from their soles. I took exaggeratedly high steps as I tried to extricate myself from the gooey mess, to the jeering amusement of the paying passengers who were having a drinks party on the deck above me.

I've stuck with handmade shoes to this day, albeit now from a rather more professional source. I have tended to favour those crafted from pejorative descriptions of yours truly: snake, alligator, lizard, and latterly, a horse's arse. There's this African despot who's on the books of one of the country's leading shoemakers. Me and Mr Despot have almost identical feet, so sometimes there are pairs going spare. I pick them up for a fraction of the true price. I find £1,000 shoes make it easier to stagger between crises.

CHAPTER FIVE

Death in a French Garden

Between the release of The Stone's 'It's All Over Now' and 'Time is on My Side' I headed for Estartit for the first of many long hot summers of mischief and mayhem. Jagger and Richards were right. Time was on my side. I was twenty and the real Sixties was under way. I didn't know it then, you never do, but it was a good time to be alive.

I was travelling alone, hitchhiking through the Dordogne, tired and thirsty with Spain a distant dream, when a Citroen DS-19, then positively futuristic, pulled over. The driver was the sort of flamboyant figure whom, as a Manchester lad, I'd half expected to meet in France in those days. His name was René Flourins, a Parisian GP and Left-Bank intellectual in his early forties. His companion was a young man, Jean Pierre. René had to be the most exotic figure I'd yet encountered in Europe, habitually attired in a faux Roman toga. A bloke in a frock might not be a natural for a Saturday night out in Manchester but he was somehow perfectly in keeping with the summer heat of France. I was offered lodgings for three nights. Six weeks later I was still there.

It soon became apparent that René and Jean Pierre were more than just good friends, but no matter; they were the most charming companions, especially René. He was from a world I then barely suspected the existence of. The three of us would sit up all night discussing Sartre, Camus, la philosophie. To me then, this was heady profundity.

Meeting up with them became a regular event. At the beginning of the next summer I again stayed for several weeks. René introduced me to his friends on the Rive Gauche in Paris. I even toyed with the idea of a black beret and I became no stranger to Pastis and the proffered contents of René's medicine chest.

When I made my third trip there was just René waiting for me at the station. "Ou est Jean Pierre?" I asked, surprised to see René alone. They were inseparable.

"Il est mort."

"Dead!" I was incredulous. He was only twenty-two.

"He … he took his own life …tablets … barbiturates. He overdosed in the garden, under the fig tree. You do remember the fig tree?"

"But he had everything to live for. I never knew he was so unhappy."

"He was killed by jealousy."

"But I thought you were devoted to him. Who was he jealous of?"

"You."

It's strange. I hadn't thought of that incident for forty years until a friend had phoned me about something quite different. I had put it all to the back of my mind, too painful to recall. My relationship with René, and with Jean Pierre for that matter, had been based on my hunger for perceived sophistication, me then being so young and in the first flush of my generation's new-found social mobility. If I'd been older and wiser I would probably have read the signals. But then again, being older would have been a cushion against such an experience. Jean Pierre had died so young. Mick and Keef were wrong. Time doesn't take sides.

CHAPTER SIX

Pissy Meets Quasimodo

Now there was to be no going back to humdrum days and humdrum ways. There were the long Sixties summers of southern Europe to be enjoyed and I intended to make the most of them. One adventure went something like the following (I write 'something', because where booze is involved who can trust their memory?) –

Pissy Percy ambled along a Spanish beach in his usual get-up, day or night. It was his grandfather's evening suit, with the customary loosened bowtie; how louche it must look to those poor fishing folk. The suit had seen better days, but so too had Percy. At twenty-five he looked forty, and as his grandfather had been some six inches shorter than he the effect was more Chaplin than Bond. At least he was better off than his mate, Mudguts, whose worn cowboy boots could be seen sticking out from under an upturned rowing boat. It's where he lived. Pissy had a proper home, on my balcony. But Mudguts wasn't welcome there. Perhaps the name's a clue. Percy dragged him from under the boat and slapped him awake. "You really should go en-suite, old chap." Mudguts wasn't so bad if you kept upwind of him. As they walked together Percy languidly dangled a champagne bottle. Only it contained the cheapest gut-rot in the whole of Spain. Percy used to top up the bottle; always the same one. Must show the 'peasants' a touch of class. We were hungry, so made our way to a simple beach café where the locals of this quiet fishing-village had gathered, it being a Sunday. The only problem was, Pissy and Mudguts had no money and I'd grown tired of funding them. "A mere detail, my muddy-gutted chum. Just leave it, dear boy, to the Percival charm. We'll be feasting on fresh sardines, olives and Rioja before …" Mudguts grabbed the bottle from him and took a swig.

I sat with the locals, using the broken Spanish I'd picked-up in the Merchant Navy to keep a semblance of conversation going. Through a growing fog of beer and wine I was vaguely aware of the arrival of my two friends. Then I heard shouting as Mudguts tried to grab a plate of food from a table. In the confusion, Percy made *his* move, only in his haste he tripped and fell onto another table, where a large family was seated, bringing it crashing to the floor. I soon became aware of a flurry of arms and feet as a group of young fishermen started wading in. I couldn't understand why, but these eight Spaniards were now attacking me. Damned by association, I suppose. One minute I'm sitting in the Spanish sunshine enjoying a cool beer or two and a bit of friendly conversation when it all seemed to come from nowhere. I wasn't twenty-three stone then, but my seventeen-stone of muscle came in handy from time-to-time. On the ships my mates had teased me over my weight-lifting – "Who's a pretty boy then?" If they could have seen me now..

The Spanish guys seemed to be crashing over the tables as I swung about me. So far so good. But the watching Guardia seemed to be less than impressed. Generalissimo Franco did not like this sort of thing in his country. They made a move in my direction, so I made a run for it, sobering fast. Of course, I had a plan. I'd swim to Africa. Thirty-minutes later an exhausted figure crawled ashore. The Guardia had enjoyed the entertainment during their cigarette break, as had my victims in the fight. So too had the watching fishermen, and most of the village. The Guardia had seen my treatment of the eight young men, so they were taking no chances. A couple of cracks to the head from carbine butts ended all potential resistance.

I couldn't decide which was worst. The headache from the carbine blows, my hangover, or Mudgut's odiferous demonstration of the origin of his name. Pissy wasn't helping the situation. The clue to his nickname was in the ubiquitous champagne bottle, although now he'd added another possible origin, one from which his grandfather's suit might never recover.

We were taken in a battered old van to a compound in the hills. The gaol we were there put in clearly dated from the Spanish Inquisition; water ran down mildewed stone walls from which hung rusted iron rings, and there were even rats to make Pissy and Mudguts feel at home. I looked for a rack. This was pre mass-tourism Spain, a country which had barely altered since the Civil War less than thirty years earlier. But it was a French, rather than a Spanish figure, who turned the key in the lock, or so it seemed: a Quasimodo look-alike. The war had left a generation of cripples, but Quasimodo's disfigurement was an act of nature. The judge and his two fellow members of the bench, though, were clearly victims of the war; they could barely muster an eye, an ear or a leg between them. These proud Spanish veterans were none too pleased to be confronted by these disrespectful young foreigners who had shown their countrymen such scant regard.

We were fined and admonished in Spanish, some of which I understood. We had got off lightly. It was deemed an Escándalo Público. The judge and his bench had seen far worse things in their lives than a fracas on a beach.

Quasimodo escorted us to a gate leading out of the compound under the gaze of a deceptively casual group of Guardia Civil. Pissy made to take a drink from his bottle, having had his sole valued possession returned to him after the trial. Quasimodo grabbed it and took a deep swig. It looked for a moment as if he might fall under the weight of his hump as he leaned backwards to eke out every last drop. He swayed, satisfied that there was no more, and smashed the bottle against a wall. "Bloody hell," whined Percy. "That was a Bollinger '57!"

"Never mind, Pissy old son," I said to him. "Plenty more champagne in the sea. Just stick with me and I'll make you a star."

With that, we jumped onto a horse-drawn cart for the four-mile journey back to a village where we were made to feel less than welcome.

My first trip to the South of France since Craigie's dad's yacht at Menton had been in my Bullnose Morris, even then ancient in an age when old was less-appreciated than now. Big Johnnie Marsden, of Mombasa fame, was with me. He was six-four and the 'big' came solely from his height rather than his girth. He was so ashamed of his thin legs he always wore two pairs of trousers, whatever the weather. Whilst driving, Johnnie had this little trick; he'd make two holes in a newspaper so that he could see enough to drive while pretending to read. I sat in the passenger seat and looked out the window, enjoying the view. Approaching motorists would stare horror-struck as we sailed past.

The car held up well but we ran out of petrol about thirty miles from the coast. What money we had was intended for life's luxuries rather than life's necessities, so after we'd had the tank filled at one of those small petrol stations you still find in rural France we casually drove off without paying. A few seconds later I was less casual when Johnnie screamed – "Look out! He's throwing something" It was a pitchfork aimed right at the car. He'd meant to get us. Fair enough. The price of the petrol hadn't been much but selling it was the business he, and no doubt his family, depended on. I took evasive action and accelerated away from the scene of the crime as fast as a Bullnose Morris would allow. "He'll call the cops," said Johnnie. "I would in his place. A couple of big fucks like us in this car'll stick out like dog's bollocks."

"Elegantly put, Johnnie. Any ideas?"

"That riverbed. Saw it done in a film once."

"What, so their dogs can't follow the scent? The old girl's not that slow." I bumped down the riverbank anyway, and we bounced along in a couple of inches of water, the river being nearly dry in the summer sun. Finally we made it to the coast, dipping our toes in the Med as proof to the rest of our bodies that we really were at that much longed for Shangri-La, the south of France. Johnnie was taking the baggage out of the car when he burst into laughter. "I've found the fucking pitchfork." Sure enough, he had. It was stuck between the underside of the car and the exhaust. That petrol guy had really meant it.

Johnnie was a swordsman. If you send someone out to buy a pint of milk you expect them to return with a pint of milk. So I sent Johnnie out to find us some women and within the hour he was standing there beaming, having bagged a brace. The south of France was shaping up nicely but, as always in those days, money was a pressing problem. Fortunately we had brought sheets of tonic mohair with us from Manchester. We set out to find a tailor and as quickly as Johnnie had found the girls we found a likely target. After a brief negotiation we sold him a roll containing dozens of sheets of the old Mod favourite. The tailor put it in a batch.

Later, Johnnie went back to the tailors and nicked the roll. The next day we returned with it. "Would you be interested in another one?" He was. Now he had one roll for the price of two. We thought it a bargain.

Always one with a keen eye for sartorial elegance on a shoestring, one of my better buys when working on the boats had been a sheepskin coat I'd bought in Montevideo. It was like having a flock of sheep on your back. The problem was that I'd never got around to wearing it as I'd had no excuse to do so, my Union Castle Africa run coming up just a couple of months after its purchase. Wherever I went never seemed cold enough. Then one day my opportunity came. I was in Glasgow and decided to try my luck in Iceland.

In those days I tended to travel everywhere without a thought of how I'd get back. I was then an optimist; somehow I'd always find the money for the return fare. I was late for my flight to Reykjavik so I started running towards the departure lounge. My ticket was non-refundable and I was hard-up; there was no way I was going to miss that plane. I was wearing my flock of sheep and the sweat was pouring off me, so much so that I was virtually blinded by it. Whenever I've told people this story they always insist I must have been pissed when I tripped and fell into an ornamental pond. I made the plane and for some reason I kept my soaking wet coat on for the entire flight. It's quite a short trip, I had reasoned, and I thought that my body heat would help dry the coat. In the confined cabin space the smell was horrendous.

When I left the airport terminal I walked into the coldest weather I had ever experienced. Maybe that's why they call it Iceland. I couldn't afford the fare into town so walking was my only option. It hadn't occurred to me that in sub-zero temperatures water freezes. The coat became so stiff that after a short while I was walking like a toy soldier.

Of course, in Iceland you do not have to go far before you meet a drunk. They all seem to drink like frozen fish. So I met a drunk. Not just any old drunk though. This one turned out to be the Icelandic Prime Minister's son. After that it was up north to Dalvik, where I managed to land some work on a fishing boat, my National Union of Seamen's card opening the door. I made enough money to get me and my coat back to Scotland, the coat having earned its keep in the Arctic wastes.

This reminds me of another fashion fiasco. I was with Pissy Percy taking the train down to the coast for yet another of our Sixties summers of fun. Unfortunately, Pissy Paul became more appropriate, and worse. It must have been those dodgy hot-dogs in Paris. Whatever, it was trouser-washing time, the light-coloured ones never being practical. Into the train's lavatory I went, shutting the door against Percy's giggles. Soon I was almost ready to once more face the world. But, with them being light-coloured, I needed to first dry the trousers. Reasoning that the speed of the train would do the job I hung them out the window. What I didn't reason on, though, was that a passing train would catch them and return my only pair of trousers probably all the way to Paris.

In those days I travelled light, working on the wash 'n' go principle. Every item of clothing I had I was wearing: one T-shirt; one sweatshirt, and that was it. I was 'going commando'. Now this may be more detail than a sensitive reader may relish, but it helps to explain my dilemma. It was either going to be a 'one for the ladies' moment or I'd have to find a solution; someone was already banging on the door. You've guessed it; the sweatshirt became my 'trousers'.

I was slimmer then, but it was still tough getting my legs through the arms, and the waist was way too big for the thing to stay up. Luckily, there was a grubby rag on the floor, and I managed to tear a strip off it to make a belt. When I re-entered the carriage, Percy, himself no stranger to mortification and with his embarrassment horizon lowered to limbo-level by his experiences with Mudguts, sat in his seat wearing an expression as though he'd just seen Adolf Hitler enter carrying Mother Theresa on his back. French sophistication somehow made it worse. In England it would have been either averted gazes or ribald jeering, depending on one's travelling companions. The French came up with knowing smirks.

I had to go through customs at Port Bou, on the Spanish border, and then make my way through town to find a cheap hotel. Pissy either walked ahead or behind, I don't know. I'm not the shy type, but I endured that walk with a thousand-yard-stare, eyes wide shut.

CHAPTER SEVEN

The Pain in Spain Leads Mainly to My Gain

The Escándalo Público with Pissy and Mudguts wasn't the only time Spain has given me pain. Or should that be the other way around? I was in a Malaga bar in the Sixties when the man standing next to me grabbed my money from the counter. He legged it. It wasn't much money, next to nothing really, but it was the principle. Even though he had a head-start I managed to catch him. I hit him too hard. As he crashed to the ground his face hit the pavement. He was in a hell of a state; it later turned out that he'd had to have his jaw rewired. The police arrived and, not knowing the facts, they arrested both of us. We ended up in the same clink, the thief being brought in later after hospital treatment. His face was heavily bandaged, but in spite of this he appeared to show surprisingly little resentment towards me, or as far as I could tell, since so little of him was exposed under the wrapping. Maybe he accepted his injuries as a job risk. Of course, all this was before Elf 'n' Safety.

Once the facts became clear I was released. I heard around town that the thief, an Arab, was dealt with harshly. I can't remember the amount involved, but it was probably no more than a fiver he'd tried to nick. But to repeat the point, it was the bloody principle. Like in Morocco recently when they tried to charge me double fare in a shared taxi because of my size. I refused to pay and there was a stand-off. The extra amount involved was five Dirham, about thirty-five pence, and my friend couldn't believe that I would create such a fuss over such an insignificant amount. But It was the principle! And, of course, the fact that I'm as careful as a Rabbi with a Scottish accountant.

A couple of years later more trouble came my way under Franco's Spanish sun. I was in Torremolinos, long before you could get a full English, and found myself involved in a serious Poker game. Years before the coast had become known as the Costa del Crime it even then had its fair share of villains and chancers. I'd never played cards much, yet I got lucky. The pot was a shoebox. It was some time later when I heard the story of how it came to be at that table.

One of the players, Otto, an Austrian bank robber on the run across Europe, had acquired the box as part of his haul from when he'd raided a Lebanese pimp's flat. He'd heard from a hooker that this Beirut woman who ran a string of girls kept gold trinkets under her bed in a number of shoeboxes. So in he went like Flynn. He was in enough trouble already, and although he always carried a gun he'd vowed not to use violence.

The luxury flat in which the woman lived was in a large apartment block with locked glass doors giving entrance to a communal marble-floored hallway. Otto and his accomplice waited outside the doors until a resident came along. The pair had dressed in suits, which still get you in anywhere. Oozing charm and with disarming Germanic heel-clicks, Otto and his partner in crime entered the building. Once upstairs on the first-floor, they kicked open the door to the flat, knowing from their informant that the Lebanese woman was out doing a heavy night's pimping. In they went, straight to the boxes.

They'd brought along large suitcases in which to carry

the swag to their waiting car. It was only when they'd dragged the heavy cases downstairs to the entrance hall that their seemingly perfect crime went wrong. It was now two a.m., and although this was Spain, where they keep late hours, it seemed that no-one was coming back that night. Keys were needed to exit the place and all the windows were sealed. There they waited for nearly three hours.

The tension, Otto later said, had been unbearable. He'd done a good few blags, sure, but these had been in and out and into the car. He knew that the Lebanese was always accompanied by two armed bodyguards and that the clock was ticking close to the hour when she could have returned at any moment. The bodyguards had a reputation around town and would have been likely to spot strangers, especially those with over-heavy cases. Otto said he would have shot his way out, but that was the last thing he wanted. He'd been living an ostensibly quiet life in Torremolinos, and as far as he knew none of the many police forces hunting him had a clue he was there. Finally, a young couple came up to the door and the man started fumbling for his keys. The woman was very pretty and carried balloons. Otto said, when I by chance met up with him years later, that because of the intensity of the situation, everything about that woman was imprinted on his memory. Not wishing to reveal that they didn't have keys, Otto and his friend began dragging their cases towards the door. The young man obligingly held it open for them while his girlfriend giggled prettily and said he should help them take the cases to the car. "Have you a body in here?" laughed the young man. "No, but I carry my entire future wherever I go," heel-clicked a smiling Otto. "We have an early flight to catch."

He knew that this was an un-reportable crime, given the genesis of the gold, but, just in case the feds did find out, they'd now be looking out for him at Malaga airport. He blew the senorita a kiss as they drove away. If it sounds like a scene from a film, it's how Otto lived his life. I suspect he no longer has a future to carry around in a case.

I was pissed and paid little attention to the contents of my shoebox. Sure, I'd opened it and glanced inside and had seen all the bracelets and necklaces, but it hadn't registered. I later realised that Otto had put it on the table as an act of bravado, showing off to his fellow members of the demimonde. Some of those there would have known the provenance of the box, but Otto knew them well enough to know that they wouldn't be talking, at least while he was in town. He also knew there were plenty more boxes where that one had come from, so he could afford to make a grand gesture with just the one. And that one I had.

I was with Joke who, although as previously mentioned was not overly approving of my way of life, quickly came to an accommodation over a shoebox full of gold in that way women have of turning a blind eye where money is concerned, on the credit side of course. She enjoyed being in Spain, and thought I did too, so she was surprised when I suggested we drive to Geneva in my much-loved Triumph TR2. By the time I'd sobered up the next morning I'd realised that I had something special on my hands and it didn't come from Freeman Hardy Willis. But if the shoe was on the other foot, what would you do? I also knew that in the Generalissimo's Spain, being caught in possession of such trinkets could mean a longer stay in the sun than expected. I didn't know then that whatever Otto had done to obtain the gold could not be reported to the police.

The drive to Geneva was tense. I hoped my English plates would give me some protection from being pulled over in a random police check. Things went well until we got to about twenty miles outside Geneva. There our petrol ran out, as had the money to buy more. By chance we met a Swiss butcher en-route to Spain. He went into a huddle with his wife after I tried to sell him some of the pieces. Eventually he produced his butcher's scales and agreed to buy some of the gold at troy weight, disregarding any aspect of workmanship. Fine, if that would get us on the road again. He weighed the total haul, then his wife chose a few pieces she could flash whilst on holiday away from the smell of blood.

We got back to Geneva and holed up in an hotel. This was in the days before I had connections in the city, before the Rubens. Even so, I managed to sell the contents of the box around town. "A gift from my mother" – that sort of thing. As the money came in bits and pieces I never totalled up exactly how much I'd made; my mind doesn't work that way. But it was enough for Joke and I to live the high life for quite a while. Probably it was about thirty grand in today's terms, but 'found' money is always easier to spend than when it's worked for. It went all too soon as we roamed Switzerland and meandered back to Holland, where my brush with artistic notoriety awaited.

Trouble used to creep up on me uninvited then. Still does, come to think of it. There I'd been at another time, aged about twenty-two, setting off to travel around Europe alone. I made it as far as Estartit, there meeting up with a couple of young women; Joanne and Lennie, from the wealthy New York suburb of Sutton Place. They'd been sleeping on the beach, more for the experience than through necessity; their parents were loaded. When I realised that this was with a capital 'L' I thought I might have a couple of heiresses on my hands so I took them back to my place and popped them in the bath. They scrubbed up nicely.

A couple of nights later Joanne and I were taken in

a police van to Port Bou, where we were invited to leave the country. My car followed behind, driven by a cop. The Guardia had even filled the tank. Actually it was only me who was asked to leave. The cops put it more tersely. So terse were they that one of them even pissed on my passport. I cannot see through the mists of time clearly enough to recall exactly what I had done to warrant a subject of our gracious Queen having his passport treated in such cavalier fashion, but I suspect I had been naughty. The usual Escándolo Público.

Once free, Joanne and I jumped in the TR2 and headed for Rome. From Rome we went to Bournemouth, in those days some leap of the imagination. There we got wind that the police were interested in Joanne so we headed for Cherry Hinton in Norfolk. Why there? It just seemed a long way from anywhere, but not so to the police. I was arrested and held in custody on suspicion of abducting a minor. We're not talking Gary Glitter here; she was at least seventeen. But her parents had put out a search on her, she being technically a minor under US law. That was the last I saw of her. I learnt a lesson there that I should have remembered two years later: hotel receptionists do refer foreign passports to the police.

That incident aside, those Spanish years were among the most carefree times of my life as me and my fellow Northern lads grew our hair long through bronzed, hedonistic summers. There was one young lad in our group, smaller than the rest of us, but he knew how to knock back the beers and make people smile. Thankfully he kept his guitar intact through those boozy sessions, because little did we know it at the time, but Davy Jones was destined for greater things. Sadly, he took an early ride on The Last Train To Clarksville, it having arrived a tad soon, offering a reminder to us all that we are never as young as we think we are.

CHAPTER EIGHT

Every Picture Tells a Story

It's 1969, and I'm taking a few cracks over the head from machine-gun butts. Maybe that's why my judgment's been a bit flawed of late. I'm in an alleyway in Marseille's North African quarter, with the French CRS asking questions about a missing Rubens and my having just legged it from the local nick. Fair enough. I have to put my hands up to all that. Except I can't. They're chained to shackles around my ankles, which is painful, considering one of them is broken. My art gallery research with Joke referred to earlier had borne fruit. I'd better start at the beginning –

In the late Sixties I was now in the habit of spending every summer in Spain, usually with Pissy Percy and Mudguts. Whenever I hear The Stones now I think of those times, especially 'Paint It Black' and 'Satisfaction'. That's exactly what I got with Joke. In '68 I'd gone to Sitges, in Spain, and had met up with this beautiful, elegant Dutch girl. I liked to think that I knew how to treat a woman, so I suggested to her that we check into the best hotel in town. I'd better not mention its name as I believe there's still an outstanding bill.

Eager as I was to impress the lovely Joke I didn't let the little matter of my being skint stand in the way of my lady's comfort. She had been sharing a room with a girlfriend in a one-star establishment and when I took her into the foyer of what was to be our home for the next ten days I was quite dazzled by her happiness. My ploy worked. We fell in love.

Even though I knew from the outset that I wouldn't be paying the bill, I lacked the chutzpah to go for the bridal suite or even a sea-view. Not that we spent much time looking out the window. Every night I would extend our stay but I sensed that Reception was getting suspicious. We were living well, too well, like you do when you're about to do a bunk; by casually overspending you try to make the staff think you don't have a care in the world, but I felt we were too young to carry it off and decided we should leave. "But Paul, I do so love it here." I was afraid she might say that. "Why don't you go and buy a nice souvenir for your mother?" That seemed to do the trick, as off she happily went. Unfortunately she returned just when I was tossing our luggage out the window. I forgot to mention, we were on the tenth floor. "Paul, I want you to help me choose a ..." She froze, suddenly aware of what I was up to. I managed to calm her down just enough to get her to stroll hand-in-hand with me out of the hotel, her head nestling into my right shoulder, as were her teeth. Luckily our luggage had landed in soft sand, exactly where I'd aimed it.

There's something to be said for not having the sea-view; it was nice and quiet around the back. The luggage survived the fall and so too, just, did our budding relationship. Joke was from a good family and this well brought-up girl wasn't used to such tricks of the trade. Yet.

We made our way to Haarlem in Holland, where Joke lived. She was busy with something or other, so to kill time I hitched to Sweden. I'd never been there and Sweden meant beautiful women. Sorry, Joke. Mudguts and I hid on a freight train like hobos in the American Depression. We were heading up to Stockholm in some style, well at least the straw was clean, when a uniformed man's head appeared over the side of the truck – "Lifter, ya?" Others joined him. We were taken to the nearest police station where our passports were examined and we were then led to a cell. They kept the passports and we thought a similar fate awaited us. To our surprise, though, our cell door was left open.

After about thirty minutes food was brought to us by a policewoman, confirming what I'd heard about Swedish girls. After we'd washed and eaten we were taken to the nearest road and dropped off, with advice on how best to hitch. The police smilingly handed us our passports. All in all a minor incident yet it has always stuck in my memory for the humanity shown to us, especially in contrast to the behaviour of the many policemen I was soon to encounter. Then again, maybe they would have a point.

We stayed a couple of weeks in Stockholm then drifted back to Haarlem, where Joke was waiting for me. Absence had made the heart grow fonder. I stayed with her at her mother's house. The old dictum that women end up looking like their mothers meant, for once, that Joke and I should have stayed together.

I soon got a job in freight at Amsterdam's Schipol Airport. I don't know whether Schipol had a euphemism, like 'Thief-row' for Heathrow, but given what was going on there at that time I'm surprised anyone ever saw their baggage again. Now I had money coming in, Joke and I rented a flat in Schveringham, near the coast and not too far from the airport. The work there was very interesting; you never knew what the next package might contain. My first real touch was a box of diamond-encrusted watches; each would be worth about £20,000 at today's prices. But I was too keen and sold them for next to nothing to the first buyer who made an offer. The next valuable item to pass through my hands, though, was a bit of a one-off. It was a present from the one-day king of Spain, Juan Carlos, to the Queen of the Netherlands. The gift was a pair of antique hunting pistols in a mahogany box. I took them home and then to the nearby beach. Mudguts managed to load them and there we fought a duel. We stood back to back in time–honoured fashion and took the obligatory ten paces. I fired first, aiming straight up. Then I remembered that Mudguts owed me money. He aimed straight at me with a glint in his open eye. He had me sweating, but at the last moment, as he fired, he thrust his arm out to one side. Honours were even. I managed to sell the guns through a dealer and gave up lending money. Soon after that the police arrived and searched our flat, which did not please Joke. They didn't find anything nor did they suspect me directly. But, just for working freight at Schipol I was suspect. It went with the territory.

I left the airport and met up with a new friend, Hans Maas, and his stunningly beautiful girlfriend. She was very much of her time – a cool Dutch girl with long, shiny blonde hair and legs up to her armpits; a hippy-chick with shampoo and conditioner. 'Where Do You Go To My Lovely?' could have been written just for her. I was still in love with Joke, but as a man is a polygamous creature and only as faithful as his options, we had an affair. Hans didn't seem to mind. Dutch liberality, I guess.

That summer I took off to Spain with Joke and became embroiled in the affair of the golden shoebox. It had been that brief experience of having some decent money on the hip that firmed my resolve to carry out something spectacular. Back in Holland I resumed my association with Hans, a fellow chancer. We often met up for a drink and it was never too long into a session before conversation drifted towards The Big One.

Although I had already visited several galleries with Joke I didn't want to involve her in this kind of caper for a number of reasons: I loved her; the risks were high; she was too 'good'; I did not wish to tarnish her innocence. Also, I was not certain she could carry it off. Maybe I had some kind of Madonna-whore thing going on there.

When I'd visited those galleries with her I'd been only half-joking. Now, encouraged by the experience with the future king's hunting pistols I saw myself as a credible art thief, a glamorous Raffles figure cutting a swathe through Europe. We weren't art experts but we knew what was practical. Our selection of a painting was driven by this need rather than by choice of artist, and we found the ideal picture in the Singer Museum in Laren. There was a Ruben's exhibition in town.

Hans and I visited the gallery countless times, day by day narrowing our choices to a handful of likely candidates. We knew, without knowing much about art, that with a Rubens we were taking a major work which was going to be valuable, if not priceless, and that the theft was going to attract attention, hopefully after the event. We needed a painting that was easily transportable and hard to damage. Peter Paul Rubens' wood panel version of a stigmatized St Francis might have been painted by the artist just for us. Thankfully it wasn't the wall-sized canvas on the same subject. If Rubens had known that another Paul, four centuries later, would be slipping it under his coat, he would have painted it on a piece of wood twice the size.

The Singer Museum, like most art galleries, was divided into several rooms. The guards would slowly roam through them, doing a job in which little happens. Well, usually. Before the days of CCTV this left each room unguarded for several minutes. Using one such opportunity I moved the painting slightly away from the wall, checking how it was mounted and were there any wires.

We took the painting in the Autumn, making our wearing of raincoats plausible. We hadn't decided beforehand which of us would actually lift it. The theft had to be opportunistic, inasmuch that a guard may have randomly appeared on the scene, his position favouring one or the other of us. As we walked into the museum, though, we had decided that one of us would grab the painting. We weren't leaving without it. To sit in a bar that evening and discuss what might have been was not on the agenda. When the moment came, Hans spotted a guard coming towards the room in which 'our' painting hung. He engaged him in conversation about another painting he knew to be elsewhere in the gallery. This was my chance.

I would like to say the theft had involved a Rififi-style midnight descent by rope, with a great soundtrack (I know, the heist scene in Rififi was near-silent) and nail-biting tension. Reality was more prosaic; I simply grabbed it and slipped it under my coat. The snatch, in real time, took no more than a couple of seconds. It seemed like many minutes. The previous evening we'd discussed the possible consequences of what we were planning. Hans and I, with our beautiful friend, had sat up half the night too excited to sleep, our wine-soaked conversation reiterating how our lives would never be the same again, whichever way things went. I have kept our girlfriend's name out of the frame, for although she was in on the research and our getaway driver, her name was never put forward as a suspect, and I'd like it to remain that way, particularly as she later found public fame and fortune. I know where you went to my lovely.

Hans and I, though, were convinced we were facing two options. One was that we would be caught in the act. We had resigned ourselves to the possibility of long prison sentences and although a bit handy we had promised each other not to use violence even if trying to evade capture, knowing this would go heavily against us in court. The second option was success. Either way, this would be a life-changing experience. The sheer magnitude of what we were doing guaranteed us, in our eyes, either a long custodial or undreamed of wealth for the rest of our days. Goodbye, rat race. Not that I'd ever said hello.

We were convinced that if we could find the right buyer we could command a fortune, with Hans and I fifty-fifty. This was before I knew such thefts are usually done to order, a collector naming his piece and his price. Now art thefts are frequently used solely to blackmail insurers, in profit terms second only to drugs in the crime league.

It was a long walk from the snatch to the gallery's exit and our waiting car with its ticking engine and beautiful chauffeuse. She had no idea of what was happening inside; would we come out, would it be the guards? Would we find the right exit? How long should she stay there? What if she were moved on? Would the police shoot them? Can you get hair conditioner in prison? If so, would it be wise to look her best?

The museum was once the rambling home of William Singer, an American artist and philanthropist and its 19th-century layout was confusing. We were young and the young don't usually plan ahead. Sod it, we were lost! At least this forced us to take deep breaths and walk slowly rather than stride too obviously straight for the street. So we strolled through the gallery's rooms, pausing occasionally before a painting, while being unnecessarily discreet in following the exit signs. I spoke to a guard – "Excuse me, where please is the Rubens' Exhibition?" Hans stood behind him, making faces.

Maybe we overdid the casualness, because the painting's loss could have been spotted at any second and the sooner we were in the car the sooner our pulse rates would return to double figures. Finally we were outside in clean air, into the car and away to a life at the end of the rainbow.

I have never since experienced such elation as when we drove through the streets of Laren, but an elation tempered by fear. It was a small town and if the theft was spotted it would not have been too difficult for the police to close off all exits. Even our driver's shiny hair began to look lank as she drove too carefully during the thirty-five mile journey back to our apartment, terrified the slightest error would attract attention. I had an ear on the sky, listening for helicopter rotors. You always hear them before you see them.

We made it, alcohol now a primal need, but maybe the TV even more so. It's one of those clichés that villains in films always switch the TV on just as their piece is about to begin. That's exactly what happened with us. But then they always turn the TV off when their item's over. We didn't. We kept it on, waiting for newsflashes, there being no rolling news then, bathing in our notoriety. Call me morally reprehensible, but that day must rank as the happiest in my life; here we were, young, free and rich beyond our dreams, the perpetrators of the perfect Sixties heist.

CHAPTER NINE

The Emperor's New Clothes

We hadn't researched our market so we hung the painting on the lavatory wall. I'd heard there was an antique dealer down The Lanes in Brighton who could help me find a buyer, so I flew to Heathrow with St. Francis in my hand-baggage. Hans and I had agreed that I'd be the one to sell it, the trust of friendship allaying any fears that I might do a runner. Before going through Customs I looked at my hands. Some sweating but no give-away stigmata. Aside from a bit of sphincter-twitching I was soon trundling into town on the never-ending journey that is the Piccadilly Line. I met my fence, Peter, a respectable-looking, tweedy type who offered me a cup of tea. In exchange for an agreed commission he put me in contact with a potential buyer, a Fernand Legros, based in Geneva. I set off there to find him, all eager anticipation. To me then, Legros was just another name.

Fernand Legros was the 'business partner' of Elmyr de Hory, art forger extraordinaire. Clifford Irving, himself to literature what de Hory was to painting, and later Orson Welles in the film 'F for Fake', chronicled the exploits of Legros and de Hory, the latter one of the most talented artists of his generation. Where most painters have an identifiable style, de Hory had every style: Chagall, Toulouse-Lautrec, Matisse, Degas, Modigliani, Picasso – and the rest.

Perhaps all talent offers easy money, but that of the art

forger more than most. In the Sixties Legros once took a De Hory Picasso to Pablo Picasso to ask him to authenticate his 'own' work. Picasso couldn't remember doing it, but once Legros had lied that he'd paid US$100,000 (over a million now) for it, Picasso willingly added his signature, his reasoning being that if it was worth that much it must be his. On that day Legros had spent maybe thirty minutes, no more than that, in the artist's company. In that time Picasso could have done five, maybe six, similar drawings. Whenever he had a drink, a fag or a frequent frolic, instead he could have made an even greater fortune. There was me thinking it's just about art.

I met Elmyr de Hory through Fernand Legros, the former visiting Geneva from his home in Ibiza. Legros was a ruthless, self-centred exotic, a hybrid of Egyptian, Greek and French. He was diminutive, elegant, usually dressed in skinny suits with rock chic accessories and enough bling to turn P Diddy, or whatever he now calls himself, green with envy. Legros' long hair was topped by his trademark fedora and he cut a rich boho dash around Geneva in his Silver Shadow, a successful art dealer out of central casting. His charisma and money ensured he was always surrounded by beautiful women, attracted like moths to the flame of his fame and fortune. Although gay, through marriage he was a naturalised US citizen. He'd always been a talent in waiting, a superb salesman waiting for the perfect product. As an ex-ballet dancer he had artistic inclinations, and in Elmyr de Hory he had found the greatest art forger in history, a man who'd spent thirty years at his lucrative trade.

The business relationship between the pair had begun when Legros met de Hory in a Miami flat owned by a mutual friend. Legros saw in de Hory the opportunity he'd been waiting for all his life. Well, what he'd so far spent of it, he then being only thirty-two. A personal relationship blossomed between them and they travelled the States together selling the master forger's works. Legros negotiated half the profits, but half of what? He never revealed to de Hory what the true selling price of a painting was, so Elmyr quite happily accepted what he was given. Legros was even happier, pocketing the lion's share of the proceeds. Then Legros picked-up a male lover, Real Lessard, ten years his junior.

Legros had pulled a master stroke. Going through US Customs he'd declared a consignment of de Hory's paintings as fakes. There was a tax to pay on original art, so Customs weren't playing. They were real, insisted their experts, so duty had to be paid. A smiling Legros complied. It was a small price for stamps of authentication. Hello Texas.

Come in Houston. Where there's oil there's money. Where there's money there's art. Step forward one Arthur Meadows of The General American Oil Company of Texas, who was to put together a considerable collection of Elmyr de Hory's finest works. Houston, we have a problem.

On another occasion, Legros went to see Van Dongen with one of de Hory's samples of his (Van Dongen's) work. Van Dongen was a libertine who usually slept with his models and was drunk when Legros pointed out to him that he'd forgotten to sign the picture. Like Picasso before him, he duly did so, and it was soon in the Mellon Museum in Texas, worth a small fortune. At a later stage the curator of the Mellon got Lloyds of London to value the collection for insurance purposes. Within days they came back. About ninety percent were fakes.

This trio of grifters drifted around the States, but despite the money they were raking in things didn't run smoothly. Legros was promiscuous, and this often led to physical violence between him and Lessard. These were early days in the relationship with de Hory, who, tired of the squabbling, severed his working relationship with Legros. He tried to go it alone in Europe, but his brilliance on canvas did not extend to a similar brilliance in business. He ticked over, but could not pull off deals in the way Legros did. Purely by chance, de Hory and Legros ran into each other in Paris. A nearly broke Legros, his cash cow cut loose, attempted to rekindle their previous relationship. De Hory agreed to this, but there were difficulties as his paintings were locked up in a New York hotel in lieu of an unpaid bill. Legros went to New York and, being Legros, somehow got the paintings out. Also, being Legros, he sold some of them. Elmyr de Hory was unaware of this as he'd virtually written them off. After all, he could reproduce similar work seemingly at will.

A year later the pair met again. This time, unlike in Paris, Legros was wealthy, now an established art dealer on the US scene, mixing originals with fakes. He was still with Lessard, and the pair began to fleece de Hory. They paid him a monthly stipend, but de Hory appeared not to be too concerned at this. The business flourished as Legros sold dozens of paintings, commanding masterpiece prices. But de Hory's interest began to wane as he found himself unable to live in the style to which he had previously grown accustomed.

Aware that they might be killing the golden goose, Legros and Lessard built de Hory a house on Ibizia. For a while this rekindled his interest, but he grew bored again. His work started to get sloppy. Legros, maybe unaware of the finer points of the pictures he was selling, continued to tout them around. These sub-standard works came under the scrutiny of the experts potential buyers hired to authenticate them.

The Feds started to sniff around. Fernand Legros and Real Lessard were arrested.

I don't know what happened to Lessard, but when Legros came to trial in France he was immediately released on the excuse that he'd served four years on remand in various gaols. But in reality the French didn't want him shooting his mouth off in open court. His success had been founded on De Hory's extraordinary ability and his own talent, sure, but without the worldwide complicity, knowing or otherwise, of dozens of dealers, owners and galleries, they could not have succeeded at such a level. There were too many influential people who did not wish to see the golden egg do a Humpty-Dumpty for a show trial to have been even an outside possibility.

Elmyr de Hory was investigated by the Spanish police. He served only two months inside, on charges of homosexuality (Franco's Spain) and having no visible means of support, there being no direct evidence of fraud under Spanish law. After he got out in '68, De Hory became a celebrity, it being the golden era of the lionisation of criminals; like Henri Charriere (another faker) of Papillon fame, and our own national treasures, the Krays. This was the period of Clifford Irving's and Orson Welles' interest. De Hory took to painting under his own name and began to receive due recognition for his talent. But by '76 his past had begun to catch up with him. The French police were nosing around and he'd been driven to leaving his beloved Ibiza home by the untenable behaviour of Legros and Lessard, who there had become cuckoos in the nest. He committed suicide. Or did he, as some say, stage his own death; the ultimate fake? Fernand Legros went on to become a creditable artist painting in his own name.

Their plan had been ingenious, not only in the technical execution of the paintings but in the fact that the crime effectively protected itself. If you're a collector of such pieces you're on a roller-coaster ride to nowhere if you so much as hint that you have doubts as to the authenticity of your picture. You stand to lose millions, or, to put it another way, taking the art world as a whole, billions. So the cycle of deception had to, has to, go on.

At a deeper level too, it speaks of the unspoken, laying bare the 'emperor's new clothes' nature of the international art trade and asking what is real and what, indeed, is fake. In real terms De Hory and Legros had perpetrated the financial crime of the century, maybe of all time, and that crime is still taking place.

I had met Legros at a café by Lake Geneva, near the Jet D'Eau, the fountain which shoots water one-hundred-and-forty metres into the air. It was the perfect backdrop to the world of international intrigue into which I had found myself catapulted. "Where is the painting please?" I told him. I also told him I knew of his background, by now having made enquiries. I asked him why he would want to risk handling a famous stolen painting, given that he dealt mainly in fakes. "Those days are over. I was busted. De Hory's out of the game."

"Do you have someone in mind, a buyer?"

"I do."

"Who?"

"You don't need to know that. It is better for you that way. And for me."

The plan was that I would return to England and collect the painting. I should lodge it in a Swiss bank vault, for which Legros would pay. Once he had his potential buyer tied-up he would contact me via a post-restante address and we'd take it from there. We sat awhile, chatting, parting on a handshake. We met for lunch the next day and that was when he took me to meet de Hory, a rather kind-looking, white-haired old gentleman, I thought. "So, this is the young man you were telling me about? Such hard work, stealing a painting. In the old days I would have painted it for you. Still, a big boy like you could probably handle a bit of hard work." He winked in a what-an-old-rogue-am-I sort of way.

A postscript to my association with Legros is that a friend and I hatched a plan to kidnap him and take him over the border from Switzerland into France, where he was wanted. We spent a lot of time researching this: how best to take him, ideally without violence, where the best unguarded border-crossing points were, how to get our hands on the $2-million we were going to demand for his return. It came to nothing. I can't remember why. I like to think it was from some latent sense of fair play, but I suspect the plan just fizzled out because some other crazy idea had come along.

It was only recently I discovered that maybe I, and not Legros, was the one who got lucky because of my distraction. Rumours abound as to Legros' interests outside the international art world. If he was the lover of the late Secretary General of The United Nations, Dag Hammerskjöld, and a personal friend of Henry Kissinger, then that could explain the rumours that he was in the pay of the CIA. The Moroccan dissident, Ben Barka, was kidnapped, tortured and murdered, some say with the connivance of Legros, and he was also said to have been behind the kidnapping of the African leader, Moise Tshombe. He'd even spent time in a Rio prison in the next cell to Ronnie Biggs while under protective custody for fingering the French gangster Christian David. I was going to kidnap him?

I flew back to England but soon heard that my man in Brighton had been arrested. I too was arrested, but not for the theft. I'd been fussing and fighting down London's Bayswater

Road, as was my wont in those days. They got an ID on me and as far as it looked, that was it. But they couldn't do me for the theft and for handling; it had to be one or the other. At this stage they had no proof I'd stolen the painting, although they knew that I had. They also knew, through the Brighton fence no doubt, that I had handled it, but they didn't want to go down that route. They wanted me for the theft, so they would let me run. I thought they had let me go. I went back to Geneva.

Coincidentally, Joke was working there for IOS (Investors Overseas Services), an investment fund for expatriate Americans, especially those not on nodding terms with the IRS. The company was run by Bernie Cornfeld, who had been born in Istanbul some forty years previously. After having tried his hand at many things he was then in Geneva at the height of his powers, running an international financial empire.

He had the sort of wealth where he could afford to try to hire the Stones to perform at a private Christmas party and by 1970 he had acquired two Boeing-707s. When I later got to know his chief pilot he told me that Bernie used to keep both aircraft on permanent twenty-four hour standby at Geneva's Contrin airport in case he needed to fly somewhere on a whim. Sometimes he did, only for the aircraft to briefly touch down at its destination before the pilot was ordered to return immediately to Geneva. These whimsical notions were not city hops, we're talking long-haul here.

He had homes all over the world. Apart from a Geneva Villa, there was a 12th-Century chateau in France, a Belgravia mansion, a permanent luxury suite in New York and a Hollywood mansion where he entertained. His girlfriends included a young Victoria Principal, later of Dallas, and Heidi Fleiss, one day to become the 'Hollywood Madame', supplying hookers to stars like Charlie Sheen, et al. Bernie used to have a dozen or so girlfriends at a time, claiming that polygamy was less complicated than monogamy. That made sense to me. If you can afford it. Small, bearded, balding and softly-spoken, all in all Bernie exercised great charm, except when anyone got on the wrong side of his temper.

IOS was selling US Mutual Funds. Here's how it worked: you continually offer the investor new shares and buy existing shares back at the request of the shareholder. The capital raised is then used to invest in diversified securities in other companies. Effectively, for IOS, it was a bulls and bears pyramid scheme and it attracted huge interest. Unfortunately, one interested party was the US Securities Exchange Commission. Bernie was ultimately found guilty of selling fraudulent investments in US Mutual Funds, for which he served a spell in prison, but he had been a victim of another's double-dealing.

There was a good life in Geneva then; a crazy town with crazy people. The place was full of high-living ex-pats, celebs, and every night was party night. One was Victor Emanuel, then living opposite the Mövenpick. His family used the surname 'Regina' in the Geneva phone directory in self-recognition of their claim to the Italian throne.

Victor had been a boy when his father had been stripped of the crown in 1946 when post-war Italy had declared itself a republic. This historic blip did not deter Victor, who lived his life as though still privy to the 'divine right of kings'. In 2006 he faced 'influence-trafficking' charges in Italy involving, among other things, prostitution and the Mafia. However, his insouciant amorality had marked his card long before then.

His full name is Vittorio Emanuele Alberto Carlo Teodoro Umberto Bonifacio Amedeo Damiano Bernardino

Gennaro Maria Savoia, the last reflecting his status as heir to the House of Savoy. His friends call him Victor. A tall, maybe six-six (one metre-ninety), imposing figure, he certainly looked the part of king-in-waiting, and in his unflinching amorality he would have been a fitting monarch in a country where in some quarters God sits at Berlusconi's right-hand.

One of his brushes with the law involved his shooting dead, with a rifle, a German tourist (yes, it is a crime!) in Corsica. The matter remained unresolved for thirteen years until he was acquitted of manslaughter in Paris.

When I first knew him he had, as a visible means of support, the local Bell Helicopter concession; a tacit arms dealer in true Sixties Geneva style. When, in 1970, he married, against his father's wishes, in Vegas and again in Tehran, a biscuit heiress and water-ski champion, he became involved in a scandal over the sale of helicopters to his friend the Shah of Iran.

In later years I used to visit him at his Leicester Square offices where he operated in a haze of booze, marijuana and whores, his daily business life accompanied by a constant backdrop of blue movies. He had the predilections of a true royal.

He had been forced to live in exile for over fifty years, unable to return to Italy until 2002, but had always retained the native Italian's love of the good life. After being given his first prison meal he was quoted as saying – "It really is true what they say; in Italy, you can eat well everywhere."

It seemed to me that the main line of business in Geneva wasn't cuckoo clocks but arms-dealing. Victor was in the right place. Perhaps it was a throwback to the war years, when Axis and Allied officers alike would drink at the same bars in the city, creating an ambience of intrigue, like where parts of London have retained their area-defining trades down through the centuries. Anyway, in Geneva it was arms, whether covert or overt, the latter dealers being international players with HQs there. Swiss banking laws and tax breaks didn't harm trade either. You needed good hearing to know what was going on there in those days. Everybody whispered.

I found a job at the Hotel Beau Rivage by Lake Geneva in the early summer of '69. Much of Geneva's louche society gravitated towards the hotel's pool and, being naturally curious, I wasn't shy in coming forward, being by then on speaking terms with Bernie Cornfeld and his soon-to-be nemesis, David Vesco. They were international tycoons. I was a swimming-pool attendant. With his Zapata moustache, Vesco, looked like a Mexican bandido, and was soon to play the part to perfection. I like to think that I played a small part too in one of the biggest strokes of financial infamy on record. " Paul." I went over to Vesco's sun-lounger. Bernie was on an adjacent one. "Yes?" "Get them out of the pool please. Bernie and I need to talk. That's the only place we can get any privacy 'round here." I looked at Bernie, who was nursing a drink. He winked up at me. The pool was soon empty.

After their chat in which the seeds of a chain of events had been sown, Vesco came over to me, extending his hand. I thought he wanted to shake mine, so I reciprocated. We did shake hands, but his contained a gold Rolex, my reward for having cleared a pool. I've still got it, my back-line insurance policy against the rainiest of days.

If in later years my experience with JP was to be an expensive plate-throwing exercise, then it was nothing compared to the £200-million-plus that their swim had cost Bernie Cornfeld (at least ten times that in today's money).

David Vesco, I later found out, was thirty-five at the time, yet to my twenty-five-year-old self he seemed much older. He was a family man in public yet spent much of his time gambling. After a seemingly amicable start to his relationship with Bernie he made a hostile move on IOS. Bernie tried to block it. It got worse, not helped by Bernie's addiction to the pleasures of treasure as he happily lazed on the lilo of life while the Great White circled. Vesco took over IOS and began to milk it, in the process taking down several European and US banks. Bernie was thrown into gaol and Vesco went on the lam, accused of owing several hundred million US Dollars. It wasn't a quiet affair and it looked for awhile as if Vesco might drag down several leading names of the day.

He began a complex operation in which he placed IOS investor funds into an international string of dummy companies, one of which, based in Amsterdam, allegedly involved Prince Bernhard of the Netherlands.

Stories about Vesco's dealings were rife. One involved his breaking into a Swiss vault to steal incriminating share certificates. He didn't waste time there on mere money. But he did spend it. When he moved around it was as often as not in his own Boeing-707, complete with on-board disco. He holed up in Costa Rica, which had few extradition treaties, most notably not with the USA, and from there embezzled $220-million from over a hundred IOS funds. A friend of Vesco's, Donald Nixon Jr, tried, in '73, to broker a deal involving illegal re-election contributions to his uncle, Richard Nixon, and clearly the very man to grant Vesco US immunity. It didn't work. Richard Nixon had other problems.

Another president, Costa Rica's Figueres, was more co-operative. In return for a substantial payment he granted Vesco guaranteed immunity from extradition for the duration of his presidency. Vesco passed his time in the country in some comfort, surrounded by bodyguards at his sumptuous villa. He even had time for a hobby: cocaine trafficking. However, the 'Vesco Law' was repealed in '74 when Figueres's term ended, but Vesco managed to hang on for another four years. But that was it, and our friend was once more on his toes.

He had few problems finding new hosts. Small countries welcomed him on the principle that he'd either bring in investors or he'd dispense bungs. When neither was forthcoming, though, he was usually asked to move on. He tried Nassau in the Bahamas, then Antigua. After that he spent time in Nicaragua, then under the Sandanistas, before finally settling in Cuba. He knew he'd get excellent medical treatment there for his urinary problem and that Fidel Castro was unlikely to agree an extradition treaty with the United States. The deal was that he'd be a good boy and not get involved in any more scams while under Cuban protection. It all went well for awhile. He married a Cuban and seemed settled. He lived the good life, armed bodyguards and the Cuban intelligence service ensuring the curious never got close.

There are differing versions of what happened next. One is that he was trying to push a fake anti-cancer and AIDS drug called TX, using Donald Nixon Jr as his contact with the outside world. Now, although there might be some cause for disquiet at the number of luxury homes Fidel Castro saw fit to own while espousing the cause of Communism, few could dispute the excellent healthcare that Cuba provides for its citizens. If the allegations were true, Vesco had not only broken his promise to the Cubans, but had done so in a way guaranteed to annoy them. Nixon got thirty days house arrest while Vesco and his wife received thirteen and nine years respectively. That was in '96. The other possibility is that he was plotting a deal with the US. In exchange for clemency he would reveal details of the levels of corruption within the Cuban government, telling of things that wouldn't have gone down too well among an impoverished, Castro-worshipping populace. Death silenced him in 2007.

All this was to come later. I gave up the pool and found a job with IOS targeting clients to invest in the 'Fund of Funds'; known in the UK as 'The Dover Plan'. Ben Dover plan? Armed with Bernie's catchphrase – 'Do you sincerely want to be rich?' – I'd be sent all over Europe, staying away from the UK for an obvious reason. I often went to Italy, being put up in top hotels so I had a good front when meeting a potential investor. I also went to France, where I was asked to see a wealthy woman who lived in the old port of Marseille. To me then she seemed old. Now she'd seem young. We had a fling. I remember her having a huge flat full of genuine antiques and paintings. I wasn't tempted, by the paintings. We got on well and she was happy to invest in 'The Fund of Funds'.

CHAPTER TEN

Tequila Slammer

Relaxing in my hotel room before meeting her to close the deal I was feeling pretty pleased with myself as I prepared a Tequila Slammer. It packed a hell of a punch. As I took my first sip the door crashed in off its hinges. There stood five or six CRS, the French special police, the sharp end of their machine-guns pointing my way. Cuffed and shackled, I was pushed towards a meat-wagon under the eyes of neighbourhood kids who jeered 'les flics' every move.

The Dutch had exercised an extradition warrant. Looking back, it's hardly surprising they'd found me. I mean, I'd stolen a priceless painting, the fence in Brighton knew I was off to Geneva to see Fernand Legros, I'd hung out with high-profile international tycoons and a set that probably had an entire Interpol office-block staffed in its honour. I might as well have laid a paper-trail across Europe. I was even travelling on my own passport, under my own name.

I was taken to the Marseilles police headquarters, the one later used in 'The French Connection'. Expecting rough stuff from CRS goons I wished I'd had the chance to down the Tequila to numb the pain. Instead, it was – "Café?"

"That would be nice."

"Fume?"

"Please." This was going well. "Now, Monsieur Brennan

(as I then was), you do understand why you have been brought here?"

"Non." Best Gallic shrug. The cop smiled. I was escorted to a room off a second-floor landing. No cuffs or shackles; just a cigarette, a coffee, and me. They showed me to a room where a young cop was already seated at a table. I was invited to sit opposite him. He had his back to the window. I had mine to the open door. We exchanged pleasantries. "You are an art lover?" This cop was about my age. "I've visited a few galleries. I heard it's a great place to pick up women. Shows you have a sensitive side."

"You like your women big?"

"Eh? Non."

"Me neither. Unlike Paul Rubens." I wanted to tell him that fat women were only part of Ruben's oeuvre. But then he probably wanted me to refer to his religious paintings. I wondered why they had put such a young cop onto interviewing me over the theft of so priceless a painting. Even though I was young myself, I remember being offended. Then I thought perhaps they'd found the only cop in the station with a passing interest in art. I felt better at that. So it went on, this chit-chat. Pleasant enough, but I wondered when he might cut to the chase, all the while aware of the nearby open door. Another cigarette was offered. I accepted, and my interrogator distractedly searched his pockets for a light. Well, in a situation like that there's no point in hanging around. Just to be sociable. "Au revoir."

"Arrêt! Arrêt!"

I hope he didn't get into trouble, but I wasn't staying for anybody. Out the door and down seemingly endless spiral stone steps I flew. Never moved so fast, before or since. Then I was on the street, running for freedom. I'd make sure that I'd never leave a paper trail again.

I can't walk on cobbled streets today without thinking of what happened next. Down I went. My ankle. Damn! I couldn't run. I couldn't move. Then the CRS arrived. "I can't move," I said in French, so they whacked me over the head with their guns anyway, over and over. I was taken in chains to hospital and my ankle proved to be broken. I was in plaster there for nearly a month, the pretty French nurses being a consoling factor as I put on my very best garçon méchant act for their benefit.

Then it was eight weeks of virtual solitary in a two by two metre cell, they were that unhappy that I'd legged it. I'd heard a lot about the high standard of catering in French prisons, so maybe thin cabbage soup every day was a local delicacy. That was a long eight weeks, helped neither by the diet nor the blinding headaches I was still getting from those rifle butts.

I was later taken to Baumettes, the notorious Marseille prison, then still full of OAS political detainees from the war with Algeria and the usual quota of murderers and Legionnaire deserters. Built on the outskirts of the city in 1936 to hold six-hundred prisoners, it today holds eighteen-hundred, without any building extensions having taken place. Each three by three metre cell holds two prisoners.

Many French prisons are the cause of national outcry, with Baumettes considered the worst. Torture is allegedly still carried out, although execution by guillotine was abolished in 1977. Renovations are now being carried out. Well, I had complained about the colour scheme.

Escapes are rare, although in 1990 there was an attempt by helicopter. Of the five escapees, two were wounded by gunfire while trying to climb a rope-ladder to the helicopter and another was found dead at a nearby landing field. Two got away. Forty percent. Bad odds.

On my way there I remembered the prison from a previous trip to Marseilles. Now, instead of being in the company of a young American woman, I was with five men in the back of a police van as we hee-hawed through bumpy cobbled streets. I could catch glimpses of the outside world as it sped past: la Belle France now a cliché of cafes and elegant women. All the sights I'd so long taken for granted were soon to be taken from me, but for how long?

Two years earlier the American woman and I had looked up at the forbidding walls of the prison and wondered what it must be like in there. Her eyes had grown wide with excitement when she'd imagined all the thieves and murderers within. Soon I would know the answers to all her eager questions. I must remember to write to her. I tried to remain outwardly calm as the van entered what I took to be the prison gates. Jesus, this was really happening. With my fellow inductees, I hobbled into a reception area, our shackles and my injury impeding free movement. The others looked tough, but maybe so did I to them. I was unshaven. Good that. Always adds a few years. The next thirty minutes were a blur. It was just as I'd expected from countless films: kit off; brief medical; prison issue clothes; possessions logged. It's funny, but whenever I read memoirs of people who've been in the slammer, they often remember their prison number. I've never remembered my numbers. Also, I knew I wouldn't be in here for too long, Baumettes then being used as a holding prison for many categories of prisoner. I knew I'd soon be swapping Camembert for Edam.

I was led to my cell amid all the bangs and shouts of prison life. It was now hitting home. Another fine mess. Although I knew I'd surely be extradited to Holland I did not know, or could not anticipate, what kind of sentence I might receive. I'd only gone and nicked a bloody Rubens.

At that stage I had no legal representation so my imagination passed sentence. Ten years, it said to me. My inner judge told me that the gendarmes wouldn't have gone to all this trouble for nothing. They wanted justice, or revenge. There'd been so much media coverage that surely the authorities would want to make an example of me as a warning to others that you do not march into a Dutch museum and pluck a priceless painting from the wall like an apple from a tree, then do a runner from a French police station. Ten years! I'd be old. Thirty-five! Oh how my perception of time has since changed.

My cell door was held open by a guard while two more hovered behind me. I half expected a kick, or at least a shove in the back that would send me crashing into the far wall. Another filmic preconception bit the dust as I was politely ushered into my new home from home. My cellmate looked up at me from his lower bunk, his eyes betraying that he was as fearful of who might be joining him as I was of whom I might encounter. It turned out he was a baker; and a murderer. Me, I could have murdered a slice of cake.

My new companion had worked every morning until two a.m. preparing bread and croissants. One night he finished early, went home and found his wife in bed with a man. So he blew the man's head off with his shotgun. He never mentioned what happened to his wife. I later found out that he'd got a token sentence. It was deemed a Crime Passionnel – a very French law.

In Baumettes there was, maybe still is, a system of communicating from cell to cell. If you wanted to move something, info or drugs, say, to someone twenty cells down the line, all you needed was a stick and some string. First you bang the pipes to alert the next cell, then you poke your stick out with your item tied to it. You'd get a swing going and the man in the next cell pokes his stick out and your string entwines it. And so on, until it reaches the intended recipient. All co-operated. You never knew when you might need it yourself.

You never met people in other wings, even those next to you, as wings weren't opened simultaneously. You could be in there twenty years and your best friend or brother could be in a neighbouring wing and you wouldn't see them. There were some hard people in Baumettes, and divide and conquer was the rule of the day.

They moved me to a gaol in Draguignan, the capital of the Var region. Early one morning soon after that I heard keys in the lock. My tendency to leg it meant I got the shackles and manacles. I should have been ashamed to travel under such circumstances but from the smiles I got from gamine young French women, to my young self it was well worth the discomfort. Two especially pretty ones were on the seat in front of us on the run to Paris. I was chained to a big guy on my left, another across the aisle. No chance of escaping. The girls kept popping their heads over the back of their seat. We stopped somewhere and they jumped off the train, but within seconds they were back on again and handed each of us an ice-cream. So sweet. Maybe they thought that by being nice to the cops they'd appeal to their better nature and the blue-eyed gangster would be set free. The girls bade their farewells and les flics and I travelled through the night across Belgium before rolling into Amsterdam. A bumpy ride over cobbles and I was soon tucked up in my new cell.

CHAPTER ELEVEN

No Joke

The Dutch authorities didn't hang about. My time in court was not much longer than it had taken me to lift the painting. But all my prior fears were confounded when I was sentenced to just two years, reduced to eighteen-months on appeal. I have to say I was shocked at the brevity of the sentence, feeling in the arrogance of youth that it somehow demeaned the status of my crime. But then again, it was June '69. The Swinging Sixties was almost over and I was missing the party.

If the French have a legal system which takes into account that people are human, have passions, then the Dutch have a system which judges fairly in other ways. I had taken the picture, sure, but had used no violence in doing so. Also, it had been daylight robbery, which in most legal systems carries a lighter sentence than a crime committed after dark. The judge had also taken into account my statement that we had expressly chosen a painting which would be resistant to damage. I also learnt at the trial that I'd left a thumbprint at the scene of the crime. It was from that time I'd moved the painting to check for attachments and wires. Bang to rights, your honour.

Joke came to the court. I discovered that she'd been to Brighton at the request of the police and had been called as a prosecution witness. She had told them everything she knew, but I didn't blame her, not then at least. What else could she have done? She knew what I'd been up to and she knew I was trouble. At only twenty-two she had moved on. She was with another guy. Anyway, Hans Maas had pleaded guilty and I had left my dabs, so Joke wasn't required to testify in court.

When I got to the prison the tolerant guards allowed her to visit me in my cell. It was nice of her to come. But it was goodbye, although I did see her once again. It's interesting how life's patterns are repeated. Here I was with a woman I loved who'd become a key prosecution witness, and many decades later it would happen again, only the second time I contend it was with malice aforethought.

The prison, near Amsterdam, was liberal and semi-open, but relatively easy as it was compared to Baumettes, it wasn't freedom. Given my youth, I had time on my side. Unlike that later sentence of unspecified duration when I could never see myself getting out sane or alive, this time I should have relaxed and gone with the flow. But of course the one time in your life when you should realise that time, for now anyway, is your friend, is the one time you are most unaware of this. I was desperate to be free. Joke was out there somewhere, and although I did not blame her for what had happened there was a nagging sense of betrayal at work. I did love her and now she was gone. Of course, I was the architect of my own misfortune, but being banged up, with all the spare time that confers, does not always enhance objectivity. How much had her testimony landed me, and Hans, right in it? The more I turned things over in my mind, the more depressed I became. I cheered up when a fellow prisoner told me of a flaw in the prison's security, via the hospital wing.

I tested the system. First off I faked a suicide attempt. I 'threw' myself from a second-floor balcony. In reality I lay prostrate at the foot of the balcony after asking a fellow inmate to hit me in the face as hard as he could. I thought a drop of blood might convince them I was at risk. I was taken to hospital for X-rays. "Not a thing," in Dutch. I knew what the doctor had said because I spoke the language. Joke and I had sat on a riverbank in happier times, with her repeating hundreds of words over and over until I got the hang of them. She thought I wanted to learn the language to get closer to her. I did, but not solely for that reason. I was so in love with her and so jealous that I wanted to know what she was saying when she spoke to her friends; a precursor of my later obsession with JP?

Desperate as I was to get into the prison's hospital wing, I swallowed a biro casing. I don't know what I expected to happen, but whatever it was it didn't. There was a medical every six months, but I was still two months short of that and impatient for freedom. I needed money, so I talked to a guy on day release. He had access to funds and would get me one-hundred Guilders on a promise (about £20).

Having the money lent me patience but also brought anxiety. I'd made my mind up that I was getting out of there, come what may. I'd watched the hospital buses leave over a period of time with their usual quota of twenty prisoners to two guards. No radios. I confirmed this with a couple of trusted inmates who said that I was right, there was a flaw in the system. The accompanying guards would have a dilemma. Do they run after an escaping prisoner and risk losing a bus load, or do they keep an eye on the majority?

I bought a medical from another prisoner who had an earlier appointment and got on the bus, seating myself near the front. Throughout the journey I was sizing up the guards. They looked fit enough, but much lighter than me. Also they didn't look like action men. They wore their hair long, as did virtually every young Dutchman in those days, and this gave them a slightly hippie look. Peace man. Then I saw they were carrying truncheons. I'd become so used to seeing these every day that I had almost come to forget they were there.

We pulled up at the hospital and the two guards made to get off. I'd been told their style was to stand either side of the only door, at the front of the bus. I didn't want to give them a chance to do that. If they were off the bus, in spite of their need to keep an eye on the majority, they might be tempted to run after me, and given their lighter build they might just catch me. No point in evening the odds any more than necessary, so I pushed them aside and off-balance while they were still at the top of the bus's steps. I was away. I could briefly hear the whoops and yells of encouragement from the other prisoners as I made my bid for the rest of my life.

It was late on a winter's afternoon as I ran through the streets of a small town near Groningen, but scared I might raise suspicion I soon slowed to a walk. Back in the slammer I asked a day-release prisoner to research train services to the Hook of Holland. I couldn't afford to wait around. If it had been British Rail I might have had problems, but the train was right on time. I'd kept quiet in prison about being able to speak Dutch, knowing the police would be looking for an Englishman, and my relative fluency allowed me to pass as a native, certainly long enough to get me to the coast.

Maybe my friend's train research hadn't been so good after all as I had to walk miles to the docks from the station. As long as I kept walking I was OK, but whenever I stopped the cold wind sliced at me like razors. It was about one a.m. when I saw a British ferry at its mooring. I got as close as I dared but couldn't get aboard at that hour. There was a caravan, maybe a makeshift office. I slipped under it, my coat wrapped around me, missing my warm cell.

It was a long, cold night. I slept fitfully, ever aware of the possibility of hypothermia and the constant security dog-patrols, which my exhaustion convinced me were there solely for my benefit. Then I imagined the entire Netherlands being combed by armed police, with every large blond man in the land being a prime suspect. I felt a little better at that. At about five the ship started taking on provisions, the noise waking me. I saw the gangplank come down and lorries arriving. My chance.

For three consecutive early-Sixties summers I'd worked cross-channel ferries, making so much on tips and extras that I could spend the rest of the year wandering. So I knew the score. Plucking up courage, I walked onto the ship as casually as my fear, exacerbated by fatigue and cold, would allow. I hid in the gents. I can't describe my relief when I felt the ship moving, although I had no idea of what might await me on the other side of the North Sea. I had no passport and had decided to give myself up once outside Dutch territorial waters. I was debating with myself how best to go about this when I was spotted by a cleaner. "Wha ...what are you doing here?"

"I'm in the shit. Shush!" I suppose I could have tried to bluff it, but the cleaner must have spotted something was up when he'd looked over the partition and had seen me standing on the seat. Maybe I should have said I was scared of mice. Anyway, what sort of cleaner was he anyway, looking over partitions? Pervert.

I let myself be taken to the captain and I told him my story, playing down the escape. Expecting the boat to be turned around, instead I was given the run of the ship. "Drink? I bet you could use one, eh? Hot meal? Got any money? No, on second thoughts, hang on to what you've got. Just sign for anything you need. OK?"

When the ship docked at Harwich the cops came aboard, alerted by the captain, as was his responsibility. They made a few phone calls. This took no more than fifteen minutes. I waited, outwardly insouciant, but inwardly all vital organs were on overdrive. Then, after a whispered discussion between them, I was a free man. "You got lucky, me old son," said a winking cop.

All I had were the clothes I stood up in and the few quid I'd exchanged from Guilders on the boat. I took the train to London. Tomorrow I'd sign on, then make my way down to Brighton to see a man about a painting.

There are not too many things worse than going to your fence's premises than to find them boarded-up. I mean, really boarded-up. Crisscross planks held by six-inch nails. To quote John Lennon – "The way things are going, they're gonna crucify me."

I knew, I just knew, that my painting was where Peter had put it, behind the false panel in the back room. After all, it was the dream that had kept me going. I also knew that there was no point in going in through the back-alley. I'd have needed a JCB to tear away the bars at the rear. No, a full frontal approach was called for here. I went to a pub and waited until I heard those distressing words – "Laydeez an' gen'l'men, 'aven't you got 'omes to go to?"

I strung it out. The later the better would suit me. Not too much post-pub brawling, vomiting and pissing in Brighton in those days. People just went home to bed, so my halcyon memories tell me. It was nicely quiet down The Lanes as I clutched my jemmy in a Woolie's carrier-bag, but when I saw a pair of beat bobbies I kept on walking right past Peter's, returning only when the coast was clear.

I broke in, taking the planks of wood inside to allay the suspicions of any more passing coppers. The place was empty down to its stripped floorboards. Gutted. No panel. No back room. I sat on the floor and silently wept.

I don't know why I had nursed the dream that the painting would still be there.

Thinking about it clearly in the bright glare of disappointment, Peter would surely have returned it in mitigation. But my twenty-five-year-old optimism hadn't made allowances for that one. Where was Peter? Maybe he'd sold the business. Optimism returned. Next day I asked around town. I tried the pubs first but nobody seemed to know much about him. Obviously he wasn't much of a drinker. Then, remembering his tweed jacket, I went to a tea-shop. It was an odd intuition, driven also by my pressing need for an Eccles cake. There they gave me Peter's mother's address.

"You're that young man with the painting, aren't you? You do realise, don't you, that you've destroyed Peter's life?" He knew what he was getting into, I thought, but didn't say so. "Don't expect to find the painting. They've taken it back. And they've taken Peter. Are you happy about that?" Happy? I'd lost a Rubens, and was I happy? Ho bloody ho. If I hadn't been nicked then Fernand Legros would most certainly have found a buyer and Peter would have got his cut. So no tears for him then. I made my excuses and left his mother, remembering her words – "You've destroyed Peter's life." Well fine, but I wasn't exactly thrilled with my own life at that moment. Then again, maybe he'd lied to her about having returned the painting, just to keep her sweet.

Over a few pints, though, I allowed myself to accept that the dream was over. I even rationalised that I'd never really expected to find the painting. I mean, it didn't make sense. If the Dutch hadn't got it back I would have got a longer sentence and there would have been more questioning. Peter could have moved it to a safe place, given the opportunity, but then the mitigation factor meant that surely he would have surrendered it. Then the drink started to talk to me. I began to rekindle the idea that there was a possibility that he had stashed it somewhere. Tomorrow, I decided, I would find out from his mother where he was being held, telling her that I wanted to see him to apologise. But next day I saw the situation with morning clarity. The painting had gone back, if not to its rightful owners (but that's another issue), then at least to its legal custodians. This adventure was over. Time to move on.

I heard that Hans Maas had got a stiffer sentence than me. Probably to do with his being Dutch. I never heard from our beautiful accomplice again, but I knew she hadn't been apprehended. Good. I wouldn't have liked to see her go to prison. I did get the chance to say a final farewell to Joke, if 'say' is the appropriate word. She came to London and somehow I found out where she was staying. I went to see her. It wasn't that I wanted to talk things over; I just wanted a shag. So I shinned up a drainpipe outside her room and entered an open window. During the act she barely awoke and never spoke.

I recently contacted her at her home in Geneva. She didn't want to see me, though. A friend pointed out that it would be wiser for the young art thief and his twenty-two year old lover to stay where they belong, in that other country called the past.

My branch of the Brennan family hails from County Cork. It's odd how the English, and Americans, are so often pleased to discover there's a touch of the Irish in the blood. Maybe it's the disquiet we feel at being linked to Anglo-Saxon Protestantism, with all the yeoman solidity and emotional baggage that implies. To us (seeing myself as English), Ireland is a freedom of spirit, the blood of Finbar O'Toole coursing through the veins, whimsical charm and the kissed

Blarney Stone oiling the highways and byways of life. Little did I know when turning my back on my Irish roots that I may one day need to invoke the Little People in seeking my pot of gold. But Brennan now carried its own baggage. It was 1973 and time to draw a line under that period of my life.

I've never paid much attention to what day of the week it is, other than that I've never really enjoyed weekends or public holidays because the world slows down too much, so when I wandered into a crowded West End bar to meet a girlfriend I wondered what the hell was happening. The place was rammed full of shiny happy people jostling each other for the bar-staff's attention as though Prohibition was about to descend for all eternity. Any normal person would have known it was six pm on a Friday. My girlfriend hadn't arrived, so I made to leave, but at that moment the music started: The Eagles' 'Outlaw Man'.

A friend had chosen the name 'Michael Grey' to avoid his issues; the Michael being ubiquitous in its many forms throughout the world, the Grey being deliberately anonymous, the colour of clerks. But I wanted a name that shouted, if not from the roof-tops, then certainly the cliff-tops. My girlfriend arrived minutes later. Our little joke was the formal address – "Hello, Mr Brennan." "Wrong man", said I. "The name is Eagles, Paul Eagles."

CHAPTER TWELVE

If You Hum it, I'll Play it

I'd had an exhilarating time in Geneva and was eager to get pack there and continue as before. But now there was no Bernie or Fernand Legros. No Joke. The scene had changed. I did now have Pam though, so that kind of made up for things. I needed work, as I'd blown my main chance. A psychologist once told me that people can be broadly divided into two types. His labels for these types were 'music boxes' and 'pianos'. The former can play but one tune and are the majority of humanity. The latter can play infinite tunes; the analogy of course being that they can lead a life of infinite variety, constantly re-inventing themselves. Anyone told of this theory would claim to be a piano, but, according to my friend, relatively few are. I cannot speak for myself on this one, but I did my bit for pianos. I started delivering the plinkety-plonkety bastards. I'd answered an ad; musical ability was not a prerequisite for the job but you had to be strong and willing. At least I was strong, although I didn't realise how heavy pianos are.

We used to wear a harness – a coulasse – a thick, buckled, leather strap around your neck, with your back and shoulders taking the strain as your legs turn to jelly. Like the many tunes of a piano there are many ways to move them. In fact, an infinite variety of ways, usually dictated by an owner who can play the piano but can lift nothing heavier than a wine glass.

Every situation is different and every home presents unique problems. Also, no matter how experienced and professional are the movers, faced with a virtually immovable object men will invariably have deeply conflicting ideas on how best to move it. It was often like that old PG Tips ad, the one with the chimpanzees – "Do you know this thing is on my foot?"

"No, but if you hum it, I'll play it."

They were a great bunch of lads to work with, but I'd come a long way from my dream as I sat in the delivery van remembering that triumphant ride through Laren with Hans, our beautiful friend and St Francis of Assisi. Here I was, only twenty-six and already getting nostalgic for the innocence of the pre-Geneva years. Life had seemed so much easier then, during those long summers back in the Sixties, before I'd even heard of Paul Rubens.

After my time as a piano chimp in Geneva I drifted into a hedonistic lifestyle of long hair and longer drinks. Our hangout then was the Lion, an English-style bar where we lowlifes would gather for debauchery and mayhem. Naturally I managed to get into a fight there. Someone said something and it all used to kick off. In those days this was a regular occurrence in my life and the violence was for real. Not for me, I have to say, all this handbags at dawn stuff that passes for a proper punch-up in too many bars these days. No, it was always straight to the point. At the end of one long day I found myself punching someone in the face. Trouble was, I'd forgotten to put my glass down and he was one of my best friends at the time. He swiftly forgave me, but it was part of a pattern which led to my being barred from Switzerland.

The cops nicked me in the Lion and took me to the airport. I had a girlfriend there at the time, a trolley-dolly (how they hate that) called Pat. They're always explaining that they're trained to do things such as rescuing passengers from sharks in the event of a crash at sea, like Mandy in the 10CC song. The problem is, that one tends to be a career-changing event, so most stick to serving drinks for the duration. This isn't sexist as cabin crews come in assorted genders. Anyway, it is true that women generally don't have the catching gene, but Pat was quick. I tossed her my Vesco Rolex just in time; I didn't want to have to explain its provenance to the police. With admirable aplomb she caught it and stuffed it in her handbag in a move that would have impressed the England cricket selectors.

I was taken to the plane in handcuffs and my passport was handed to me. It was one of those dry, crisp Swiss days, so I don't know how it came to be so wet. Another pissy insult to our gracious Queen? But before I could summon a gunboat to settle the affair I realised just how hungry I was. I had been kept in a cell throughout the previous night and had been under arrest for much of the day. Now, in my experience, cops are usually quite good at taking care of the needs of the inner miscreant, but these guys had neither fed nor watered me. To this day I do not know what I had done. Whatever it was, I don't think it had taken place in the Lion, or Pat would have known. I suspect it was serious though.

So there I was on the plane, a free man, chatting to my fellow passengers. I invented a story to cover my deportation; one where I had been picked-on in the street by some locals and had defended myself but the cops had favoured their own kind; in other words, something palatable to British tourists familiar with the wily ways of foreigners. The clucks of indignation indicated total sympathy for my plight. Everyone gathered round and offered me the portions of their in-flight meals that they didn't want. Then the stewardesses got in on the act. Seconds and thirds came along – "Another bottle of red, Paul."

"Ooh yes please," giving them the old bay-boy twinkle. The lucky gene was in overdrive on that flight, even though I suspected I didn't deserve such treatment.

When I got back to London I looked at my passport to check that it was dry and the ink hadn't run too much. That's when I saw that the Swiss authorities had given me an extra stamp. I was officially a naughty boy, unable to return to the land of the cuckoo clock for six years.

CHAPTER THIRTEEN

E = MC-Squared, Relatively Speaking

When I met Nessie in the mid-Seventies she was part Goldie Hawn, part Judy Geeson, sprinkled liberally with Holly Golightly, although she didn't share the latter's profession. Blondes don't always prefer gentlemen, so we married. But E equalled MC^2 – two eccentrics equalled mad chaos^2, relatively speaking. We were in our different ways too alike to stay together. Now Nessie remembers the bad times more than the good. Like when I left her for another woman, which I suppose is a low point in any relationship. But I remember the good times. I remember the fun. Serendipity decreed in her whimsical fashion that I should live until recently just half-a-mile from Nessie's current home. It cost her a fortune in blinds and heavy curtains as she sought to obliterate any sight of her long-lost past parking its car in the only warden-free spot in town, right outside her kitchen window where it pressed its nose to the glass to satisfy its insatiable curiosity. We'd honeymooned in Rio and travelled the world, me at spouse rates. BA long-haul was BOAC then, and Nessie was very Catch Me If You Can in her stewardess uniform with spotless white gloves and pill-box hat; that Come Fly With Me look from an era when international travel was as glamorous as a Peter Styvessant cigarette ad. In those days the majority of long-haul passengers were male businessmen, so as a stewardess you only got the job if your face, and the rest, fitted. Training standards were high (I was only joking about trolley-dollies) and the women presented as real people rather than today's rictus grins and orange faces pickled in formaldehyde. The prerequisite good looks made flying something to savour. Call me a sexist pig, but this was the Seventies and we all were. Anyway, I'm employing retrospective license here. Then we used to say what we thought. Now we think what we dare not say.

Nessie got wind that I was in the Fulham Tap with Janice. She walked in as Steve and the boys tried to warn me. Too late. It was over, not because I was with another woman, but because I was clearly *with* her. We were young. Well, I was thirty-six, but since men do not rush to embrace emotional maturity, I was but a sprog. Nessie and Janice have enjoyed a fleeting friendship over the years, but now with hindsight I understand that for a woman that kind of hurt never really goes away. Sorry Nessie. Oh, I almost forgot to mention, Nessie was pregnant with our daughter, Samantha, most of whose childhood I was destined to miss.

Whenever I think of Nessie, I think of cars. That was my game when we were first together. The used car trade was lucrative. I kept that sideline going almost up to the present day, it always being good for a bit of running-money, although now new cars are so cheap who wants a used one anymore? In the late-Seventies it was mostly bangers and screamers, the latter being the dissatisfied punters who demanded the then highest standards of Rolls Royce engineering on a rusting fifteen-year-old Mini. Still, those days in the trade helped teach me about people. You find yourself developing an instinct on how to handle different types. Most persist only so much. Nearly all go away in the end, one way or another. Some go in a cloud of exhaust fumes; some with a whimper; some, as in the case of one man, with a bang.

He'd only gone about two-hundred yards. I thought it was the IRA, but it was his engine blowing. I hid under the bed while Nessie did her wide blue eyes trick trying to persuade him I'd gone abroad. Somehow she managed to convince him I was in Antigua, even though he'd seen me only five-minutes earlier. I stayed under the bed while she worked her charm.

Usually I wore them down verbally. Occasionally a thump would suffice. I couldn't, though, bring myself to thump the one with the placard. Outside the Kensington flat day and night for two weeks he was, demanding justice. "Morning. Lovely day we're having," I would say. Then, when I returned – "Looks like rain. Still, mustn't grumble." Bizarrely, we exchanged such pleasantries as though his carrying of the placard was an end in itself and the original cause for complaint was irrelevant or forgotten.

I'd reasoned that people trust vicars and in a strange way, students of a certain kind. You don't see them too much these days, but that rather nerdy, cord-trousered, college-scarved Oxbridge look that you can still glimpse on University Challenge – think a young Stephen Fry and you've got the picture – was a winner. For this, a college scarf is de rigueur, and my affected side-parting and spectacles with plain glass didn't harm the image. I'd taken to flogging Austin 1100's, reasoning that if you stuck to one model you could interchange spare parts and also cut down on advertising costs. All you had to do was run one small ad and with a bit of thought you could flog half a dozen cars from it. Trouble was, they were often of various colours and years and I'd have six or so parked in various places around the square. When a punter phoned I hadn't kept a record of names against models, so a bit of ingenuity was called for to weed out the appropriate car. I'd get round the colour issue by inventing a state of colour-blindness. Now Nessie has to be the most colour-coordinated woman of all time, so when she was around I wasn't allowed out if the collars and cuffs didn't match, but with her flying so often I could then get away with one of my favourite tricks. Down to Mr Byrite's I went, and a combination of tangerines, lime-greens and turquoise was the order of the day. When a punter phoned me and discussed, say, a black 1100, when they arrived I had to pretend that I had only the one car; remember, I was a student. The conversation would run something like this –

"Hello Mr Eagles, I've come about the car."

"R-r-right."

"Is it here?"

"Y-y-yes. R-r-right out-s-s-side. I-I-is it ma-ma-ma-maroon?"

"No, you said it's black."

"Ah. I-I-I'm so-so-so-sorr-y. I'm co-co-co-colour bl-bl…"

"Colour-blind? Yes, my nephew has the same problem. You and he look like you go the same tailor. Ha ha." Oh, how offensive people can be.

The stammer worked wonders. There I was, clearly naïve and hard-up (college scarf, glasses), honest (side parting), and disabled (in need of sympathy, but not like being really afflicted). I got caught out on that just the once as I drunkenly held forth in a local pub when a disgruntled punter came in and caught me at it. At first he was not sure that I was the same person, but then he plucked up the courage to approach me. "Mr Eagles?"

"Yes?" I didn't know him from Adam, I was doing that many cars a week. "Mr Eagles, it's about the car…" Then it clicked. "Your stammer appears to be cured …" Nessie stepped in – "His doctor told him to drink. If only he could always be like this. It's a miracle."

Talking of miracles, the vicar ploy was used on more than one occasion with resounding success, although I once did the college-boy and the vicar at different times with the same punter. After that experience, I gave up the cloth and stuck to academia.

I occasionally met my match. I knew when the game was up. I once sold a Triumph that had been recovered from a Thames slipway. Usual story; the owner had gone to the pub and parked his car well clear of the water at low tide. Of course, the tide came in. I'd bought the car in a hurry and sold it cheap. Trouble was, the buyer complained about dead crabs in the glove compartment. So after unsuccessfully trying to convince him that the car was amphibious, I gave him a full refund. Less the price of a crab supper.

Crustaceans aside, I also had problems with a bird of prey. With a house high in the Bavarian mountains, this guy was an expert on eagles. He'd bought a used ambulance from me. It wasn't that he was a hypochondriac, perhaps needing a quick trip to hospital in an emergency. No, in Germany in the busy high season his ambulance would give him priority over other road users and speed him to his mountain eyrie. Fair enough. But the ambulance didn't work. Maybe that's why the St John's had sold it. Anyway, he got cross with me and became 'The Eagle Hunter'. He scared the life out of me and I bet those Bavarian eagles gave him a wide berth. Any man who buys a used ambulance to escape to a Bavarian mountain-top is going to be an individual, and this guy didn't let the side down. Nessie and I, to get from the flat's living area into the bedroom, used to crawl across the pitch-black hallway while my would-be nemesis screamed through the letterbox – "Eagles, this is The Eagle Hunter. Leave your nest, Eagles". We rarely completed the crawl to the bedroom, having collapsed giggling in the darkness. Eventually he went away and for a while the days felt empty. I like to think he's still out there somewhere, driving a bright, shiny new ambulance high in the Bavarian mountains while eagles soar overhead.

Sometimes clients would arrive unexpectedly early. I'd be clocking the mileage by running an electric drill backwards and the incriminating wire to the Black and Decker would still be hanging from my first-floor window. It's like when someone has a facial disfigurement and you try desperately not to look at it. But whatever your brain tells you not to do, you do anyway. That furtive glance. Did they notice? This followed by inane babble as you try to put up a verbal smokescreen. John Simpson didn't bother with all that. A fellow-trader, among other things he used to clock forward. Imported American cars over a certain mileage avoided tax. So thirty-thousand on the clock was worse than fifty-thousand. You can imagine the look on Arthur Daley's face at such flagrant disregard of the rules of professional conduct.

CHAPTER FOURTEEN

Carry on Camping

Perhaps I should have dieted before attempting to squeeze
through a caravan window, but the embarrassment of getting
stuck half-way through was ultimately worth it, it has to be
said. The long hot summer of '76 saw for me the beginning
of a money-spinner that was to run for over a decade. It was
one of those pivotal moments in life, and it arguably shaped
my entire future. It started with an ad in the late 'News of
the Screws' (sic) – '14-days in the South of France from only
£49.50'. Too good to miss. So off I went.

The convoy of coaches left London Victoria at lunchtime
on the Friday and arrived at Mediterranean Camping Holidays
campsite in Port Grimaud, across the bay from St Tropez, some
twenty-four hours later. I counted the convoy: five coaches each
carrying fifty passengers. There was money to be made here.

When we arrived, exhausted, we were greeted by a field
of four-berth frame-tents. It seems unlikely now in the age
of low-budget airlines that people would even contemplate
a twenty-four hour coach journey of this kind unless fleeing
a war-zone, but for most of the people on that trip this
was their first journey abroad and it was a huge adventure
to a place of virtually guaranteed sunshine and the furtive
possibility of sex with a stranger. All the tents were clean and
fully-equipped, and the staff were eager and friendly young
Brits and Aussies. That's when they were sober.

Large men and sleeping-bags make strange bedfellows, especially when the local ants seem to think they have the right to share your accommodation. The heat was unbearable as a high-summer Mediterranean sun beat down for twelve hours daily producing conditions under canvas which surely flouted the Geneva Convention. Fortunately, my natural curiosity ensured that I would enjoy only a short stay there.

Instinct told me that the site's administrative caravan held the key to my future. Like Indiana Jones in search of the Ark of the Covenant I started in through the locked van's open window. It was only when I was halfway through and felt a pair of hands on each foot that I realised the game was up. The owners of the hands, two big Aussies, tugged hard, and after a while I popped out, only to be confronted by a large crowd of holidaymaking families eager for a diversion. This wasn't the sort of situation to cause trouble in, so I allowed myself to be marched to reception and then off the site. I explained that I'd tripped and had become stuck as I fell forward. This obvious lie raised a laugh and defused a situation which could so easily have involved the police.

Two-months later I drove down to the South of France with Steve (Lish the Lush) Lishman and a friend who'd had some experience of selling travel. We must have checked every campsite between the Italian and Spanish borders before settling on a site at Canet Plage, near Perpignan. We naively avoided going for a site on the Riviera as we felt that Mediterranean Camping's Port Grimaud site offered too much competition. So instead we offered a resort which few in the UK had heard of.

We formed a company – Camping Club of the Mediterranean Ltd (known as CCM) – and set-up office in Nessie's and my spacious Kensington flat. For the first year we traded from there. Poor Nessie would return exhausted from one of her frequent round-the-world trips to be confronted by the chaos of CCM's office in her living-room. Apart from the office being open seven days a week, the telephones were non-stop at all hours. When you've just come back from a three-week tour of duty and the last leg has been a flight from South Africa full of arse-grabbing businessmen, you do feel you deserve a bit of peace and quiet. The days would invariably end in some sort of party in a flat that always seemed full of strangers. There'd be people sitting on the sofa whom you assumed were friends of one of the guys in the flat, a couple of rooms having been rented out. They rarely were. It was chaos and no way to run a business.

Despite that, during the first season, by advertising in the weekend nationals, we took two-thousand-five-hundred clients. It was encouraging, but against Mediterranean Camping's seven-and-a-half thousand we were not competing. We clearly had to address our marketing strategy.

For the second year ('77/'78) we opened an office in London's Holland Park Avenue and held a launch party at the flat to which was invited the PA of Mediterranean Camping's English owners. We got her drunk and made an impression in soap of her office keys. A locksmith in Paddington duly obliged and one of my colleagues slipped into Medi's offices on the Friday night and borrowed their mailing-list for the weekend. We photocopied the contents and replaced the file with seconds to spare on the Monday morning. This saved a fortune on advertising and led to Medi Camping's guys offering to put a Molotov cocktail through our window, an offer which we politely declined. That season we took ten-thousand paying customers.

On the day we were to move into the new offices I was arrested. The delightful Sally, who'd been with us from the beginning, and another of my employees, had gone to

Holland Park to find the door locked so had visited the flat to try to find me, but there was no reply to the doorbell. For once the place was empty. Then they heard heavy breathing behind the door, which of course could mean only one thing. They knew that Nessie was flying and I was the only person they expected to be in the flat. Although I was then only in my thirties, they'd deduced that I'd had a heart attack, such was my love of food. Shouting through the letterbox produced no response, so they returned to Holland Park, only to find the police waiting there. They then learned that I'd been taken to Vine Street nick for my part in an international car theft ring. There had been a major misunderstanding in which, for reasons I cannot remember, I had told a car buyer who'd complained too much that I was a DS Johnson. This had been reported to the police and they had begun a phone-tap on the flat, which, through a hilarious set of misunderstandings and misinterpretations had led them to conclude that I was the mastermind of said gang. All in all, it was an inauspicious start for the new office. The heavy breathing? It was my Cavalier King Charles spaniel, Suzy.

Our original client-base was mainly northerners: miners and factory-workers and their families. Then came an ever-increasing proportion of younger singles, an embryonic 18-30s market. That's when the fun really began.

The name's Craig, Tim Craig. His son, Daniel, was probably at home in Chester watching Roger Moore reruns of his future self and disagreeing with the Sheena Easton song that 'Nobody Does It Better' as Tim charmed exhausted young women arriving on-site after a twenty-four-hour journey to sun, sea, sand and sex. His usual daywear consisted of Speedos, shades, a surfboard under his arm (even on dry land) and (here I'm sure my memory is playing tricks) a diver's knife between his teeth. No, it was strapped to his thigh.

Tim would conduct the client induction meeting, which took place outside his caravan. The clients would assemble: singles, couples, families with children. Among them would invariably be a smattering of pretty young women. Half-way through his speech Tim would select a suitable candidate and take her into his van. As cheering, bemused, or horrified clients looked on, the caravan would rock back and forth, like in a scene from 'Confessions From A Holiday Camp'. Eventually, Tim would emerge, freshly-showered, with his wolfish grin in place, and carry on the meeting as though nothing had occurred. The women always stayed inside, probably hoping that nobody would recognise them once they had a tan.

Among the male clients Tim became known as 'The Commandant', partly because of his blond crop, but also because of his strong-arm tactics in enforcing lights-out. Ably assisting Tim in his site manager role was Dennis Norton. Bearing more than a passing resemblance to Steve McQueen, astride his 'Moto Guzi' the former East End tear-away looked every inch the south of France adventurer. When asked if he was ex-Foreign Legion he would give a non-committal gallic shrug, although even his gestures had a cockney accent, adroitly confirming what the questioner wished to hear and doing no harm at all to his hard man reputation.

'No noise after midnight' was the rule, and the witching hour was lights-out, in every sense, especially for those who disobeyed. Tim and Dennis would prowl the camp from eleven-thirty onwards, 'tickling sticks' at the ready. These were baseball bats, with the slogan 'your head goes here' emblazoned along their length. They were effective deterrents, and the only noise on the camp after midnight came from whichever tents Dennis or Tim chose to visit.

"Pssst!" From the roof of the shower-block a face wearing camouflage paint and a black woollen hat appeared. "I say, chaps, the escape committee meets at twenty-one-hundred hours – 'Greasy Joe's'. Pass it on." The voice was clipped, cut-glass. It belonged to the ever-busy 'White Rabbit', named after the character in Alice in Wonderland – 'I'm late, I'm late, for a very important date'. It was an apposite nickname for reasons other than busyness, for Wonderland was where this white rabbit lived.

Although never having served in the military, he had been 'decorated' with just about every medal ever awarded, and a few more besides. His most prestigious medal, though, was the 'Legion d'Honneur'. You do not receive France's highest honour for nothing, and in the case of 'Le Lapin Blanc' (to give him in this context his French name), it was, according to the rabbit, Charles de Gaulle no less who had personally decorated him. Soon after landing his RAF Lightning for emergency refuelling at an Algerian airfield during the OAS days in the Sixties, the White Rabbit found the base under attack. Field Marshall de Gaulle was at the time conducting an inspection. Seeing that France's revered leader's life was in danger, the one-day Camping Club of the Mediterranean's intrepid Chief Escape Officer leaped into action. Vaulting into his aircraft's cockpit he turned its machine-guns on the enemy troops. Swivelling the Lightning's nose back and forth he raked deadly fire on the attacking freedom fighters. Field Marshall de Gaulle was saved. He showed his gratitude by awarding Le Lapin Blanc the Légion d'Honneur on the spot.

Years later, when confronted by an irate Frenchman, and holder of a true Légion d'Honneur, who questioned the validity of the White Rabbit's medal, our hero responded in fluent French with true sang froid – "Sir, an English gentleman never discusses acts of valour!" When last spotted, he was driving a number fifteen bus through central London, wearing his driver's badge with pride.

CHAPTER FIFTEEN

Drowning was Popular

Throughout history, the many notable battles between France and England have usually ended in an English victory, if you discount William's trip to Hastings. However, with the Battle of Greasy Joe's think more The Little Big Horn than Agincourt. OK, Custer's last stand took place on American soil, but the end result was a crushing defeat, much like Greasy Joe's. And it had all started innocently enough.

The White Rabbit had convened the Escape Committee for twenty-one hundred hours at Greasy Joe's bar. Nobody can remember its proper name, but Greasy Joe was the proprietor of what was basically just a windsurfers' beach bar with good music and better women.

As with all great historical battles it's essential to understand the lie of the land. La Presqu'ile de Giens is a hammer-shaped peninsula with two parallel two-kilometre roads about three hundred metres apart forming the hammer's handle. The campsite was on the east road, Joe's on the west. The roads were divided by a saltwater lake which served as a desalination plant. The English army assembled on the campsite, emerging from their sea of tents like Henry V's troops before Agincourt. The French, meanwhile, were assembling in the bars of nearby Toulon. The English, to their credit, were running against national stereotype; all they wanted was a pleasant night out, a few beers and a laugh.

The French, all young men, wanted to drive out the foreign invader. This was the late Seventies and they were not used to an influx of tourists, particularly the type CCM provided in droves – loud, gauche and often drunk on beer. The locals were especially shocked by that last bit. They really had never seen anyone get deliberately drunk on beer Wine, yes, but beer-swilling was to them beyond the pale. Mon Dieu, we must teach these barbarians a lesson. They hadn't seen large northern lasses in mini-skirts and platform heels before, but that's another story.

The escape committee meeting was in full flow when they burst in, baseball bats swinging and sawn-offs at the ready. In the carnage heads were cracked and legs broken. Some of our clients got away by crawling across the desalination plant. Others made the long and arduous journey around the hammer-head while being picked off by motorcycle-riding raiding parties. It was a long night. Tim and Dennis were elsewhere, otherwise they might have helped even the odds. Throughout, the police were conspicuous by their absence, although once we started giving them regular gifts their standard rose.

The White Rabbit could, although a florid Anglo-Saxon, easily pass as a Frenchman from the north, thanks to his fluent French. This he did, displaying the same level of heroism that had 'saved' De Gaulle's bacon – "Les Anglais. Pah!"

Most of the clients involved in the battle were due to go home the next day, which is what they did, apart from those detained in hospital. I was in the London office at the time and was amazed by the lack of reference to the event, both in terms of phone calls and letters of complaint. I can recall us receiving only two which referred directly to the 'Battle of Greasy Joe's'. People, even then, were more used to a hard life and were brought up not to complain. That's the only explanation I can give. Imagine that happening in today's rampant compensation culture. However, although there was only scant mention of an incident which would nowadays merit week-long tabloid coverage, we did use to receive complaints on remarkably trivial issues. Some people found it genuinely shocking that the locals had the temerity to speak French, and who would have thought that there were ants to be found on Mediterranean campsites? Squirrels were once flippantly described by a staff-member as 'tree rats'. That little comment resulted in a deluge of the 'how-dare-you-expose-my-children-to-vermin?' variety. But in a strange way, these were not complaints. They were people's way of dealing with the unfamiliar, 'abroad' then being totally foreign to many.

To return to the matter of clients not complaining over serious issues, there was one letter which would make even the most jaded complaints department suffer a collective jaw-drop. A woman had written in to complain that she was unhappy with this, that or the other. So it goes. Then on the second page, about paragraph three, she 'mentioned' that her thirty-six-year-old husband had died of a heart attack on the coach. The callous drivers (French, natch) had left his body by the roadside (by a ditch, natch) and driven off, ignoring her cries and those of her weeping children. That bit took about three lines, then off she went again, about how angry she was that a crab had bitten little Jimmy's toes, or some such. No mention again of the dead husband. She concluded her letter by asking for a full refund because of her 'disappointing' holiday. Of course, it was a clumsy attempt at getting a refund. Clearly she needed to hone her communication skills.

Over the camping years we took a few casualties. Drowning was popular. So too was falling off mountains.

Heart attacks were not uncommon. Early on, at Canet Plage, we had a death which was somehow not sad. A man in his mid-eighties, still sprightly, had taken his younger (early seventies) girlfriend on holiday. He'd wanted to show her where he'd fought with the Republicans in the nearby Pyrenees during the Spanish Civil War. He also wanted to show her something else. So enthusiastic was he on the latter that he expired on the job. We obtained permission from his distant family and carried out his last wish that his ashes be scattered in the mountains so he could be with his fallen comrades at arms.

We had a young Pole working on the site at the time. The Iron Curtain was still tightly drawn, yet somehow he'd managed to escape to the West. He was white-blond with a distinctly Slavic cast to his features, yet in order to throw off the scent the secret police he was convinced were watching his every move, he called himself Hank. He was, he also said, an Egyptian from Cairo. Because of his haste to leave Poland he had few possessions. So when the old Republican died, 'Hank' was in his tent in no time, helping himself to any item of clothing he could lay his hands on, ignoring the fact that the tastes of men in their mid-eighties tend to differ from those of young men in their early twenties.

On our advice 'Hank' became Dutch. At the end of that season he travelled up by coach from the South of France and waved farewell to the other passengers at a service stop near Paris before 'departing' for Holland. While the passengers were otherwise engaged he hid himself under the coach and clung on for dear life all the way to London Victoria. The coach drivers had told him of the best place to hide; somewhere where he had an even chance of not falling to his death. We picked him up from Victoria, shaking and filthy. He was stone deaf for three weeks. He met a woman and entranced by her friendliness he soon married her. He now had the right to stay in England.

A friend with a campsite just up the road from our place had an unusual experience. One weekend his coach company had supplied vehicles with upright seats (much like standard bus seats) rather than the advertised recliners. Naturally, after a twenty-four hour journey, his clients were none too happy. A mob gathered, seeking justice. Like a sheriff confronting a lynch party, my friend, ably assisted by beer with vodka chasers, stood down four hundred yelling clients. Eventually, after much bantering (some wag even produced a noose), my friend selected six people as representatives. Each of these were then 'consulted'. One man, whose diabetic daughter's life had been saved a week earlier by Dennis (then working with my friend), was given a 'talking to' behind the gent's shower-block. No witnesses. Others were consulted in sundry fashion. My friend elected to take one out to dinner, intending on charming her into dropping her complaint. They ended up married. The thing is, she wasn't even staying on his site. She had just happened to be passing through.

After his General Gordon at Khartoum moment, my friend organised a stone-throwing contest between his staff and some of his happy campers. The prize was a bottle of champagne. One staff member and one camper rowed a suitable distance out to sea and acted as judges. There were some impressive attempts, and a camper won. It turned out that he was a county javelin champion. The spot where the stone landed was duly marked with a buoy. After that my friend used to charter a yacht and hold lavish lunches offshore, just beyond the marker buoy, and bombard the site with increasingly impolite megaphone messages as the afternoon's drinking wore on, secure in the knowledge that no-one could touch him.

Another time he tried to put into action what he'd heard about subliminal advertising. He was convinced that if he set up speakers hidden in trees around the site he could bombard the sleeping campers with whispered messages to their subconscious so that on a given day the following season they would all collectively book for another two weeks of torment. His advertising agent dissuaded him, as did his wife when he tried to persuade her to dress as the Virgin Mary and stand on the roof of a barn in the Pyrenees in the hope of attracting paying pilgrims.

We were aware that the campsite was a little isolated out there on the tip of a peninsula. True, there was Greasy Joe's and a couple of beach bars, but unless our male clients wanted to spend their days drinking ice-cold beer in hot sunshine watching topless French nymphets play beach-volleyball there was little else to do. Anyway, everywhere closed at seven, apart from Greasy's, so we had to, as my mother would say, make our own entertainment.

London buskers couldn't believe their luck when one of our management team passed by. There they were, down in the tube station – 'Let me take you by the hand, and lead you through the streets of London …' Next thing – "I left my home and my family, I was no more than a boy …" This to a crowd of five hundred jeering, drunken, happy campers. A total lack of talent was no bar to employment. The only criteria was a need to keep the onsite rioting to a minimum. Far better the mob's ire be directed at one hapless soul was our philosophy. The conversation in the tube station would have gone something like this – "Hi. Fancy playing a gig in the south of France?"

"Fuck off, man."

"No, I'm serious. Do you?"

"Yeah, but …"

"Be at Victoria Coach Station tomorrow at noon. Here's my card. What's your name?"

"Stewart."

"See you tomorrow then, Stewart. Be on time." Even with beer cans whistling around your head at least you were getting attention. From sleepwalking clerks and secretaries, to find yourself in front of five-hundred screaming punters must have felt like playing Wembley Stadium. Some of those guys may be still down there on the Croisette in Cannes – 'Yesterday, all my troubles seemed ...'

We found this concert pianist tinkling the ivories in a Toulon three-star. He'd modelled his appearance on Beethoven and was deaf to any criticism as he strode in a state of long-haired intensity through the campsite in his dated evening wear as though en-route to the Albert Hall. One night we'd arranged for him to give a concert, backed by local musicians, in the campsite's restaurant, attended only by Steve and his wife, Miss Ellie, me and Janice, and the local Huissier and his mistress of the moment. We all wore full evening dress, not, I think, as a piss-take, but because that is what we felt the occasion demanded. Outside the firmly-locked restaurant a raucous mob was gathering, their sun-reddened faces pressed against the window panes. As the evening wore on and Beethoven came to the 1812 Overture, we could barely hear the music over the howling of the mob as 'The Night of the Living Dead ' came to life. In the interests of political correctness I'll draw a veil over the dwarf-tossing and wet T-shirt competitions. Different times.

CHAPTER SIXTEEN

She Liked the Penguins

We persuaded some Page Three girls to come down to Les Cigales in the early Eighties. The Sun's Page Three was then new and the girls were household names. They also hadn't all succumbed to an identikit look of fake tan and girl-band hair, not to mention the dread silicon implants. They were also capable of fluent speech. I was quite taken with Sian Edie Jones and Jilly Johnson and I still have shots of Sian and I swimming from a boat. She was naked. I sometimes look at these photos. When I'm alone.

I often wonder where some of the characters of that period are today. There was 'Animal', a six-four Aussie 'Okker' with a heart of gold; 'Karate John', who for obvious reasons was always good to have around. Then there was Tony Glenn, a giant Glaswegian who'd served twelve years in the Guards. It was never a fair fight for Tony unless he had at least seven or eight on to him at a time. Sally? Perhaps you had happy little Sally's, although so much time has passed they could well be years older than the young and free you of those distant days. Then there was Leigh, a mainstay for many seasons; a Kiwi, who during quieter moments we used to tease by getting her to say 'pen'. It comes out as 'pin'. Try it with a Kiwi. Hours of fun for young and old alike. Cathy? Where are you and far too many more to mention? Oh, what happened to you, although I know what happened to me, what became of the people you used to be? Oops, that sounds like plagiarism. Better move on.

The guy who'd worked for me at CCM from the beginning went out on his own. This set our 'dirty tricks department' in motion. We managed to temporarily stop his business partner's source of finance thus preventing them from securing their chosen campsite for their first season, forcing them to seek a compromise. This was a site at Argelès sur Mer, in the south of France near Spain. The problem was, the Dutch businessman they'd rented it from was double-booking, so every week six coach-loads of people would arrive there only for them to be forced into temporary accommodation. This was an adjacent site. Now, if I thought I'd received unusual complaint letters, how's this? – 'Dear Sirs, We had a very nice holiday, but there was a small problem. A Grizzly Bear kept trying to put its claws through the side of our tent. This kept my daughter awake all night. So did the roaring lions. She liked the penguins though …' Wrong country? No, a travelling circus had pitched camp next-door to the temporary site. The next week, under media pressure, French cops ringed the town to keep my friend's coaches out. He managed to get them diverted to another site we'd found for him several hundred miles to the east. He flew down there and was in the bar when they arrived. But they were later than expected, so he hit the beers to pass the time, and instead of telling it like it was he tried to blag his way through the situation, saying that the hills behind the site were in fact the Pyrenees. This didn't go down too well with some of his better-educated clients. He managed to barricade himself in the bar while an angry mob tried to get at him. He phoned our site, Les Cigales, and we dispatched Animal and Karate John to help Tony Glenn, who worked for my friend. In like Flynn they went, burning rubber on the gravel outside the bar. They cleared a path for my friend and got out of there in a cloud of dust.

When some of the people who'd been on that site eventually returned to London they came into my friend's office while he was at his desk. Fortunately these were Christians, so instead of starting any trouble they simply sat on his office floor and sang – 'We Shall Overcome'.

My friend wasn't a Christian. He sent Tony Glenn to Argelès-sur-Mer to 'talk to' the Dutch businessman, Franz Harrivan. After having his head held underwater by Tony a few times, Harrivan saw the error of his ways. He soon coughed up, in more ways than one. That's how it was with us then. A bunch of cowboys who'd perform dirty tricks on each other then meet in the bar later and have a laugh about it. At times it was more like the Wild West and it was a lifetime away from today's over-regulated age.

It was around this time when I had a life-threatening experience in a small car every bit as deadly as my earlier encounters with bubble-cars. The Seventies Matra-Simca Bagheera was unique in that it had three front seats with a mid-engine. This was the Courrèges-themed limited edition and it matched its owner's hat and handbag. A business rival, Patsy had suggested that she drive us from La Presqu'ile de Giens to Monte Carlo. On the way we were to check on gear stolen from our respective campsites. We suspected one of our staff members, we weren't sure whose, had been selling the stuff down the coast. Near Sainte Maxime was a lock-up guarded by a young Moroccan. With a wad of money under his nose he named the culprit. Then we changed the padlocks, threw a few theatrics to persuade him not to change them back, and sped off. This was strictly business, so what happened next surprised even the man who thought he'd already had all his surprises. We were driving down the broad sweep of La Promenade des Anglaise in Nice when Patsy asked me to be quiet. "Belt up." I hadn't said a word. "Put your fucking belt on. Now!" With that she threw the car into a sharp sideways left-hand turn. "Don't look! It's Tom." Now, I'd briefly met this Tom. Broad at the shoulder, narrow at the hip, charming, dead eyes. When he'd left I'd asked Patsy about him. "E's one of those ex-'usbands who don't do 'ex'. Even Ray's terrified of 'im."

Ray was her current squeeze, an East End hard man who wasn't scared of anyfink (sic), except dominant women. But who isn't? We called her Modesty Blaise, this Patsy; all flash and Costa Del Crime, with more rings than a New Delhi call centre, the boutiques of Porto Banus her natural habitat. Her ubiquitous fake tan came in a choice of two colours, orange or orange. She dressed like it was always Ladies' Day at Ascot, the modern no-knickers version, always topped by a wide-brimmed hat. What was 'class' in Marbella caused a few pert noses to be raised on the French Riviera. Think Ronnie Knight-vintage Barbara Windsor. This gave rise to a great line from a friend of mine, a rival campsite operator called Nick, ex-Cavalry, founded Fired Earth, very South Kensington – "My dear chap. She simply isn't of our seed." Please excuse my apparent sneering, as I'm here laughing at Nick's attitudes as much as at Patsy. Then too, she later robbed a good friend of mine of a large amount of money and an even larger part of his future, so she deserves a lot worse than that. It was the guy who employed Big Tony, that one.

By now we were sliding around the back streets of Nice while I remembered what she'd told me after I'd met Tom. That he was a Karate Black Belt, a feared enforcer, that he ran prostitution in Nice, that he fought for the British in Malaya in the Sixties. That there, especially at Full Moon, they used to let him roam the jungle alone at night, hunting for prey for his knife. I remembered being shocked when I'd heard stories, apocryphal or not, of how British Paras in the Falklands used to wear necklaces made from the ears of enemy dead. Tom had been at it twenty years before. He killed like a fox, for pleasure. "Patsy. Slow down! Casn't we just stop and have a chat? Does he like beer? Ice-cream? I mean, he's met me on the campsite. He knows there's nothing between us."

"If he sees me alone with any man, they're dead. You don't get it do you? 'E's always tooled up and 'e's got the Gendarmes in 'is pocket. You ain't got a prayer. Me too."

"Ah." Another screech and slide and we were on a fast straight. "Which car is it?" I asked, not unreasonably, peering in the mirror. "Does it matter?" Silence. "OK, it's the red Jag." I saw it then, slewing from side to side behind us, trying to overtake humble Renaults and Citroëns. "What a beauty." It was an XK150S drop-head Coupé, with the hood up. "Is it the 3.4 or the 3.8?"

"What?"

"Only asking."

"The 3.8, one-hundred-and-thirty mph. Happy?" Mmm. Fast then.

"What's it worth?"

"Shut it." It was late afternoon, the traffic building. The Bagheera was named after the panther in The Jungle Book, one cat against another. The Bagheera's nimbleness won the day. Aided by Patsy's feline driving skills it finally bested the power of the Jag and its psychotic driver. She then took a circuitous route to disguise the fact that we were heading east to Monte Carlo or bust. On the Corniche just outside Monaco we were caught in a jam, down to walking pace. So it wasn't a stone that hit the passenger side-window. "What the hell was that?"

"Probably an air rifle," said Modesty Blaise with admirable

sang-froid. "Kids." I felt it just wasn't my day. But then again, I hadn't been shot. Mustn't grumble.

The later camping years coincided with 'The Boys from the Blackstuff' era of high unemployment in the early Eighties. We found ourselves taking on a lot of staff from the north of England, suffering as it did more than the south. Although doing what could have been described as a dream job, with little real work, constant booze and sunshine and sex on tap, some of the staff were still disgruntled. To them, we campsite owners were loaded, and they seemed to imagine that we had come to this position because it had dropped off the nearest tree. To them we were exploiters, a philosophy much in keeping with the times. Many of the staff were wonderful, staying with us for years, but there was always a small clique which was out to make mischief.

On some crazy whim I had taken to collecting stuffed animals, so it became an ongoing game for certain workers to hide them when we weren't looking. The stuffed bear would pop up in the most surprising places. One day he'd be sitting on a bar-stool, another day in the women's showers. But my real favourite, which the dissenters knew, was Onze, my stuffed owl, so named because he cost the equivalent of eleven quid in a local flea-market. I was very attached to old Onze, and so he would disappear even more than the bear. Being a bird, he usually found himself in high places, and I once found him sitting on the roof of the complex, another time up a tree. I let all this mischief go, reasoning that it was an outlet for the staff's frustration and harmless enough.

A parting gift was when they put sugar in the petrol tank of my old TR2, the car that had seen me through many earlier scrapes. But even thus violated, the old girl came good. Unaware of her plight, I drove from Toulon with Onze and the bear, up to Geneva, over the Jura, and back to England. I almost made it to the office, but blocked injectors finally got to her in Park Lane.

It all came to an end after eight good years. The miners' strike and its knock-on effect among our main client-base gave us two lean years, and when the market returned it soon became pretty clear that people no longer wanted to sit on a coach for over twenty-four hours in extreme discomfort. They wanted to fly. But it had been fun, and there were still the grapes of wrath to come.

CHAPTER SEVENTEEN

Grapes of Wrath

Each September, the coach/camping holiday companies, which by 1985 were several, needed to run empty coaches down to the South of France to bring back their last clients of the season. They had to pay for fuel, ferry charges, drivers and motorway tolls, so they were willing to sell their empty seats at a rate which just covered their costs. Put bums on those seats and you have a profit. September was grape-picking season. We'd pay up-front for fifteen coaches (seven-hundred and fifty seats) and advertise grape-picking holidays in the press. One-way only. That's the deal. It could be argued that we were exploiting gullible young people, but we were young ourselves then and to us this was just another angle. The coach/camping holiday business was running out of steam and here was a chance to squirrel away some running-money for the winter. In spite of this, we took care not to guarantee jobs; we'd simply take you to the grape-picking regions and then you're on your own.

We rented a short-term serviced office in London's west end, put in the ads, and waited for the phone to ring. It never stopped. For a couple of weeks it was fine. The coaches would roll out of London's old Gloucester Road Coach Station full of eager 'grapies'. We should have stopped then, but, I thought, just one more week. It was the third week when that scourge of Eighties free enterprise struck. Esther Rantzen and her

'That's Life' team rode into town on their white chargers. There we were, at the coach station with hundreds of grapies ready for the off, when suddenly all hell broke loose. Cameras were everywhere; shouts, confusion, chaos.

We'd had wind of it. The red-tops were on the case. A few days earlier, the Sun I think it was, had run a story which showed a rat in a ditch eating a slice of birthday cake as large as the rat itself. There was another shot of a sad young woman. It was her twenty-first birthday, and the rat, her sole companion, had stolen a piece of her cake. I always remember the solitary candle sticking out of the slice as the rat tucked in. Anyway, she was one of our grapies. We were fair game. Rantzen had something to get her teeth into.

I was prepared. My disguise consisted of a long mac, a Sherlock Holmes hat, fake glasses, you know, the kind with eyeballs on the end of springs with a fake plastic nose attached, and a Groucho Marx moustache. I could look the world squarely in the eye. The other guys in the scheme were kept busy. One was Bill Prosser. He was deeply involved in a lifelong love affair with his favourite person, himself. No accounting for taste, as some who'd met him might say. So, he was the ideal man to front the cameras and deflect flak. The other guy, when questioned by reporters, simply said – "I'm sorry I don't have time to talk to you, but I have a responsibility to our paying customers." With a wide-eyed, earnest delivery and frowning over a clipboard, he knew they wouldn't show that bit – they needed to feed off aggression. I later learnt that when confronted by confused grapies he'd diverted about two hundred of them onto coaches that were heading for Spain. That meant oranges. A few quid in the pockets of grateful drivers and they were off.

In case at this point you feel I'm gloating over exploitation, I should point out that many people who'd turned up on spec booked and paid under the noses of Rantzen's crew. Someone shouted – "Where's the sweaty fat man?" So I'm on the big-boned side. So I was sweating. 'That's Life' put that down to a guilty conscience. I put it down to an aversion to paying back several thousand pounds in readies. Naturally, the majority no longer wanted to travel. "There he is!" went up the cry, as a less-than-svelte man slowly drove his turquoise convertible Roller through the coach station. I don't know what he thought was happening as he was pursued by a mob of some two hundred people, many with cameras. You need an ego to drive that car in that colour; maybe he thought he was getting the attention he deserved. I used the diversion to ditch the disguise. I carefully folded the raincoat over my arm and strolled off to the pub, unrecognised amid the mayhem.

I'd got the idea for the glasses on springs a week earlier. There'd been a small hitch in getting some grapies off from another coach station, Kings Cross. They were waiting for three coaches scheduled to pick them up. We were there too, waiting in the wings. The only one they knew by sight was our man from the office, Andy. He was tiny, about five-four, and when he was under stress his eyes took on a 'Looney Tunes' look, as though on stalks and spinning at the same time. Well, the coaches didn't show, so this Andy was the focus of the grapie's wrath. Some chased him but he'd got off to a good head-start so it looked as though he'd get clean away. Memory plays its tricks, but I swear that when they caught him they stretched him into impossible shapes while his eye-stalks and tongue grew to two metres long. But that Roger Rabbit moment was soon forgotten when we arrived back at the office to find a mob trying to break down the door. To have furtively slunk away would have been a sign of guilt, so one of our guys acted on instinct. He took a running-kick at the door screaming – "Come out you bastards, we know you're in there." He got so carried away that he nearly kicked the door off its hinges. On this occasion it was the coach company that took the blame. Their drivers had forgotten the pick-up, thinking they had an empty run. We, and in turn, our clients, were refunded.

I remember Prosser chasing Andy around the office when something had gone wrong, slapping him like Manuel in Fawlty Towers. I wonder where Andy is now. Probably making a fortune in IT. He was a bright guy. Just had these funny eyes.

Talking of characters from those times, there was another, but I won't use his name. Suffice to say he had this knack of rubbing people up the wrong way while remaining convinced he was the epitome of urbane charm. Since you either have charm or you don't, it's wise not to fake it. We can all see through that at about three-years-old. He hadn't spotted that one. Some camping customers had. They threw him from the top of Calais harbour wall. It was a long way down and they didn't even bother to ask whether he could swim.

CHAPTER EIGHTEEN

From Your Own Correspondent

In between all these activities I further amused myself by expanding my already varied CV: RAF signaller (AWOL); merchant sailor; lifeguard; used-car salesman; doorman; minder; bent baggage-handler; art thief; fund salesman; rock impresario; entrepreneur. Then I had my imaginary jobs, like the one where I was a roving international correspondent for The Sunday Times. The pay wasn't so good, as it was only imaginary, but the perks were excellent. With Nessie a long-haul air stewardess, as her spouse, for now at least, I could travel the world at ten percent of the going rate. As an imaginary Sunday Times reporter, a forged press accreditation and a bit of blarney opened all sorts of doors.

It was the early Eighties when I found myself in Haiti during the Baby Doc years, a place still full of suited, shades-wearing Tonton Macoutes, the ubiquitous private army of the late dictator, Papa Doc Duvalier. It's estimated that during their decades-long reign of terror they were responsible for the at least sixty-thousand deaths of their fellow Haitians. They still guarded the new dictator, Baby Doc, but when I met Monsieur Jolieville at the bar of the Oluffsen Hotel they were nowhere to be seen. I felt like a correspondent in a Graham Greene novel as I stood next to a character straight out of the pages of one of his books.

The hotel was the finest in Haiti's capital, Port Au Prince, and Jolieville held court there. I knew him immediately, simply from a written description. He was dressed like an Edwardian English gentleman, complete with linen suit, panama hat, a cane and the bizarre affectation of spats. "Ça va, M. Jolieville." I offered him my card. "Ah. The Sunday Times. A fine newspaper." We got talking. He was as charming as a Minister of Information and court jester should be. Even now that Papa Doc was gone, Jolieville still enjoyed an untouchable status under Baby's regime. Though the bodyguards were nowhere to be seen, I felt that they would soon appear if he seemed to be under the slightest threat. "So, Mr Eagles, you are a journalist. Would you like to hear my story?" I kept up the lie as he spoke of the days under Papa Doc, his unguarded comments demonstrating that he felt he was beyond reproach from the current regime. He talked of the disappeared, of the cult of Voodoo. How Papa Doc would walk into, say, a jewellers, and virtually strip the place bare, with the owners pretending to be pleased that he had bestowed his patronage on their establishment, but knowing in effect that they were ruined. How his 'taxmen' would collect duty from anyone who seemed to be making a pile and then take it in suitcases straight to the dictator. Yet while he talked of the misdeeds of another, you sensed that this urbane man had somehow had an extraordinary influence over that very dangerous man.

I don't know why, but I suppose I somehow took it as my due when, after we'd chatted awhile, he offered to show me around. He arranged to meet me in the hotel bar the next day. He would take me to Sans Sourci, the ruined palace at Cap Haitien, modelled on the Palace of Versailles. We drove there, his driver the only other occupant of the car. I'd blagged my way into a few situations using my fake press accreditation, but this was proving to be my strangest 'assignment'. Close to

Sans Sourci, there is another folly, this time a castle built in late Victorian times by the self-styled Henri 1, a 'king' who'd set the template of cruelty in a long line of rulers destined to keep Haiti virtually the poorest country in the world while they got rich. The castle was on a hill and Jolieville and I each sat on a donkey to take us up a track which was inaccessible by car. Henri used to have, according to Jolieville, a novel form of torture, one that certainly wouldn't have appealed to me, given my appetite for food. He'd had a pit dug adjacent to the castle's kitchens and into this he would throw prisoners. The pit was covered by a metal grill, allowing the starving prisoners to smell the roasting meat above and to be occasionally tossed bones on which were the most meagre scraps of meat, enough to remind the soon-to-die of just what they were missing. They also had the added pleasure of being pissed and shat upon.

We then moved on to what, for me, was an even more extraordinary location. At Cap Haitien was a compound of fading villas dating back to the early-Forties. The more astute Nazis had clicked fairly early on that the war was not winnable so they had drifted over, the navy guys being among the first for obvious reasons. There they had built a village, paying their way using looted gold from Europe, more than welcome in another cruel regime. In this political no-man's land without extradition treaties the exiles could continue their Germanic lifestyle untroubled by advancing allies and the court of Nuremberg. Jolieville seemed to know everyone there, and although the ex-Nazis seemed to treat the locals mainly as servants, he enjoyed high-standing. He seemed to sense my surprise. "Haiti welcomes all, whatever their persuasion. We are a very tolerant society. Beer?" The oompah music started up. I was sitting in a place which replicated a Bavarian village, albeit one surrounded by dense tropical jungle and graced by the odd Swastika, with lederhosen and dirndl-wearing locals. I haven't been back since. I suspect that as the war generation dies off there may no longer be Swastikas fluttering in the tropical breeze, but history teaches us that we should never be too sure.

I got around Port-Au-Prince in a battered and borrowed old Merc, keeping my eyes peeled for zombies. I had imagined the place would be full of the undead, lurching every which way in a Voodoo trance, so you can imagine my shock when one appeared in my rear-view mirror. But I was reassured when this one spoke to me in pidgin French. In my experience the average zombie maintains its right to remain silent. She had great big eyes and a wide friendly smile and over the next few days proved to be very much alive as she became my constant companion. She had sneaked into my car while I was in a bar. It was her way of saying hello. About three days into our friendship I had a business meeting at my hotel with a German, one of the Nazis from Cap Haïtien. I had convinced him that I was indeed a Sunday Times reporter and he wanted to tell me his story. Marie, for that was my little zombie's name, was determined to leave me in peace to conduct my 'important' interview for the famous newspaper. I say 'little' because she couldn't have been more than four-eleven, five max. The Nazi and I had barely begun our chat when, before you could say 'Hitler's only got one ball', there was a huge commotion outside. We ran to the pool to find little Marie had been fished out and someone was breathing life into her, she more dead than undead. Thanks to the man's quick response she made a full spluttering recovery, and I carried her back to my room. "What happened?" She began to cry. She was so sorry that my interview had been ruined. "That's not important. What's important is that you're ok."

"But your interview ... I interrupted it. You ..." Then the

truth came out. She had gone into a swimming-pool for the first time ever. She couldn't swim but had seen people walking on the bottom and so thought it wasn't very deep, even for her. Then she decided to walk to the other end, unaware of the slope. Once she was in the deep end she naturally got into difficulty, but didn't want to scream in case she disturbed my interview. So out of respect she thought she'd better die quietly.

CHAPTER NINETEEN

It was Only Rock 'n' Roll, But I Quite Liked it

I was at a stage where I was starting to poke my fingers into many pies, at least those I hadn't already eaten. I had the camping operation, my Harley Street clinics, of which more later, and was soon to move into the care home business, my long-term future. So why not become a rock impresario too?

Steve Lishman had run a club in Antigua and had an ex-wife and two sons there. Reggae was his thing. So he and Doghouse (on account of his habitual hangdog expression) Dan arranged a Reggae night at Bow Town Hall. There were bins full of jerk goat and other Caribbean delicacies, so convinced were Steve and Dan that this event was going to be big.

I got there to find that three bands had turned up and about thirty members of an audience that clearly had nothing better to do. Steve, Dan and I sat around, had some goat, chatted a bit, got pissed. We'd lost money on the night. Still, there were always the balloons, hundreds of them above a net ready for the big moment when they would be released onto the heaving, happy throng below. Well, the dozen or so who had stayed the course. As Dan had said – "At least we've still got the bloody balloons." This thought cheered him up so much he actually looked for a moment as if he wasn't praying for a lynch mob to ride over the horizon and put him out of his misery. Then he almost came to life as he saw through the glass doors that the roadies were about to release them. It was one of those 'you-were-only-meant-to-blow-the-bloody-doors-off' moments as he lurched into the hall trying to somehow push them all back up to the ceiling, screaming – "Not the bloody balloons!" They were only balloons, but their release underscored that the evening had been a dismal failure. Clearly we were not cut out to be rock impresarios. Still, making the best of a bad job we dove in among the balloon-bursting Rastas, they and us giggling like kids in the ganga air. I don't know how much we'd dropped on that Bow evening, but we would come to never forget those bloody balloons.

We went to a Soho club after that to drown our sorrows, there for our idea to be born. Steve had co-produced Mungo Jerry's 'In The Summertime', and he, Dan, and I, had tried our hand at producing another one-hit-wonder. Over a few beers we came up with the idea of running a competition to find a hot new band. As with all beer-induced inspiration it's hard to pin down exactly whose bright idea this was, so we can all claim bragging rights. 'Battle of the Bands' was born.

Most drink-fuelled ideas never make it through the next morning's hangover, but this one had legs and the tapes flooded in, hundreds daily. We'd put ads in the NME and Melody Maker, asking for demo tapes from bands wanting to enter a national talent show. It had to be original material. The idea was simple: we held heats at major nationwide venues, aiming to get six bands from each area. The ultimate winners would get to cut an album and the runner's-up would earn a place on a compilation album. In those days there was a lot of Punk and Ska, with the Rude Boy sound coming through. We got Waxy Maxie to do PR. Waxy was pure rock 'n' roll, a real Denmark Street hustler, and in his element. He got RCA to take-up the recording rights, and we were under way.

All this was funded from Camping Club and even in year-one we got some money back. The events were hugely successful at a provincial level as our bands played to packed venues. It was quite a scene. We had huge trucks touring the country and all our families and friends came along as the circus rolled into town. The Dominion in London's Tottenham Court Road was the venue for the first Final, then it moved to the Hammersmith Odeon in the second and third years.

We'd had a real stroke of luck. TDK Tapes, then one of the biggest and best-known cassette tape manufacturers, was looking for high-profile exposure in the music business and our plan fitted their brief perfectly. They offered us a three-year deal. I had money tied-up in CCM, Harley Street and my new nursing homes business, so I was fighting on many fronts. TDK's offer was manna from heaven. Battle of the Bands took on a life of its own and our sponsors were delighted. Hundreds of tapes flooded in, and we had one man, Duncan, whose sole role was listening to these tapes every day in the basement of my Harley Street slimming clinic. Steve helped him. As a contestant you were probably better off if Duncan and Steve caught your tape early in the day rather than when 'rock fatigue' had settled-in later on. How many would-be rock-greats are now stacking shelves just because the boys caught up with them too late in the day?

Established stars got involved to give their support and stay in touch with their grass-roots: Phil Lynott of Thin Lizzie; Kevin Godley of 10CC and later 'Godley & Crème'; Alsion Moyet and Vince Clark of Yazoo, and every red-blooded male's hot tottie of the day, Kym Wilde. Then there were DJs Paul Gambicini and Mike Reid, and Jimi Hendrix's former manager, the ex-Animal, Chas Chandler.

Although during the Battle of the Bands era I rubbed shoulders with rock and pop royalty of the day, it wasn't a milieu with which I was overly familiar. A case in point is when a thin, long-haired and frankly unusual-looking man asked for a lift to Birmingham (where unknown to me he was to judge a Battle of the Bands heat) in our company Austin Princess. He seemed like a nice guy and I asked him what he did, as you do. He said he was in the music business too, so I blurted out my usual 'stick with me, kid, and I'll make you a star'. It was only when we reached the NEC and my new friend was mobbed by autograph hunters that I thought to find out what his name was. I asked my driver. "Robin Gibb, mate." I was still none the wiser.

The quality of the acts was high. Duncan 'Dunking Biscuit' and Steve didn't let much rubbish through, if any. Thanks to Waxy, the UK media got involved and national TV took a keen interest. The first Final made prime-time BBC on a Saturday night, kicking a major soap off the top spot. It was raw, live TV, and this was helped by the strict formula of seven bands with only two-minutes between each set. The actress Rula Lenska supplied the links. It was the 'X-Factor' of its day, the first competition of its kind. But where X-Factor is arguably a Karaoke show for the occasionally talented, Battle was a real contest in which bands played their own material and created their own sound.

'The Crack' won the 1982 Final. Simon Cowell may now be one of the world's highest paid entertainers – then a lowly record plugger – but if he'd been on the judging panel back then he probably wouldn't have made it through the night. Rick Wakeman was on the panel and he nearly didn't survive The Crack's unique vote-catching technique. They were a mod band with a skinhead following and raised the bar of the punk/Oi! scene. Their Doc Martyn bovver boy fans in

Hammersmith that night took no prisoners. While the band threatened Wakeman and other dissenting panel members, their fans threatened the audience. No-one there felt safe and even the cameramen were intimidated, their shaking hands creating a cinema verité effect that was certainly not intended. Slade's Noddy Holder was one of the few who voluntarily voted for them, the lead singer Steve Jones's raw voice reminding him of his own. They stayed together as a band until '89, lamented now for never achieving the massive recognition their talent warranted, but then again, the scene had moved on by the late Eighties.

Rocket Records threw a bash at their Bayswater Road offices, where gold discs covered every wall. Me, Steve and Doghouse Dan got invites. Elton John was there with his manager and then boyfriend, John Reid. Being Elton, he was dressed in his usual flamboyant style, and this being the Eighties, it involved huge shoulder pads. Doghouse Dan was pissed, and seemed fascinated by Elton's leather jacket. He and the former Reg Dwight had a lot in common, both being North London boys. Somehow though, Elton became convinced that, because the dark-haired Dan looked Irish, he was a member of the IRA. The more Dan denied it, the more Elton became convinced that Dan was indeed one of the boyos. The talk became conspiratorial, with Dan increasingly tactile with every drink. The whole room had been watching them talk, most wondering who this important new face was who could so effortlessly command Elton's rapt attention. Convinced now that they were soul mates, Dan leant on one of Elton's shoulder-pads. But each pad protruded some six inches either side of the real Elton, and Dan fell through air and leather, grabbing Elton on his way down and sending the two of them crashing over a sofa and into a tight embrace as they rolled across the plush carpet. The astounded onlookers had assumed they were close, but not that close.

Elton's reputation made a full recovery from the ordeal and the next year his latest album was released, the one with the perfect track to remind Dan of his time as an Irishman. In The Fulham Tap, me, Steve and Phil Lynott were enjoying a freshener at the bar when Dan and his hangdog hangover walked in. "I'm still standing better than I ever did", came from the three of us, with Phil Lynott giving it his full Whiskey In A Jar rasp, startling the early morning punters and doing that rarest of things, getting a full-beam smile out of Doghouse.

We had our main offices on the Fulham Road, and Noddy and Phil used to hang out there soaking up the energy of the place. There were always kids from competing bands hanging around there too, all doing their surly rock 'n' roll thing, that weird act that talented, articulate guys feel they have to affect as soon as they join a band. All very Spinal Tap.

I think it was the second year, when I was at home getting ready for the Final and excited at the prospect of a great evening. I was about to leave for Hammersmith when Nessie announced that she had something better to do. There we were, off to a televised final, to be in the company of all the top stars of the day, and she had something better to do. It hurt me terribly and was the beginning of the end of our marriage. I would have been so proud to have had her there. True, she had caught me unawares in the Fulham Tap with Janice just a couple of weeks earlier, so maybe she had a point.

In year-three we tried for Europe, the long-term plan being to go global. You never know, but had it taken off we might have changed the face of Euro rock. Our producer, an actor called Tony Forrest, went with Duncan to make a presentation to the Japanese suits at TDK's Dusseldorf headquarters. But Simon and Duncan got pissed, so when they put stickers on a wall-mounted map of the world, showing all the projected venues, they managed to get most of the cities in the wrong place, Sydney becoming Melbourne and so on. The businesslike Japanese were less than impressed and the game was up. TDK pulled the plug. But they had one last contractual obligation, an end of deal party. We held it at Heathrow's Skyline Hotel, famous for its pseudo-tropical pool area. It turned out to be one of the wildest rock parties of its era, with bemused Japanese gleefully hotographing the mayhem. We'd hired Shakatak for the finale and they ended up thrown in the pool.

We should have gone for another sponsor, but there was so much going on elsewhere, what with the camping company and the easy money of my burgeoning Harley Street clinics, that the sheer hassle of dealing with up-themselves bands who were often as high as kites meant that we lost our enthusiasm and the rock 'n' roll years came to an end.

Steve and Dan had their own pressing issues and it all just drifted away. None of our featured bands are still around, but many names who've since made it big got their first break in the original 'Battle of the Bands'. We'd made our mark and had three years we'll never forget, thanks to jerk chicken and those bloody balloons.

CHAPTER TWENTY

Harley Street Fat Cat

Today in England I am dismayed at how so many people under forty or so have a tattoo. What a great way to demonstrate your individuality, when most of your peers are similarly afflicted. It's not that I've got anything against tattoos. I mean they're fine if you've fought your way through a war or maybe ended up drunk in a Shanghai whorehouse when you've jumped ship and the local Tongs are on your case so you get Suzie Wong inked on your arse to match the Mum on your arm as a momento mori. You know, a proper adventure, like black sheep uncles used to have. But somehow I feel uneasy with young people who've done nothing more exacting than getting a watered-down degree after a gap trip to Thailand, doing a De Caprio at The Beach and acting as though they've lived the life.

There was a time not so long ago when people were actually embarrassed by their tattoos and wanted their momentary indiscretion obliterated forever, especially when they got to that stage in life when the canvas is not as tight as it once was. Step forward Uncle Paul. People come from all over the world to Harley Street to get just about everything fixed. And they're willing to pay. I, of course, have no medical training, so I fitted into the environment perfectly. In the Duke of York some of the finest medical minds of their generation used to gather. People like Dr. Blood, so-called by the red-tops because of his penchant for storing blood for transfusion in buckets. I was more professional; I had the Professor. I'd bought two lasers, pioneered by the Greek brothers, Dermis and Epidermis, as we came to call them. These devices were the cutting-edge of modern technology (we're talking early Eighties here). The anti-wrinkle one used by Janice in the hairdressing and beauty salon she ran on Fulham Broadway promised everlasting youth. That'll be the day. But it did no harm. If a client, invariably a woman, left the salon with a new hair-do and her perceived wrinkles miraculously erased, then even if the illusion lasted only for an afternoon's shopping on the King's Road, if she felt good the laser had done some good.

The other laser, the Litechnica C02, we used for tattoo removal. I flew to Israel and bought it direct from the manufacturer. The professor modified it so that it was a serious piece of kit. Put it this way, if an alien death fleet was threatening our planet with destruction then the Ministry of Defence would have called in the Professor. It was a bizarre Heath Robinson affair, with lots of whirs and flashing lights. It scared the life out of me, but being in Harley Street was one-half of the healing process. What could possibly go wrong at such a salubrious address?

The C02 used to burn off the tattoo and then a vacuum-extraction system would suck away the loose skin left behind. Well, the tattoos went, so I earned my fat fee. Trouble was, the Professor's laser left a blistered scar on more sensitive skin, and it was difficult to judge beforehand who was likely to suffer an adverse reaction. Luckily in those days my clients were mostly men, and big boys didn't cry then, otherwise the law-suits would have been worse than they were. They'll possibly be a revival of the tattoo removal business when overuse of tanning booths, bingo-flaps and gravity lead a generation to reconsider the wisdom of their youthful follies. Hopefully by then the technology will have improved. A misguided attempt at counter-culture will no doubt meet compensation culture and it could be a very expensive business indeed for future professors, and people like me.

One sector of our clients who weren't men were the women, mostly from Holloway Prison, who were brought in under guard to have their tattoos erased. Nowadays we're all familiar with the sight of young women walking down the street in summer with the ubiquitous tattoo on what is often a very broad expanse of flesh above the 'whale tail' of their visible thongs. But these women are for the most part 'nice girls'. Back in the Eighties only 'bad girls' had tattoos. I had signed a contract with the Home Office. The thinking seemed to be then that if you remove the tattoo you remove the criminality. It was regular business, but the Home Office were lousy payers. They should have been banged-up.

There was a serious, and very unfortunate, spin-off from all this. The Harley Street area was home to many people who had fled Nazi persecution and had found themselves in the medical profession. Some had been in concentration camps, and the smell of burning flesh was a sickening reminder of what they'd been through. This smell permeated the entire area. We put in new ventilation systems but still it persisted, so we put a stop to our operations.

My previous medical venture had been 'The Harley Street Diet Clinic'. At the time weighing twenty-stone and counting, I was clearly the ideal front-man: follow my diet and you too could be just like me. Our doctor prescribed a high protein diet, with amphetamines to speed up the metabolism and diuretics to get rid of excess liquid. It was effective, except for the giveaway rattle as my rake-thin clients zoomed up and down Marylebone High Street with fixed grins on their faces as they desperately searched for the ladies.

In the early Eighties my system was the acknowledged way to slim fast, with some clients losing a stone a week. It was a precursor of Atkins, and we've since learned that the good doctor died relatively early from a fall allegedly linked to his obesity. In those days Dr Tom's diet was commonly used on film and TV stars by their studio bosses to get them ready for a shoot and to foster the illusion that they are perfect people.

Although Dr Tom was the acceptable face of the clinic, ably assisted by Annette Gardner-Smith, the only way we could keep up with a growing demand was by employing agency doctors on a per diem basis. We were making quite a name for ourselves and there was a growing list of celebrity clients, from the Duchess of Kent to Gary Glitter. I'm not saying the following technique was applied to these two, but one of the agency doctors had rather unorthodox and unfortunate modus operandi. He was a committed exponent of aversion therapy – "You're fat, aren't you? You're ugly, aren't you? Come on, get fatter," he would scream at his sobbing patients. He'd leave them in a room while they were observed unwittingly on camera, a plate of cakes on the table. Somehow he wired up the cakes to deliver an electric shock.

Dr Tom's character, a Frenchman, had been hired in the south of France when he'd been working on the beach adjacent to my campsite as an ice-cream seller. He did seem to have full doctor credentials though, for without these Annette would not have taken him on, but he did have some unusual tactics, I have to say. He brought his technique to my spin-off business, an anti-smoking clinic. He'd get clients to sit in a bath full of dog-ends and, unknown to them, there was a pad under the butts that delivered a shock. There was no water in the bath. He didn't practice what he preached though. Before meeting clients he'd chain-smoke Gauloises. One day, when Annette was doing the accounts, she noticed that the books didn't quite balance. "I've sent nearly thirty people down to you and all I've got to show for it is fifteen pounds and a pile of cancelled cheques. What have you been doing?" What he'd been doing was falling in love. Most people, if lucky, manage this rare feat two or three times during their adult lives. Our friend managed to fall in love several times daily. This lurve machine had a simple technique; he used to tell women, in his most charming French accent – "I love you. I do not think I have ever come across anyone like you." Oh yes, and there was his other technique; that of giving them their money back, or should I say my money? I spoke to him. He left. Quickly.

Later I heard a little more about 'Le Docteur' from one of my fellow fat cats of Harley Street, as we were once titled by the media. It turned out that he'd done the rounds of the local clinics. But like so many people who've crossed my path the good doctor was heard of again. He turned up in a Bath paediatric ward delivering babies. He probably helped to make them. His love-life was put on hold during a spell in prison, the authorities not being overly keen on fake medical credentials.

Around this time I was using London's Marylebone High Street area as my adventure playground. Anybody who frequented West End hostelries then might have clinked glasses with Ronnie Fraser, the squashed-nosed character actor who usually played, in forty-odd films and TV shows, a suede-shoed cad or cheeky Tommy, with a full range from priggish to dodgy. In real life he was neither. Stephen Sheppard, a friend of mine and an enemy of Joan Collins, formed the third member of our lads who lunch trio. Stephen has since made an early departure, as those who celebrate life too much often do. Back in the Eighties though, he was in his pomp, garnering plaudits and money for his writing and film work. He then held the record for the biggest advance of all time, US$1-million from Warners for the film rights to his novel, The Four Hundred, and had an on-set bust-up with La Collins while making his TV mini-series, Monte Carlo.

Resplendent in his trademark white suit and fedora with the obligatory fat-cat cigar, Stephen ran an open-house policy at his Harley Street home. Ronnie was around so much I thought he lived there. This of course was the same Ronnie who was a wild goose in The Wild Geese, with his mates Harris, Burton and Moore. "Roger Moore, he could drink 'em all under the bloody table, old boy. The lot of 'em." That was Ronnie.

We'd all crashed at Stephen's one night. At about three in the morning I got up for a drink. Women were all over the place, like scatter-cushions. Maybe they were scatter-cushions that happened to look like women. I don't know. It had been that kind of night. Ronnie appeared. "Drink, old chum?" It was a rhetorical question. We were both raising glasses to our lips when we heard a mournful wail. Ronnie's small eyes were like saucers. More wailing – "I've lost my head!" "How's he bloody talking then?" This from Ronnie. "If I don't find my head I'm dead. Has anybody seen my head?" As lines go, it wasn't quite 'My Kingdom for a horse', but it did have a certain poignancy. Then the headless one appeared. It was David Gallagher, then head designer at the Royal Opera House and, as they used to say then, a confirmed bachelor. There was a major production tomorrow and it depended on this head. He'd been designing a wig for the leading lady and without it – "Without it, my dears, we simply can't go on." Now, I knew from hanging around these luvvie types that

The Show Must Go On – "Has anybody seen David's head?" None of the cushions replied. "You know what, old dears, I think we might have left it in the King's Head. I thought it was part of the pub's décor. Ha ha. We left the queen's head in the King's Head." DV was too relieved to be offended.

He hugged Ronnie and sat to await the dawn. At that moment Sheppard staggered into the room, still in his white suit. "My fucking head!" Ronnie nearly choked on his brandy, then walked over to the mirror and put a hand either side of his head and wobbled it to make sure it was attached. It was all in the twinkle of those little eyes.

This had been around the time Janice ran Marloes, a hairdressing salon on Fulham Broadway. Her most colourful customer had to be John Bindon. Apart from his infamous party trick with beer glasses, there was his reputation for ultra-violence and an affection for the Caribbean island of Mustique. Janice kept John looking good for his assignations with Princess Margaret and his acting roles in films like Get Carter. He was a charming geezer whenever we had the odd beer together, but this was someone who'd once sliced off a man's arm with a machete, so I always broke my notorious short arms, long pockets, habit whenever it was my round. Feather-cut, I think Janice called his hairstyle. A bit soft, if you ask me; the haircut I mean. I blame Janice and that haircut for his popularity with the ladies, though maybe his charm and the ability to balance several half-pint glasses on his schlong may have contributed to his success. He died young. Well, fifty is young, isn't it? Never used to be, but things change all the time.

CHAPTER TWENTY-ONE

The Thirsty Woman and the Honey Monster

The old Bristol 411 did ten miles to the gallon but I was still at my stage of enjoying status cars so I stuck with her. She was a stately, heavy creature, known as 'the rich man's Rolls Royce'. Her thirst, though, drove me into the arms of another woman. It was 1982 and, being careful with money, I took a train from London to Redditch. Ronald McDonald (no, not that one) had told me that the way to go was into care homes, a generic term covering both residential and nursing premises.

I had been sitting in one of the UK's first McDonalds, on Kensington High Street, with Ronald (I should have told the staff what his name was; we might have got a free meal). As a result of our discussion I found myself on the train, and there fell into conversation with Margaret. What is it with me and my need to discuss my forthcoming business plans with every passing stranger? Margaret was a case in point. By the time the train pulled into Redditch, Margaret was already hired as my manager. She had no experience of the care home business and neither did I, but I've always worked on the principle that if I like someone then they're in. Anyway, Margaret had great skin.

When our train pulled into Redditch we went to see what was to soon become my first care home. Ronald McDonald had introduced me to a bank and in no time finance had been arranged. So when our taxi arrived at this fine old house outside town I knew that I had the funds to purchase it and so began the most profitable period of my life so far. The house had been owned by the founder of BSA. I followed his example in terms of speed and within one month Margaret was installed as manager of my first care home. She and I were having an affair.

The then Tory government, under Margaret Thatcher, was offering state subsidies to private care homes and it seemed that every entrepreneur in the land had jumped on the gravy train. All I had to do was provide the facilities and Mrs T would cough up the money.

I was then still in my thirties and old age was to me as remote a concept as England once again winning the World Cup, so I was then less taxed by standards of care than was later the case. Initially I just looked at the money, as did we all. At first, Margaret was stretched. She had assistance, but as well as being Manager she was also Head Cook, and being my lover is a full-time job in itself. So, enter the Honey Monster.

He'd gained the tag from the fact that he'd flogged honeycombs on the Portobello Road, and although it was the early Eighties and we were all beginning to squeeze into navy double-breasted suits, the Honey Monster was pure late Sixties counter-culture. His real name was Alex, and with his mane of long hair, wildly staring eyes and crazed grin, if Charles Manson had set eyes on him he would have thought he was staring into a cracked mirror. He was the kind of guy who you sensed that, if he flipped, he'd come at you with anything to hand and wouldn't stop until you were dead, or worse. So I hired him. Head Cook.

If you had found yourself in a care home in the early Eighties you would have been born in Edwardian times and you'd have hit adulthood around the era of the Charleston.

So when Mad Alex, as he came to be known, force-fed you video clips of The Old Grey Whistle Test at a volume so loud that even 'Whispering' Bob Harris appeared to be shouting, then you would probably have looked with longing to see the Grim Reaper at the foot of your bed. And when you'd been through World War Two and had become used to spam and tinned peaches as luxuries, then a maniacally-grinning Alex feeding you a diet of macrobiotic brown rice was not what the doctor ordered. You would rather have eaten the carpet. If there had been a carpet.

Fortunately we soon acquired some qualified nurses who started smuggling in food parcels and then imposed a regime of meat and two veg. Outnumbered by these matriarchs even Alex backed off, snarling in less than honey-smooth fashion – "They don't know what's good for them. No wonder they're all so fucking old."

He was out of there, but not before he'd made his last stand. Well, his last but one actually; more on that later. By this time my relationship with Margaret was strictly professional and Alex had taken my place in her affections. As his protest at being sacked, Alex locked himself, with Margaret, in the on-premises flat. We smashed the door down about four days later. She of the silky skin emerged, covered in psoriasis sores, whilst Alex was high on Acid, his eyes spinning like the rings of Saturn.

I forgave Alex. I've always had a soft spot for people who are characters, although I haven't always been able to spot those who have character. I like the curious, in both senses of the word. He would say something completely innocuous and then throw his head back in maniacal laughter. You know that way drunks hold your eye that bit too long when they're trying to make a point? Well, Alex did that too, but his eyes seemed twice the size of normal peoples'. You always found yourself looking away, and then glancing back. The stare was still there. Unblinking.

Back to forgiveness: I rented him a flat in the basement of my diet clinic. Trouble is, he didn't pay the rent. I let it go for months. Then, troubled by my suggestion that a few pennies coming my way might not go amiss, he barricaded himself in, history repeating itself. Then, cheeky bugger, he took out an injunction against me. Oh well, don't they all? I wanted him out. He'd fallen off my Christmas card list, but with the injunction against me I couldn't make contact. I don't know how he got food in, but I laid siege and never even saw so much as a light go on. I couldn't get the utilities cut off without affecting the clinic, and for awhile I couldn't think what to do. Then I had an idea.

It was a Sunday morning. Trying to be a responsible citizen, I'd worked out that that's when the fire service would be hopefully not too busy and the traffic wouldn't be so bad. I didn't want to waste too much of their time. I therefore didn't think I was compromising the emergency services when I told my manager that I'd smelt smoke coming from under the door of Alex's flat. I also mentioned to the police that drugs were involved.

For someone who had offered the health-giving malnutrition of a macrobiotic diet to elderly care home residents, Alex also followed the inconsistencies of the counter-culture ethos; he was drugged up to his spinning eyeballs. The firemen and the police arrived simultaneously and forced their way in.

Alex had been holed-up there, in a W1 flat, terrified that he, the Honey Monster, was at threat from the big bad bear, namely me. The police searched the flat for drugs while the bear eyed Alex hungrily. There were, amazingly, no drugs on the premises. Maybe they were all inside Alex.

This had really been the best possible conclusion to the affair, both for the Honey Monster, who was free to go under the watchful eyes of the police, and for me, who had been unable to do anything to someone who had lived scot-free in my expensive West End flat for six-months. To put it mildly, I wasn't too happy, but the presence of the police prevented me from getting myself into trouble. Instead, Alex and I shook hands. One last stare and the crazy laugh and he was gone. That was the last I saw of him, but not the last I heard.

Two days later he'd acquired a Chopper motorbike and had gone up to the Scottish Highlands to find a woman and hole up with her in a remote shack for the winter, like a latter-day Jeremiah Johnson. Some years later I heard that Alex was in care for full-blown schizophrenia.

Back at the Redditch home, the staff were having a hard time keeping control. There was one old lady who saw herself as some sort of latter-day Scarlet Pimpernel. One of my senior staff had a policy of encouraging some of the more vulnerable residents who were making their way to the dining-room to place a hand on the shoulder of the person in front. This was because that particular home was full of labyrinthine corridors, and if someone had become lost they might not be seen again until a cleaner next went to a broom cupboard. The Scarlet Pimpernel was clever. She usually managed to get to the front of the queue, and on one memorable occasion she went through an open outer door and the Great Escape was on. She made a run for it across the fields and others did their best to follow, exhilarated by their daring. I don't think it was any form of protest, just a way to remind themselves that they were still alive, people with pasts, if not much of a future.

From my stuttering start I managed to build up a professional care home business. It had to be professional. At one level, with elderly, vulnerable people in care, rightly so, but it was also becoming a highly-politicised industry. I was building up a chain of homes, piggy-backing on added value.

By '87 I had eighteen or nineteen homes. Please forgive my vagueness, but I was finding it hard keeping tabs on them all, and one day I mislaid one. I had them all over the place – Torrington, Swansea, The Wirral, Yorkshire, Liverpool, the West Midlands. I was driving to one of my homes in the company of a bank manager, a humourless soul. Finding this particular home was like trying to find a rented silver car in an Asda car-park. "I'm sure that the last time I looked it was here in Pontefract, or somewhere like that."

"Mr Eagles, my bank has lent you several million pounds. Surely you cannot lose a home of that size."

One home I do remember was in Smethwick. I'd agreed to buy it in principle, so the owner upped roots and moved lock stock and barrel to the Isle of Man even before the deal was completed. He bought a home in Douglas on the strength of a gentlemen's agreement. Maybe he thought that having a pre-ennobled Digby Jones as his business advisor guaranteed completion. I arranged a Saturday morning meeting with the business guru's guru in a Happy Eater near the NEC. He arrived wearing his customary knitted-leather shoes, an elegant affectation I vowed to emulate. Shoe chat over he wasn't too impressed that I'd tried to knock fifty-thousand off his client's price, but the seller, in being a bit previous, had given me two loaded barrels to point at his head. For him, this was a deal that had to go through.

I knew Digby Jones and liked him. He was clever and fun and probably still is. As a future business advisor to the government and the opposition he was nobody's fool. I knew I was up against a top-flight brain and fifty grand was worth a lot more then. So we negotiated. He was big, but I was bigger.

Startled happy eaters scattered, as did tables and chairs. It was more briefcases at dawn than a fight to the death, and it ended on a handshake and I was fifty thousand to the good. I'd given it my best shot against one of the finest business minds of our generation. My barrels were smoking.

CHAPTER TWENTY-TWO

Gin, and Tonic Mohair

I was born in Maghull, near Southport. I suppose when I went back there in the Eighties to look at the possibilities of starting a local nursing home I was doing what so many who've made a bit of money do; it's the local-boy-made-good syndrome. It's not far from Liverpool so I took the train to Lime Street. I checked into a railway hotel, can't remember the name. Whenever I arrive in a strange town I just grab the first person I see and start asking questions. He or she might not know the answer, but they think they know someone who does. Try it. It works. Before I'd knocked back two gins in the hotel bar I had arranged a meeting with Derek Hatton, the leader of the local council and a man who was no stranger to tonic mohair. All I'd said to the barman was – "I want to open a nursing home in the area." Hatton sent the local head of education. There was a recently-closed school in Kirby, one of those Fifties-style 'To Sir With Love' places on the edge of a sink estate. Maybe no-one needed an education now there were no jobs to be had. I went to see it on a hot August day, all broken windows and doors off their hinges. It had only closed down at the end of the summer term and it was full of the echoes of children who had been learning to operate a lathe over in Birkenhead, but it was on prime land. I spoke to Hatton. He said – "It's up for tender, but it doesn't necessarily go to the highest bidder. It goes to whoever we feel would be best for the region." I got it in one. I had myself a school.

By the time all this had gone through a few months had passed. I had so many homes and so much money passing through my hands that I'd almost forgotten the school. The local kids hadn't. Come Guy Fawkes' Night they showed their affection for their Alma Mater by razing it to the ground. I rang Derek. "Shit! There's asbestos on the site. We've got to get it cleaned-up." I had been planning to refurbish it. Instead the insurers paid £400,000 straight to the builders.

Even though the local kids had burned their school down it did not mean they left it alone. We had to build a three-metre fence around it to keep them out and the pre Elf 'n' Safety workers wore hard hats to protect their heads from stone-throwing mobs. It was like Fort Apache The Bronx as our big black minder, Jamaica, worked virtually twenty-four-hour shifts.

Eventually, though, I had a brand new home for a £120,000 outlay. As soon as the first local granny had moved in the attacks stopped and the home became the safest place in town. The kids never did get those lathe jobs in Birkenhead. They closed down the shipyards.

The Honey Monster wasn't my only residential tenant. Around the time Alex was holed up in my London flat, I had another rental on the go near Ilfracombe in Devon. This one was a standard three-bedroom terraced house I'd acquired as an investment. The sole tenants were a woman of about forty and her teenage daughter, according to my care home manager who'd arranged the letting. Like Alex, the woman got behind with her rent, like a true a hippie-chick child of the Sixties. I'd never met her, so I went to the house with a Yorkshireman, George, who used to work for me as a general factotum. We rang the bell. There were some odd sounds coming from inside. "Sounds like bloody farmyard," said George. "It's probably Emmerdale Farm," I replied. "Wrong bloody time," said George. "The Archers?"

"Wrong bloody time." George knew his soaps. I pushed the front door. It opened. Inside it was neither Emmerdale Farm nor The Archers. George was right. It was a bloody farmyard. Chickens were running around and I counted at least six sheep. Remember, this was a bog standard three-up, two-down. We stared in amazement. I knew the house had no rear entrance as it abutted a factory wall, so the sheer illogicality of the situation struck me almost more than the fact that there was a farmyard in the sitting-room. How had she got all these animals into the house without the usual curtain-twitchers spotting them? It was like a scene from 'The Good Life'; at any moment I expected to see Felicity Kendall. Then there she was, only I hadn't realised that Felicity was into full-frontals. "Who are you? What are you doing here? demanded a defiant upper-class voice. George just stared. "Bloody 'eck! Bloody, bloody 'eck!" The owner of the voice was standing at the top of the stairs, completely naked save for a pair of green wellies. She was about eighteen and very pretty. "Is your mother in?" was my lame response, while George tried to stop one of the sheep escaping. He was from farming stock so might have been expected to know what he was doing. Somehow he couldn't concentrate. "Please do excuse the boots," said the girl, as though standing naked in front of two strange men was the most natural thing in the world for her. "It's just that I've been mucking-out ... oh, this? It saves on washing clothes." I had to evict them of course. I just hope she found something warm to wear.

CHAPTER TWENTY-THREE

I'm Telling Mrs Thatcher of You

In 1986 I'd decided to dip my toes into the up-and-coming Caribbean cruise business. Previously cruises had been seen as exotic, the preserve of a vanished breed: prewar dowager duchesses with prince-nez glasses playing Whist on deck with a blanket covering their knees while keeping a sharp look-out for errant icebergs. But now a new market was beckoning.

Today cruising is a huge business turning-over billions worldwide, but then it was still much closer to the traditional image. True, young Americans were starting to feature strongly among the passengers, but a large part of the market were Miami matrons, their hair turned quite gold with grief as their fingers dripped diamonds. They were all seemingly looking for a man who could dance and who, presumably, found diamonds attractive.

From my office in London's West End I started to court the great and the good, convinced that their patronage was the fast-track to big bucks on the high seas. Blue-chip company heads were favourites – take the CEO and his wife, or wifelet, on a free cruise, royally wine and dine them, and I might well get three hundred or so paying passengers when that company next held its annual conference, sales incentive jolly or product launch. Famous names and faces were in the frame too, as were the elite of the international Bridge world and politicians.

All were eager for a free trip to the Caribbean. Typical me, though. There I was, looking as always for a Unique Selling Point, when in reality I could simply have advertised and the project would no doubt have been a success. But even though I had money from my care homes, I was trying not to spend too much on this speculative venture, thinking that famous names would garner me free publicity.

It went well at first. The cruise companies were vying for business from the emergent UK market. Their freebies fell off trees and Virgin Atlantic was handing out Upper Class upgrades like they were hot towels So what went wrong? There were, of course, little blips, like when I went to this fund-raising evening at London's Guildhall. Phil-the-one-eyed-mercenary had taken me there in a then new and much sought-after vehicle, a Range Rover. I thought he was in the trade. I later discovered that he 'borrowed' a top-of-the-range model every time he wished to make an impression. This one he'd nicked from Soho. Anyway, safely inside the Guildhall I looked forward to a pleasant evening. A few friends and an ex-wife were my guests.

Earlier that week I'd had an idea, together with the Sales Director of a Norwegian cruise ship company. We managed to get the largest model we could find of their flagship and put it in a prominent position in the hall. We had adorned the display with balloons and advertising pennants and we were feeling pretty pleased with ourselves. Various famous faces made speeches until finally it was the turn of the then Princess Anne. A feisty sort, the future Princess Royal had our display directly in her line of vision as she began to speak. But she froze in mid-word when she saw how we had tried, from her view-point at least, to hijack the event for our own evil ends. Our display could have made no difference to how much money had been made for charity as guests had funded the event by paying up-front, but she strode from the podium and out of the hall, her face frozen into an 'off with their heads' expression. I wouldn't like to have been on the wrong side of her five hundred years ago, when her kin went in for that sort of thing. Then there was another little problem. Over a misunderstanding about the prize for the winner of the Lords v Commons Bridge tournament, which I had put up, I had a bit of a falling out with the boss of the army, the then Minister of Defence, Michael Mates. There he was, banging on my desk, eyebrows beetling, and threatening me with dire consequences if I did not stick to my agreement. I can't remember exactly what had gone wrong with the deal; something about an overbooked hotel in Estoril, Portugal, I think. But he actually threatened to tell the Prime Minister, using the immortal line – "I'm telling Mrs Thatcher of you." All that was missing was 'na-na-nana-na'.

First Princess Anne, and now this. I've been up against a few hard nuts in my time, but Margaret Thatcher in her 'Iron Lady' prime! I don't think so. I would rather have faced the British Army.

But these were merely diversions, and they shouldn't have affected my long-term aim of becoming a major player in the cruise business. Then along came Alan.

I was coming into the office a couple of days a week to look after the cruise business. I'd rented a suite of West End offices and Alan was using one room to run our financial consultancy. I had thought that it would be a good way to meet fellow entrepreneurs and get a bit of a buzz out of some wheeler-dealing, the care home business lacking much scope for excitement. Alan used to run an ad in The Times offering his services as a financial consultant. He would concurrently run another ad in the same paper in which he sought the services of financial advisors. That way he built up a database so that whatever area of expertise a client required we usually had someone on hand to advise them on a highly-professional basis. We got a varied selection of people on our books, including moonlighting barristers.

Alan was a true recidivist, a professional career criminal and, unusual for his calling, a man of high intelligence. If he had not had the criminal gene, if such a thing exists, he could have ended his career running a multi-national company. I did not know of his background when I met him, but if I were to have judged him purely on first impressions, I would have counted my fingers every time I shook his hand. It had something to do with the camel coat draped over his shoulders in all weathers, the fat-cat Havana, and the oversized wraparound shades of such opacity that I doubt whether I ever saw his eyes during the few months of our acquaintance. He looked like the kind of master criminal Batman would have a pop at.

I'd be there, glad-handing politicians and pillars of society, while Alan was in the next room dealing with the likes of 'Jewel Thief Dave'. One morning Dave and a mate of his had coffee with us at the office, then went out to do a bit of armed 'shopping' dahn (sic) Bond Street. They didn't get any jewels. But the Sweeney got them.

Another time there was a man who had been, according to his own legend, on the Concorde design team. He always carried a sapphire, his insurance against poverty and his entrance fee into deals. The sapphire was alleged by its owner, Peter Bray was the name he used with us, to be worth £25,000. Obviously that would be far more at today's prices. Alan had a client who was doing a deal with the South African government over some micro-lights to be used for reconnaissance purposes. Peter Bray's aeronautics expertise should come in useful. While this deal appeared to be proceeding smoothly enough, Peter, or 'The Vicar of Bray', as he came to be known, tried to broker a deal on behalf of an Austrian who claimed to be the legal executor of the last of the Krups family, the German munitions giant which was notorious for arming the Nazi war machine. The deal with the vicar was that if we could raise the funds through investors the keys to the Bavarian family castle would be ours. It could be used as an up-market hotel. We would have to pay the money into Bray's offshore bank account, but surely there would be no problem with that, would there? The castle was the inducement, but in my eyes even that prospect was bettered by his pièce de résistance: as owners of the castle we would receive a flag of honour, a 'Merito Navali'. This is an Austrian award given to only one other person in history, the round the world explorer Ivan Bisin (who?). However, undeterred by the rarity of this award, I was all but swayed by the extras that came with the package. We'd been promised a 'Mouse That Roared'-type Ruritanian uniform: high black boots, turquoise trousers, jacket and cloak, and a high-peaked cap. I suspected they'd throw in a monocle and duelling-scar gratis.

We played along with this grandiose Walter Mitty scheme. The vicar must have thought we were straight from a nursery as we showed such keen interest. The fraud squad also showed interest. It turned out that Peter Bray was one of several aliases used by our friend the vicar. With his clipped moustache he looked as if straight out of an Ealing comedy. I doubt though whether his victims ever saw the joke. I later discovered that he'd conned many a gullible old dear out of their life's savings. For a while, the Fraud Squad were convinced that Alan, and I by association, had played a part in the vicar's cons. One day they came to interview me. I suggested that we went out to a nearby pub for a chat as I didn't want the staff to think anything was up. We had a fairly informal talk over a couple of drinks and that was it. It was only later when my lawyer told me they'd been convinced of my guilt because I was so nervous I was shaking like a jelly in an earthquake. What they hadn't known was that I'd been to a party the night before and I had the shakes so badly that even with two hands I couldn't lift my pint to my lips without given half of London a beer shower.

Alan had problems with a bad deal involving a Nigerian businessman who was owed £7,500 by him (then enough to get cross about). So a man came into the office and suggested to Alan that the money be made available within twenty-four hours. There was a rider attached; if it wasn't, Alan would be shot. Dead. The would-be assassin was a casting director's dream: long, black leather coat and dead eyes. He was polite though. Yes please, he would like a nice cup of tea, with two sugars please. This gentleman assassin was at great pains to point out that there was nothing personal in all this and he was just doing his job. That's all right then. Another cuppa? When Alan told me about this later he made it clear that I too was in the frame. The next day the crisis passed. Alan found the money. I could have paid it, but I'd made a point of not going to the office on the day I was due to be shot dead. You can never be too careful.

What really set the cat among the stool-pigeons was when someone came to the office offering us a priceless painting. Could we find a buyer? The only problem was, the painting had a dubious provenance. It had been stolen by the IRA in a helicopter raid on a country house in County Wicklow, Ireland. The man who offered it to Alan was called Peter. Just that. He claimed he'd been in the SAS, but looked more like the kind of 'SAS' man you would meet in pubs throughout the Eighties, inspired as they were by the Iranian Embassy

siege and the Falklands War. Podgy and furtive, he would
have looked more at home in the old wartime Pioneer Corps
than in Mrs Thatcher's Praetorian Guard. However, Alan's
innate criminal instinct was aroused. Yes, he said, he knew a
potential buyer. He was just stringing Peter along. Then, not
surprisingly, given the political atmosphere of the Eighties, it
all came on top. Suddenly my cruise business side-bet had led
me to become a target for Special Branch or MI5, or whoever.
Dark Forces were at work. I'm sure upsetting the Minister of
Defence had had nothing to do with it. Alan had pressed all
the wrong buttons. The previous tenants of our office suite
had been a bit wide. It wouldn't surprise me if the premises
had been under long-term surveillance. Then when a grass
comes on the scene and offers a bait which Alan nearly snaps
his fingers off to take, the cops must have thought they were
onto the big one.

So it went. Alan's recidivism had given him an aversion to
prison. He was sixty-two and convinced that one more term
inside would finish him. He was in ill-health. A forty-year
addiction to cigars had taken its toll and he had a chronic
bronchial condition which reached crisis point every winter.
He needed to go to the 'Costa del Crime', but his woman
didn't want to go there and he had three kids just about
grown-up; two getting on in the world and one wrong 'un.
They needed him, so he stayed around.

I hadn't got my name on paper over the financial
consultancy, but I felt that I should somehow try to help Alan
out of his tight spot, without unduly compromising myself.
The office phone bill was high; too high not to have been
disconnected. I wasn't going to fund a sinking ship, so I went
to our tame BT engineer, of the kind who in those days you
could get to jump through hoops for fifty quid. He made his
enquiries. He came back, ashen-faced. He knew 'nothing'.

Then I knew, they were serious. Phone taps. At least I didn't need to pay the bill.

A man came to the office, dressed, now I come to think of it, like my would-be nemesis, DV would twenty years later: blazer and slacks. He said he was in the record business. In that outfit? He gave an address in Percy Street, London W1, coincidentally just around the corner from MI5's offices in Curzon Street. Was I being paranoid? Even paranoiacs have enemies. I had too much going on to get involved in all this. This was a side-bet too far.

Alan had decamped to a hotel in Thayer Street, just a few yards from the office. One night we stuffed all the office papers, everything, into the boot of his Jag, and took them to a dump. I'll always remember him dancing like a crazed satyr around the fire we'd lit. I can only think he'd been doing deals of which I was unaware. With him holed up in the hotel with his room-mate, Paranoia, the drill was to knock on the door in Morse using a three-letter code established the previous day. He'd had another idea to ensure I wasn't followed. It was like in the 'French Connection' (a recurring theme in my tale) – get on a tube train and jump off sideways just as the doors are closing. Anyone following will be bewitched, bothered and bewildered. Then, a refinement this, run up the station escalator and glance over your shoulder for a glimpse of any pursuers. This, by the way, was all meant to happen at six-thirty in the morning. I don't even walk up escalators. That's their job. It's why they move.

Despite all the drama, the affair just somehow fizzled out. Maybe the feds got their man and through phone taps realised we were just caught up on the fringes. Alan got out of town, but not to the Costa del Sol. He went to Slough to be looked after by his kind and caring woman. It's ironic really. He was terrified of going back into prison, yet voluntarily exiled himself to Slough. I doubt that he's still around. If the cigars didn't get him, Slough would.

I got on with my care homes, but I'd given up the West End office, and without it my attempts to float a cruise business just sank without trace as I closed another chapter in my life. Those dowager duchesses of long ago had got it right – watch out for hidden icebergs.

Another of Alan's ventures could have got me deep in the mire. One day he'd suggested to me that I go with him to an office on the City Road so that he wouldn't look like a one-man-band. He didn't go into too much detail; just that he was giving business advice to two young chancers from the East End. They were running a chain of photo development booths across London and were doing very well at it. Alan and I sat waiting for them in a room adjacent to that in which they were to interview one of their photo booth managers. The two rooms were separated by frosted glass. You could see the shapes moving behind the glass, but hear nothing. Soon two shapes became three as they were joined by their manager, who had been offered a chair in the middle of the room. After a while their visitor was becoming clearly agitated. Then the mime took on a darker tone as one of the men jumped at and grabbed the arms of their manager from behind while the other laid into him with his fists. This went on for a couple of minutes until the figure was left slumped forward in his chair. There appeared to be more talking, then he was dragged out of the room. Our two new friends joined us. I was introduced to them by Alan. "What was that all about?" I asked. "'E was runnin' one of our boofs up west. Bit short on the readies, innit. So now 'e goes back after a bit of a slap an' the uvvers won't get any silly ideas. Right?"

"How do you know it was him and not one of the others?" He shrugged, and then spoke slowly, as though stating the obvious to someone with learning difficulties. "E was the only black there, weren't 'e?"

We all went to a nearby warehouse. It was huge, stocked top to bottom with blank video tapes. I found myself shaking hands with the warehousemen, not knowing why and not bothering to ask, knowing that Alan would later explain everything and that any indication that I didn't know what was going on would have made us look like amateurs in the eyes of the two men. I'd come straight to the meeting from King's Cross and hadn't had time to be briefed by Alan. We left the meeting. Alan explained – "We take over the company, with their agreement, as the front men. Let's face it, we present better at a corporate level. We buy a consignment of tapes. The boys pay for it. Then we buy another, much larger. Again the boys pay for it. You with me?"

"I don't know yet. Tell me more."

"No, I mean do you understand where I'm going?"

"I'm beginning to get an inkling."

"Then we buy the big one. I mean, those tapes the boys have in the warehouse would be just a fraction of the sting we'll go for. It's our plausibility, you see, that'll swing it. You can talk about foreign markets, all that spiel. Given your approach ..."

"My approach?"

"Aren't you interested? It'll make us a fortune. We can move the tapes out fast at market value. No back-street dealing."

"So we sting the supplier? We don't pay for the last consignment."

"It's foolproof. Even the boys don't have any idea who we really are. I've just given them a potted background. You're ex-Guards, a Captain Simon Brand ..."

"Alan, I have successful nursing homes. I'm trying to run a cruise business. I've done my naughty boy days."

"Think about the money, Paul. Even with a four-way split we're talking a serious amount. Then if we pull this one off, there'll be others." Alan was of course talking about a classic 'Long Firm' scam. Build credibility right up to the last moment then run with the goods. Hard-core villains had been doing it for years. I didn't need to think about the money. Sure, this was pre-computer days, when it was possible to do business with a fake ID, but frankly it wasn't even the morality of the deal that dissuaded me. It just didn't smell right. It didn't smell right to the boys either. It was ironic that we were being brought in to add credibility. They'd apparently just about accepted me, but the real problem was with Alan. If only he'd ditched the glasses and camel coat he could have made it as a conman. The boys, they were still in their twenties, knew enough about life to know that if Alan was prepared to stiff the supplier he could do the same to them. The deal was off. Who knows? If it had gone ahead would I have been tempted to take a bite of the apple?

Another vignette of Alan's life involves his domestic arrangements. Whilst living in the family home in Slough he would often go away on business trips 'abroad'. These trips involved taking a train for all of the twenty minute journey to Paddington and then a short taxi ride to Mayfair. It was here that he kept another home, and another life. No-one there knew his real name and even I do not know the name he used as he built-up an impregnable firewall between his two existences. Somehow he'd managed to fund a town-house in one of the world's most expensive real estate areas. Now I'd never seen Alan with real money; just a wallet-full of running money, so I suspect he must have borrowed the house. However, he managed to live a parallel life in Mayfair, taking mistresses and being invited to all the top parties. His main love was playing Bridge and he went to every game he could. This also made him valuable 'business' contacts. The rogue from Slough fitted perfectly into this milieu. Where he couldn't pull the wool over the eyes of a couple of East End twenty-something wide-boys, with the Arab high-rollers of Mayfair he was among his peers.

CHAPTER TWENTY-FOUR

Hello, Dearie

I got into the letting business in London during the boom of the late-Eighties, using loose money from the sale of the campsite. It was the usual buy-to-rent deal of the times, with rich-pickings to be had from Gulf Arabs. Just before Ramadan was a busy time for high-rent, short-lets. I was always amazed at how many family members and servants could be crammed into a three-bedroom flat.

The women would venture out in the chauffeured limo for their daily trip to Harrods' perfume counter; otherwise they would dwell in traditional isolation as their men-folk did the rounds of Mayfair hotel bars, casinos and hookers. I charged high rents for my three properties, but no-one pays a rent they can't afford, at least not for long. On professional advice, I used to take a fat deposit up-front to cover the ravages of domestic cultural differences; hot pans on unprotected carpets, that kind of thing, but these issues aside, it was a lucrative business to be in. I had one tenant, an attractive young Dublin woman, whom the neighbours complained about. They didn't like all the screaming, so I went there and rang the bell. "Hello, dearie. Is there anything special you'd like?" This in her rich Dublin brogue. Then she stepped from behind the door. It occurred to me that the red basque and the riding crop were unusual. "We've had a lot of complaints from other tenants in the building. Do you think you could keep it down a bit?"

"I'm only here for three or four hours a day, love. Give a girl a break."

"I'm sorry, but any more and you're out." There was more, so I went back. She wasn't having it. OK. I watched the place and waited for her to go out. Then I climbed the fire escape and slipped into her flat and changed the locks. She got on the phone and offered me free regulars if I relented. I explained that I had regular access to such delights and no noise meant no noise. So she called the police and accused me of harassment, and she was back in business. Soon after, though, she disappeared, and I rented the flat out to some peaceful Arabs.

When I finally had a good look around the place I realised what she'd been up to and why there'd been so much noise. She was into S&M, and the three wardrobes in the flat had been used as makeshift dungeons. She'd lock her punters in for hours on end, and then entertain clients on the bed while the masochists were locked in the cupboards. She was a true exponent of what most women claim to be, a multi-tasker.

One of my flats, in Bryanston Court in London's West End, was reputedly the place the then Prince of Wales had used when courting Wallis Simpson in the Thirties. Meanwhile, I was on the verge of abdicating all involvement in the property business, as interest rates were hiked sky-high in the early Nineties. But not before I'd met up with Mustapha, a Saudi letting agent who made me look like I needed a square meal.

Mustapha was larger than larger-than-life, nicknaming me, for some reason, Tiger. He had an interesting property-acquisition technique. He would go to Harrods' letting division and express interest in a property, usually on the Hyde Park Estate, near Edgware Road. They would give him the keys and that would be that. Once in, he'd change the locks, and then draw up a contract which he'd post on the door. This made it a civil matter and the police couldn't get involved. For some reason, although he repeated this process several times, the busy Harrods office didn't seem to catch on, maybe because they had so many empty properties on their hands and because Mustapha was such a familiar figure to them that it was almost as if he was one of their team.

He was letting these properties out for thousands a week, even in those days. Then he received a complaint from a Gulf high-roller. There was no carpet for his wives to pray on and the stripped-pine floorboards just would not do. This was easy for our Mustapha to resolve. He simply went with me to a Belgravia mansion he had the keys to and took a Stanley Knife to the carpet there. This we rolled up and somehow managed to manhandle to a waiting truck. I say 'manhandle', but he got his six daughters involved too. Back in Hyde Park Square we unrolled it and hammered it to the floor using six-inch nails and a bit of subtle furniture-shifting. Job done.

CHAPTER TWENTY-FIVE

I'm Telling You Man

If it's true that diamonds really are a girl's best friend then I'd have an interesting social life if the next venture came off. I was sitting in a pub in London's Bethnal Green when I got talking to Freddie. I never did get the hang of his African name but he was big in Sierra Leone. According to Freddie, his status as a Paramount Chief meant that people felt obliged to bow and kneel before him on the streets of his capital, Freetown. He had been offered the role of Chancellor of the Exchequer of Sierra Leone but his accountancy job in Leicester Square was better-paid so he stuck with that.

This was in 1992, before the bloody war in what is one of Africa's poorest countries, this an accolade not to be wished on any nation state. It was also before we became generally aware of the concept of blood, or conflict, diamonds. Freddie's dreams were modest; he simply wished to help his people and have a statue erected in his honour as a benefactor of his country. Oh yes, and he wanted his very own diamond mine. I bought him another pint of Guinness and listened to what he had to say. He was talking my kind of language. "I'm telling you, man," – this a phrase I'd hear many times over the next few weeks – "there are diamonds there on the ground, just waiting to be picked up."

"I'll have some of that," I thought, not for the first time.

I must have put on a couple of stone during our meetings

as I matched Freddie black pint for black pint as the plot unfolded. It was simple really; we'd just go in there and fence off a few diamond-studded hectares and we'd be as rich as Croesus. I wondered why everybody didn't do the same. I contacted a friend who ran a London diamond company. Yes, he'd fund it if it all stacked up. "Get a geological survey done, Freddie."

"I'm telling you, man," he yelled at me, somehow thinking that such a suggestion meant that I doubted the veracity of his promise that Shangri-La was there for the taking. But he went ahead and commissioned a survey. Then I contacted another friend who was ex-British Army Intelligence, a branch of the services always claimed by wags to be an oxymoron. He disproved this fallacy by introducing me to the African expert of one of the UK's top international security companies. Most of their operatives were ex-special forces. So here I was, ready and poised, funding potentially available, and a team of ex-SAS ready to take me into bandit country. Time for another Guinness or two. "I'm telling you, man."

"Freddie, this is not what I wanted. Screw your loaf."

"I'm a Paramount Chief. Show me some respect, man."

"Freddie, in Sierra Leone you are a Paramount Chief. Here you're just another book-keeper ."

"What's the problem? You wanted a geological report."

"Yes, Mr Paramount Chief. I wanted a report. On a diamond mine. This is for a fucking gold mine. How do I show this to my backers? They'll think I'm crazy." A gold mine's not so bad, you'll be thinking, but the survey had nothing to do with Sierra Leone, or seemingly anywhere else for that matter. For all the detail on show it could have been the Moon's backside. "I've got another idea, Mr Paul. Why don't we take a container ship full of rice into Freetown? I can feed my people and then they'll give me that statue. Maybe you can have a statue too."

"Great. Think how much granite they'll need to make a statue of me."

Soon after that Freddie went to Sierra Leone to collect his two-year-old adopted son. He disappeared.

The diamonds had been a diversion. My bread and butter was still care homes, but I was under pressure. The Tories had instigated the Social Services-funded care homes initiative, but then, under John Major, had begun to review their original policy. This sector was growing too large. The changing demographic was having an impact. The ageing population meant that the Social Services' bill was way too high and no government wanted to continue handing out blank cheques to every chancer who put their hand up and said – "Yes please, I'll have some of that thank you very much." The downturn began. In 1994 the government instigated a repressive clampdown on care homes in order to reduce the burden on the state. A Europe-backed Act of Parliament was passed to impose stringent standards on care homes. The gravy train had reached its final destination.

In principle I agree that standards should be maintained, but most homes did so by default. But a Brussels-imposed standard criteria put huge pressure on the owners of older buildings. I feel that older properties in semi rural areas are attractive to elderly people and provide a restful environment. But, by definition, these older properties lack the amenities demanded by the authorities.

Wheelchair access was a very reasonable demand, as were bathroom facilities for the disabled. But no sooner had you made one set of changes, and over nineteen homes that was a considerable expense, than a new set of conditions was imposed. Apart from the cost of all this, you also lost rooms. A new corridor to improve fire safety standards, extra bathrooms, or new rooms which conformed to a minimum size, meant that the overall number of rooms was reduced and thus a finely-tuned profit margin was depleted. Eventually it all came on top. In 1999 my bank called in our overdraft and the game was up. After all, a bank is a place that will lend you money only if you can prove you don't need it.

Many smaller operators who had once made a steady living were put out of business. These smaller care home owners took to re-mortgaging their houses in order to make ends meet. The only real winners were the PLCs, which had shareholders' funds to call upon. Increasingly, the smart money in the business goes into purpose-built homes which meet current standards and are of a design which can relatively easily accommodate any future changes.

I was out of business. Millions had passed through my hands and I had lived the Charlie Potatoes life for a good few years. I knew that I had to get back into business fast, before I ended up in a care home myself. That's when my troubles began. All those carefree years were soon to come to an end. I met my perfect partner.

CHAPTER TWENTY-SIX

Perfect Partners

There I was, giving my details to a dating agency. Following the rules of the game I praised my positive attributes – swimmer's physique (well, I swim); bon vivant; raconteur extraordinaire, not forgetting the inevitable V.G.S.O.H. and that size matters when it comes to a chap's bank balance. After all, if I was looking for a perfect partner, so too was my soulmate to be. Best foot forward. I saw her photo and we met up. JP and I soon found ourselves taking our first tentative steps down the road to mutual bliss. Current cynicism aside, we were both at the time taking all this seriously; very seriously indeed.

This was 1999 and I had found my perfect partner. True, neither of us were exactly love-struck teenagers with no baggage. I was two-timing my partner of twenty years, the mother of our children, Janice, who in turn was receiving malicious phone calls from the perfect one. "Is that the prostitute's house, from prostitute's money, whose children are on drugs and are sexually abused ...?" It later transpired that Janice and our children received hundreds of such calls, many of which were far worse. Sometimes they would be every few minutes, even on Christmas Day, which shows that JP has a sentimental streak I suppose. Love is blind, though, and a perfect partner can do no wrong.

When those same tapes were played some five years later,

it was pointed out to me that JP had sounded like that girl in The Exorcist when she was possessed. What, however, possessed me to gloss over the calls and fail to see what everyone else could see so clearly? But I was happy then and, to tell the truth, my happiness has always mattered to me. I moved in and set up home in her 15th-Century farmhouse.

When my care homes business collapsed I was in hock to the banks to the tune of £8-Million; not exactly small change, so I took the IVA route. This was done legitimately through my accountant, although even I came to doubt that last bit when JP's halo slipped to somewhere around her ankles. The denunciation to a disturbingly credulous constabulary could have come from no other source, but I have no proof. Put it this way, no creditors stepped forward to point the finger; the only parties who might reasonably have been expected to show an interest.

This was to come later. For now all was blue skies as far as the eye could see. We must have driven the equivalent of a couple of global circumnavigations in our search for a brace of care homes which we could operate together, with JP up-front and me raising the bulk of the finance. Although she had no business experience at the level we were contemplating, she had a proven record of dealing with elderly people, mainly women, through her flower arranging demonstrations. We finally settled on two homes, one in Somerset, the other in Humberside. These were chosen for their business potential and that they were the best the market then had to offer within our price range.

I think we had become so used to driving vast distances that we completely lost touch with the practicalities of having two homes hundreds of miles apart. That was fine when I had substantial numbers of staff within my chain of homes, but not so easy for JP having to commute across country.

Given my IVA, my usual facility for raising business funds was temporarily curtailed, but I still managed to come up with the bulk of the money through a partial re-mortgage on Janice's home, with her permission, I should add. JP, meanwhile, raised some of the finance and also presented herself as the company's officially-approved CSCI (the care home industry's then governing body) representative.

Praise where it's due. JP had excellent people skills and was always immaculately presented and totally committed; an asset to any company she was involved with. Soon, her efforts had laid the foundations of a successful business. But there were fault lines in these foundations before even the first building block was in place, for any outsider could see, especially those blessed by hindsight, that our relationship was doomed to failure. It would have taken a V.G.S.O.H. indeed for me to have endured her constant verbal sniping, and I was a long way from getting measured up for a pair of angel's wings.

JP had once told me a story – It had been a wet night as she'd driven the Holt to Bromsgrove Road. She was an experienced driver and had had little reason to trouble her insurance company since she had been in her teens. Tonight, though, she wasn't concentrating. I was back with Janice. It was 2002, over two years into our perfect partnership, and my desertion was hurting her. We'd argued; one of those can't be together, can't be apart arguments that peppered the turmoil of our relationship. I had been feeling guilty at leaving Janice alone with the children. So didn't I feel guilt at leaving JP alone? She'd driven at speed, vowing revenge on Janice for taking me away. She told me later that the tears of anger filling her eyes meant she didn't spot a bend covered in wet leaves as her Mazda flipped and rolled. Equally confused, she said, were the owners of the garden in which the car finally came to rest. I can imagine the scene – an immaculate woman in a cashmere coat dusting herself down and smiling winningly, offering of course her most profuse apologies.

JP's Mazda moment recalls yet another incident involving a car. I was telling her about the air-rifle at the end of the ride in the Matra-Simca with Patsy as we passed the spot where it had occurred some twenty-odd years before. JP had never been to Italy and as we were on the French Riviera, Ventimiglia and the Italian border were only a fast drive away along one of the world's most glamorous roads. We were heading for Genoa, the northern Italian port that I had once shipped out of en-route to Port Said. We were happy then, as you are supposed to be when you are in love. I'd told her of my first berth on a cargo ship, how I'd arrived with nothing but the clothes on my back and a toothbrush, she laughing at my pronunciation of tooth as 'tuth', my inner-northerner.

There'd also been a bottle of Sun-In, or whatever the proprietary brand of the day was, all the more to enhance the charms of the blond, blue-eyed boy off in search of dusky maidens on foreign shores. I'd told her of why I liked Genoa, of its smell. I'd remembered that time I'd walked down mildewed sloping alleyways wet with winter drizzle, yet lit by a full Moon breaking through the clouds. I'd seen cats' eyes that night: two, three, dozens, more. As I walked the cats had followed, like I was wearing a regal train of undulating fur. Who would have directed such a scene? Perhaps a Fellini. We talked, we laughed, she my Grace Kelly to my equally imaginary Cary Grant as we swept over a viaduct. I felt young. I felt as though everything had come together at last, and I was with someone with whom I could share that, my soul-mate, my perfect partner.

In keeping with the pattern of this book you might then expect fate to intervene, something bad to interrupt my reverie, bad tidings perhaps. The phone rang. It was Harry, JP's son who managed her farm. The barn was on fire and the wind had changed direction. The house was threatened. In no time we were on a plane from Nice to London, my mind turning cartwheels. I should have been interested in JP's possessions, that supporting beams in the house were ship's timbers from vessels of Henry-V11's navy, already a century old when they were used on the house, witnessed by the carved initials of long-dead carpenters. This was her family home, her children's inheritance, her life. "Jesus, what about my papers?" She looked askance. Cary Grant might have said – "You poor thing," flicking his eyes from side to side to show he was acting, all the while squeezing her hand, but we'd know he was really thinking of whether his papers were OK.

We arrived some twelve hours after the call from Harry. The barn was still smouldering, the house too hot to touch even though it was being hosed down by firemen. All was well though. My papers were safe.

JP didn't like being without a man in her life, and one on the end of a telephone wasn't what she had in mind. What was the point in talking to me when all the time she thought I'd be going home to her, to Janice? She soon found someone else through computer dating. Perfect Partners? Perfection is hard to find. He lived nearby and had money and land. That's a start. But JP is a passionate woman and her new mate came up short in that department. Still, they got engaged, so it wasn't a trivial affair. He ended it, though, when he found out that she'd resumed seeing me. She said later that her ex-fiancé was a nice man. Is that what she really wanted? Anyway, I certainly didn't fit that bill.

Apart from all the personal ads I was using around that time to meet a variety of women, there was one with whom a real relationship developed. It was Janet, who overlapped both Janice and JP. That was to be a strange affair.

CHAPTER TWENTY-SEVEN

Alienating the Aliens

I was at a loose end at home alone one day when the doorbell rang. Two booted and suited men stood on the doorstep, clean-cut and smiling and with enough apprehensiveness about them to reassure my habitually guilty conscience that I wasn't about to have my collar felt for some long-forgotten misdemeanor. They were Jehovah's Witnesses.

We've all been there on that one, and usually we suddenly remember that there's something in the oven or that the dog's about to drop puppies. Being me and ever-curious, I invited them in for a cup of tea.

When I drink I do so for England, and any other country that will have me. When I smoke I can keep an entire tobacco plantation going single-handed. In other words, the tendency is towards compulsion. So, when these two guys knocked on the door I jumped right into their world. They don't smoke, drink moderately and keep fit, the men somehow looking like astronauts and the women like Stepford Wives. Bright and shiny and clean and happy, like all people with shared beliefs they take great comfort from their common ground. Many hold responsible positions and often have a sales background. Strangely, I found a surprising number to be window cleaners; maybe because they make good money and don't have to adhere to a fixed work schedule, or maybe they've seen too many sinners 'when I'm cleaning winders' (sic). Whatever, the main difficulty all shared was the sense of trepidation as they door-stepped. They usually expected a polite rebuff but were often met with insults. I admired them for their courage in sticking to their beliefs in the face of doubt.

One of the men who visited me that first time at the house was called Steve, and he got me briefly into alternative medicine. Although I was never privileged to be one of the many who enjoyed physical intimacy with Princess Diana, we both visited the same colonic irrigation specialist in Windsor, and it is highly likely that we both made royal arses of ourselves in receiving the warm, soapy water treatment from the same instrument, although I spotted no sign of a royal crest. Apparently, analyses of waste products from the intestinal tract have shown a build-up of the detritus of undigested food, including traces of a mother's milk, even in people over fifty. It was recommended that the irrigation be repeated every couple of years, although considering the number of times I've been financially shafted recently it feels like the process has become even more frequent and, I have to say, my bank account feels thoroughly cleansed.

Back at Kingdom Hall I was beginning to find some of their beliefs a little difficult to digest. That there are one-hundred-and-forty-four-thousand chosen ones who have an assured reservation in Heaven was one of them. This elite are fast-tracked but the rest of us, the good ones, that is, will have to wait around to be resurrected. The Jehovah's Witnesses believe that the full quota has not yet been reached, and a man in Beaconsfield will be one of the last to be identified. This all seems a bit unfair on those yet to be born. Of course, this seemingly arbitrary figure is based on a Biblical reference, and was probably more arithmetically sound when the early Christians numbered relatively few adherents, but it doesn't really stack up in an age when the world's population has hit seven billion.

One part of the belief that I did find easy to digest was the unleavened bread. There is an annual conference held in Twickenham at which the bread, a bit like Melba Toast, is passed around. It got round to me, and I was starving. I noshed away for Jehovah, much to the horror of the assembly. I did not know it, but only the Chosen Ones were permitted to partake, the rest being required to pass it on. There was the most silent silence that I have ever heard as it dawned on me that they would not be upping the number to one-hundred-and-forty-four-thousand-and-one. I slipped away from their church after that, just as another was slipping into something far more sinister.

I've mentioned quite a few of the women in my life, not because I want to appear the lothario, but because I have always enjoyed being around them. I got involved with one whom I cared for very much. Her name is Janet and she fitted in between Janice and JP, with perhaps too much of an overlap for the sake of good order. She was young and I not so young. I found her extremely attractive, but she had this wall-eye. I got that fixed, as conversationally it was distracting. When talking to her I always found myself looking over my shoulder to find out who or what she was staring at, always forgetting that in her own way she was looking directly at me. Once Moorfields Eye Hospital had done their work we saw eye to eye on most things and for awhile I was extremely happy. Then she fell into the hands of the Scientologists.

Whenever I'd mentioned to friends that I was going to refer in this book to my passing interest in Scientology and the Jehovah's Witnesses they advised against it. Their point was that I would be seen as a nutter and it would make it hard for readers to take any of the book seriously in an age when even admitting to being a Christian is, to so many, like saying that you believe The Tooth Fairy is Santa Claus' love-child. But what happened was that Janet got sucked into Scientology, and I followed, to get her out.

We all know of the celebrity adherents of Scientology, the Cruises and Travoltas, where the cult, in return for donations and publicity, uses its powerful PR machine to protect reputations and thus maintain box-office appeal. Janet did not have the power to make Tinsel-town jump nor are her thoughts likely to provide newspaper headlines, but she is more typical of those sucked into the machine. Intelligence offers little protection in that the intelligent are often the most sensitive and therefore vulnerable of people.

I started my affair with her when she, a young mother of two, was married to a man some thirty years her senior. Working on the principle that you regret in life the things you haven't done rather than those you have, I instigated an affair with her. She was at the time having an affair with my company's group MD, so it's probably fair to say that if her marriage hadn't quite hit the rocks then the ship had definitely sprung a leak. The MD took ill and I jumped on board.

I must have been going through one of my less-sensitive, drink-fuelled stages because, to my current astonishment, I found myself going to her house to spend the night with her while her husband and kids were there. Eventually, even I worked out that this was impractical, so a week later we arranged to go to an inn in Inkberrow, Worcestershire, the town on which the Archers is reputedly based. That evening turned into a real soap opera. I waited in the bar for her to arrive and had a few drinks, my anxiety mounting. I sensed something was wrong. In spite of this, as she was always so punctual I ordered her usual starter in the hotel restaurant. I was ravenous and I didn't want to appear selfish at this stage in our relationship, so I thought some food on a plate for her would convince her I was the kind and caring type. Which of course I am. I ate mine and sent hers back to be warmed-up. She had no mobile and after that visit to her house I was certainly not going to phone there. Eventually I went to bed.

The next morning I phoned her office in one of my care homes. There'd been no sign of her. She was off the radar. After that I returned to the inn every night in the hope of seeing her. On the fourth night I spotted her across the crowded bar. A man, a stranger, was putting his coat around her shoulders, making that chivalrous protective gesture that shows a man cares. I called out her name. That was a mistake. They both ran and I was impeded by the crowd. By the time I reached the car park they were away.

I later discovered that Janet and the man had stayed with a near neighbour of hers. I was traumatised. The sense of loss was appalling. I was in love with Janet and in love with the idea of her being in love with me. I have already referred in this book to my reaction to loss and rejection. If I give something up, then fine. If it gives me up, then I want it back.

This chivalrous man, I later learned, was called Gary Stewart. A lot of people in the area knew him. He had a little business that involved buying aerial photos from a helicopter firm and selling them door-to-door. Most pre-Google people were fascinated at the prospect of getting a bird's-eye view of their home, and at only twenty quid a shot there was no shortage of buyers. His line of business also gave him access to bored and lonely housewives.

A familiar sales technique is to mirror your mark, using the same eye movements and facial expressions, gestures and even breathing patters. It taps into the subconscious, and the Scientologists have got it down to a fine art. People at the pub said it was peculiar, how Janet and Stewart would even walk in step.

She'd been swallowed by the cult of Scientology. Much of what I learned about her experiences came later. Like how she had been taken to a Scientologist centre in Birmingham, where downstairs they had a bookshop. Outside the shop would be smiling followers, much like charity chuggers, who'd stop passers-by, usually the young, and try to gain recruits. I remember it happening to me once, years ago on London's Tottenham Court Road – "Would you like to change your personality?"

"No, thank you so much, although I must admit it has already been suggested I should by many of my nearest and not so dearest." Above the Brummie bookshop was a sauna. There, vulnerable inductees would sweat out their impurities; their 'bad' personalities, infected as they were with traces of alien 'Thetans'. They would be steamed from dawn to dusk, then fed huge doses of vitamin B-complex, like recovering alcoholics. Once 'healthy' and receptive, they would be indoctrinated using powerful brain-washing techniques. They'd be mentally stripped bare, asked to reveal their earliest memories, with an 'e-meter' attached to them. Comfortable memories would keep the meter's needle in neutral while traumatic memories would cause violent swings, much like a lie-detector. They were then made to submit to psychometric testing, just like any banking recruit in the City of London. The avowed purpose of all this was to break down the blocks which early traumas place on a person's mind, that and their 'alien' memories, thus encouraging them to become 'clear'. Or, put another way, it is a device to break down a person's individual personalities and turn them into an amorphous whole, a single organism espousing the teachings of the great teacher, L Ron Hubbard.

Apart from having too many names, L Ron had, during his World War Two US Navy service, complained of suicidal tendencies and a seriously affected mind. Right, just the kind of spiritual leader one needs when lonely and vulnerable. In 1954, our Ron founded his 'church', the inverted commas because it still hasn't achieved the status of a recognised religion. Mrs Hubbard was sent to the slammer in the Eighties for the burglary and wiretapping of some one-hundred agencies, including those of the US government, which were looking into the 'church's' activities. Hubbard died before the IRS could do-do-Ron-Ron for tax fraud involving his illegal disbursements to worldwide offshore banks. This money came, of course, from his celebrity stooges, but also from people who'd pledged their life savings to keep Ron the con in luxury yachts, having paid up to $1,000 an hour for an intensive course that would keep them in a state of euphoria which they had been led to believe comes from having been 'cleared'. The core of Scientology's teachings is that humans are made up of clusters of spirits, 'Thetans', who were banished to Earth seventy-five million years ago by the crazed galactic ruler, Xenu, allegedly for tax reasons. Please don't ask! What a bastard. Even Gordon Brown wouldn't have tried that one, although come to think of it … It is not dissimilar in this respect to Christianity in that these Thetans are supposedly immortal souls dwelling temporarily in an Earthbound material body, but the Thetans' extra-terrestrial genesis does stretch credulity somewhat when you consider the world's population doubles in a generation. All the lonely people, where do they all come from?

Do remember, according to Ron, you do not have to be a Scientologist to be a Thetan. We are all Thetans, descendants of those primordial godlike entities who created the material universe in a time before time and succumbed to its pleasures but then try to reject the leaden boots of being and return to their exalted state. It all goes a step beyond Christianity in that we were once our own God. It's not bad, for a religious basis, in that it makes as much sense as any of the others. Now I am not one of those prone to dispute that there could be life in a galaxy long ago and far away, but consider the Warp Factors involved in getting here in the first place. True, some of the higher beliefs of Buddhism are brought into play, but by a karma comedian.

You couldn't make it up, unless you were a science fiction writer, which of course Hubbard was. He wrote Westerns too, but try making a religion out of that. I suppose he could have carved one of the Monument Valley pinnacles into the shape of Clint Eastwood as Josey Wales with Chief Dan George seated at his right hand. That would get them thinking in a couple of thousand years. But there's one even more serious flaw in all this. If you're leader of an alien cult, would you really be called Ron?

In the unlikely event that a Scientologist stumbles across Get Lucky, I should emphasise that my viewpoint is purely subjective, and I concede it is as perfectly reasonable to found a 'religion' based on aliens as it is to worship Prince Philip, as do members of New Guinea's Cargo Cult. That armed guards allegedly stake-out the perimeter of the Scientology centre, Gold Base, ninety-miles from LA, in a parody of Spectre HQ, is surely a sign that the cult's leaders fear a rush of disciples and they just wish to use the guns to encourage folk to form an orderly queue.

But it's no laughing matter, especially when you learn that Nancy Cartwright, the voice of Bart Simpson, is a cult member. Bart would soon give them short shrift, but he wasn't around to make them eat his pants, so I got myself a private detective. It cost me thousands trying to break through their defences. Once I'd tracked down Janet I joined up. I tried to play it dumb, but, as always, I talked too much and they sussed me, asking me to leave, perceiving that I was a dangerous influence. I had started to affect other recruits and the Thetans were not happy campers.

I'd thought that if they wanted childhood traumas I'd give them some. What my happy childhood lacked in drama I managed to make up for with a bit of imagination, but I think the imaginary incident with the clown at the circus was a step too far. I was asked to leave. I've always been proud of that. The Scientologists actually asked me to leave.

The police weren't interested. Maybe they were too busy down at the Masonic Lodge. I made Gary Stewart my target, applying constant psychological pressure on him, shadowing him. Funny that, it's what the Scientologists call it – 'Shadowing' – when they hit on a mark and groom them for recruitment. After three or four months Janet came round and left the cult, ultimately stronger than Stewart.

I had 'won', but at what price? My love for her had been genuine, yet I could not forgive her for the pain she had caused me. We did try to rekindle the relationship, in Malaga. I asked her about the physical side. She said that he'd never touched her. That made sense. Once the act has taken place the balance of power is changed forever. Also, by now I had met my Perfect Partner. Speculation is a largely futile activity, but perhaps without L Ron Hubbard I would not have found my PP and got into the pickles of recent times. But then again, if Janet was that psychologically vulnerable, then maybe she would have ended up enslaved to another cult. After all, if you are vulnerable enough there's always someone out there ready and willing to gobble you up.

I went to see her some time later. Remember my visit to Joke when I slipped up her drainpipe? This time I climbed a sturdy tree. She was living in Spain, and it was a bugger climbing through dense branches in that heat, but finally my head poked above her garden wall. There she was, watering her plants right there in front of me. Like the Joke visit I didn't speak during the act, although this time it was confined to tree-climbing. Janet looked up, with that sixth-sense we use when we guess someone is there. She saw me, or rather my head, as unlikely an apparition as a Thetan in Tesco, and fainted clean away. She must have been excited to see me, that's all I can think.

CHAPTER TWENTY-EIGHT

I'll Enjoy Getting You into Trouble

I later found out that one of JP's taped messages left on Janice's recorder had been the unambiguous – "I'll enjoy getting you into trouble." This was to me. She'd wrongly thought that I was staying at Janice's. This was back in '99, in our early days as perfect partners.

One day we'd gone to lunch at a country hotel. I forget precisely where, but it was a very pleasant day, I do remember that. It didn't last, though. We had an argument, or rather JP spoke and I listened. I can't remember what it was about, but it was one of those tirades that wash over you while you fake the right responses. All you're doing of course is feigning consciousness. It was probably something to do with Janice. When JP wasn't making her 'Exorcist' calls, she would content herself with ranting about Janice. Anyway, she stormed off. I suppose she got a minicab, but I was just happy to see the back of her that day.

I had a Bentley Continental at the time, a car that could all but drive itself. I knew I must be over the limit, certainly enough over not to do the sensible thing and leave the car there. I hadn't got far though, when there they were flashing me to pull over. So I did. Then I jumped out and legged it across some nearby fields. Those farmers with their ploughs, they just don't appreciate how difficult all those ruts make it for us miscreants to get clean away. "Sir. Sir! Stop! Stop now!"

I've often wondered how, in films, the fat cops always outrun the fit, young guy. Well, I wasn't either, but I outran those two. I hid in a hut As there were no windows I couldn't see outside, so I stayed in there for hours. I can still smell that hut.

Next day the police arrived at the pub where I was drinking. I spotted them early and ran into the gents to drop some Rohypnol tablets into a window-box. I'd got the tabs to help JP sleep because she had a severe back pain at the time, not to get my wicked way. I was arrested for the driving offence but got off on a technicality. When I went back for the tablets, all the plants were dead. Those tablets can't be good for you.

I should have learned two valuable lessons that day. Firstly, don't drive with two bottles of wine inside you. The second? Well, put it this way, until later events I'd put that incident down to coincidence.

CHAPTER TWENTY-NINE

Fernando Luca Swims with the Fishes

I was in Istanbul with a friend in late May, 2004. We were trying to source Rolex watches, hoping to buy cheap over there and sell dear in the UK. OK, so it wasn't the big picture and it didn't work out, but for me it was a cathartic trip. It was my first weekend away from JP. I'd left her. It's extraordinary how obsession can take many forms. From Istanbul I took a boat up the Bosphorus to Romania. I went to Bucharest, on my first naughty-boy R & R trip in many years. Tony Knight, who was to re-enter my life later, lent me his flat and his bodyguards. My friend and I had already had a near-miss in Istanbul when we'd wound-up in a clip-joint; just we two, the girls, and an army of villains. There's nothing so unusual in all that of course, except that I was carrying a small fortune in cash for the Rolexes. My friend, a fit runner, so an unlikely-looking candidate, faked a heart attack so convincingly that he was helped into a taxi. We were out of there.

Two days later there I was in Bucharest with still too much cash, a newly-purchased Rolex, no resourceful friend to hand, and surrounded by people who could have made very good use of all that money and a luxury watch. For the first night, Tony's armed bodyguards gave me reassurance, until it clicked that they posed more of a threat than the locals. I got out of there. Tony later claimed I'd welshed on the deal, having failed to pay his staff, etc, but he hadn't known the background to the story. Still, I did pay him back. Indirectly through me he met Waka Kele.

When I returned from Bucharest I still had the Rolex Submariner I'd bought in Istanbul, so I tried to sell it. First-up was this giant Mancunian. I'm six-two yet felt like I was talking to his belly. I'd driven up the M1 to meet him at a mutually convenient service area. He presented a banker's draft. The problem was, it was virtually hand-written. Then he got offended because I wouldn't accept it. It was like Waka's later righteous indignation at having been caught out. It went on. One after the other came out of the woodwork trying to scam a watch.

I was selling at way below market value, so was not conning them. I soon realised, though, that as a business idea this was a non-runner, so I sold it to a friend, Paul Downey. He'd already bought a couple of Rolexes in the Far East and had sold them on for a small profit, so he was happy to buy mine. Born in Geneva, raised in Istanbul, it had travelled via Bucharest to London and probably expected to end its days in Manchester, where its waterproofing would have been tested to the limit.

Paul sold it on eBay, using an escrow site for payment. His own buyer was in Palma, Majorca. Paul was known to me as 'Tops', because of his penchant for keeping his tan topped-up. He's travelled the world, a redhead leaving a trail of empty factor-50 sun-block tubes in his wake. So a trip to Palma in early May, although eating into the profit margin, hit the spot. He met his man, a respectable-looking guy called 'Fernando Luca', and the deal was done. Tops, always a 'fashionista', was distressed by the man's diamond-patterned golfer's v-neck, but he's willing to overlook anything in pursuit of a profit and a tan. He gave over the watch to this very personable, if badly-dressed, individual, and flew back to London waiting for £10,000 to hit his account. Nada. He'd been had. It had been a very convincing fake escrow site. For those unfamiliar with escrow, it's where funds are held until both the buyer and seller are mutually satisfied that they wish to go ahead with the transaction. How many tubes of factor-50 can you get for ten grand? But no point in crying. You have to move on.

Months passed. Then one day a look-alike escrow website popped up. Could it be? Tops followed through. He tried Interpol, the British police, the Spanish police, all to no avail. The British wanted all documentation in English, the Spanish in Spanish. Bit by bit, though, he wore them down, and a plan was hatched with the help of the Palma police. A sting was set-up. A 'watch' was sent by DHL from London to the buyer's given address. He was using a different name this time, not Fernando Luca, but the police knew it was the same man. The cops waited outside the house for the DHL man to make his delivery. Tops was in the car with them, wearing a cream Armani suit, looking like Simon Templar. But the DHL guy panicked when he saw all the guns. So one of the cops borrowed his uniform to deliver the package. It didn't contain a watch, though. It contained a can of sardines and some makeweights to exactly equal the feel of a heavy Rolex and its box and papers. As 'Fernando' opened the package he saw the message – "Fernando Luca sleeps with the fishes." He looked up to see that the 'DHL man' was pointing a gun at him, although he was laughing too much to have used it. 'Fernando Luca' was held on remand in a tough prison for several months. But then, under the Napoleonic Code, on which the Spanish legal system is based, a deal was struck. He bought his freedom by paying back my friend's money plus expenses. Tops was back in sun-block. Luca, an Italian, was part of a Europe-wide Romanian gang. Maybe the Rolex went back to Bucharest, close to Istanbul, where it 'grew up'. What goes around comes around, like the ticking of a watch.

CHAPTER THIRTY

A Beretta? That's a Lady's Gun

My first arrest through DV (again initials to obscure identity) came a few months later, in October 2004. This was for an alleged DSS Benefit Fraud and several alleged false insurance claims. I will never be able to prove it and the police certainly did their best to do so, but I and those close to the case were convinced that the whole investigation had been instigated by JP. It was also, I was convinced, the genesis of her relationship with DV, although both contend this did not take place until over a year later, several months after my imprisonment, and of course in law I bear the burden of proof.

A friend had stayed overnight at my flat after having worked late the previous evening transcribing JP's 'Exorcist' tapes. These I wanted to use to help establish whether or not she was a fit and proper person to run care homes. She was, after all, trying to take over the homes at this stage and, as the registered carer, she had the moral high-ground.

DV must have loved days like these; just like being a proper copper again. He had six or seven officers as back-up and a private insurance investigator too. Like when I got stuck in that caravan window, life for DV changed forever that day, all in the split-second between raising his arm outside my front-door and bringing his knuckles down hard in insistent rapping. That special rap the police use that lets you know it's not the postman nor are you overdue on the semi-skimmed. For me, there are better ways to start the day. DV, though, looked happy enough.

My friend the tape man had remained in the flat while I was carted off. DV asked whether I was in the jewellery business. It was a strange question until I recalled that only JP had known about my Rolex trip to Istanbul. There were too many of them, the police that is, all too big and too protected for such relatively minor offences. Clearly I was potentially a dangerous man, that old JP mantra. I possibly had a gun; after all, she put it about that a chum and I had raided a West End bank using Berettas. A Beretta? That's a lady's gun, as Q once said to Bond. Also, if I wish to withdraw funds from my bank I queue like everybody else. Anyway, isn't it a banker's job to rob *us*?

After the arrest, following which I was bailed, I started drinking heavily and resolved to do something about it. The Cardinal Clinic is a rambling old country house in a picturesque setting in the Berkshire countryside. Over Christmas 2004/5 I had voluntarily submitted myself for treatment. It's like a Priory without the paparazzi. I needed to lose weight, stop drinking, stop worrying, stop being scared. Time once was I was never scared.

The clinic is about three miles from Windsor and too close to Slough for comfort. Escapees in search of a drink are always presumed to have gone to Windsor. Those who choose Slough are given up on as lost souls.

A couple of my more cynical friends dropped by for lunch on Boxing Day. They complained the turkey and the gravy were cold. Sod them. I was paying. Or someone was, anyway. They said it was effectively a loony-bin, full of the weak and gullible. How could it be a loony-bin? I was in there.

I found the ambience excellent and the facilities, advice and care superlative, or perhaps I just liked being centre of attention. The other patients, if that's the right word, were there for two or three weeks. At that time of year it's a good place to go to avoid the season's temptations. They were largely a talented group of people who had suffered 'burn-out'; what would have been a nervous breakdown in earlier times. Some were using the Cardinal to recharge their batteries before re-joining the fray, much like at a health-farm. Some though, were genuinely vulnerable. One such was a tree-surgeon who, as the result of an accident, had been left badly disfigured down one leg and, now unable to practice his profession, his confidence was shot to pieces. He underwent treatment, and although I couldn't see much progress in him, I wished him well, and his plight somehow started to put my own tendency at that time to self-obsess into perspective.

One day a beautiful young woman arrived. She looked straight off the catwalk. It was though she had been driving to The Priory and had taken the wrong turn. On top of all their other problems, the male patients suddenly developed swivel-neck syndrome. Suddenly, people who had previously hidden their outside lives from each other started revealing the value of their properties, the size of their bank balances; all the usual male mating calls. She suffered from a chronic coke habit and repetitive action syndrome. But whatever her problem, she was vulnerable, and so too was my tree-surgeon friend. So two broken people got together and made a whole. As far as I am aware they are still together. I do hope so.

If you are receptive to psycho-analysis, then the treatment given at clinics such as the Cardinal opens you up and enables you to confront aspects of your personality which were previously hidden, even from yourself. After leaving the clinic I stayed off the booze and cigarettes for a few weeks. Then one day I saw a teasingly-priced Merlot in the local supermarket wine section. At least I'd tried.

CHAPTER THIRTY-ONE

Wasn't Me, Guv. It Was Boris

I must confess, I became obsessed with the whole JP/DV affair and was convinced I was being made victim of a conspiracy and was determined to expose it. There I'd be each morning, sitting in a greasy spoon amid all the men with rolled-up copies of The Sun in their back pockets, getting stoked-up ready for a proper day's work ahead. I'd be out early, making my endless lists of Things-To-Do, mobile poised, as much a tool of my trade as any Black & Decker, but it doesn't get your hands dirty.

Then I'd see the cleaners, the tired-looking women hurrying home to pack their kids off to school, scrubbing floors to keep their future ASBO earners in Coke (the drink, I think) and Wagon Wheels, or whatever it is children eat. They'd be all ages, these women, but many still quite young, in that old-young way a hard life confers on people. Some were probably no more than five or so years on from that magical moment when eyes had locked across a crowded Wetherspoons and a smooth-talking prince had offered the earth and the stars and a crown fit for a princess. So she got these Marigold gloves.

That day, the light-bulb that hovers above my head glowed brightly. These women might be strapped for cash, but in many cases it didn't seem to affect their ability to put food into their mouths. I bet there was a cupboard full of

XXL Marigolds tucked away in the deepest recesses of the local council's HQ. Just my ham-fisted size.

This was after my original arrest on the benefits and insurance charges. We're talking early '05. Don't get me wrong. I didn't get into drag as a cleaning lady. I got the cleaner job as me, although there was a bit of hairnet-wearing activity. I recall it was hats or hairnets, depending on which part of the building you were in. Now my shock of Boris Johnson blond is quite distinctive, and for those who have questioned the provenance of the colour I here attest that the effect of morning sun kissing a field of swaying ripe corn is au naturel. So that's settled then. And do remember, I'm a litigious sod.

The hair being covered was important, for without a net or hat DV might have recognised me when I confronted him face-to-face in his office. On this occasion I'd opted for a net pulled low, so that the sides caused my upper ears to protrude like Benny Hill's Fred Scuttle. I shoved out my bottom lip too, just like Benny. This seemed to work, because DV looked straight at me from no more than a metre away. I sensed rather than heard him coming. Of course, what I was after was written evidence that DV and JP had conspired against me.

Thankfully, DV didn't recognise me. Even without the net and facial contortions he possibly might not have done so. After all, I was out of context, and even in his wildest imaginings he couldn't have dreamt that his arch-enemy would have shown up in such a guise. It was beyond normal comprehension. Mine too, when I look back on that time. I knew I'd had a lucky break and I knew when to ride my luck and when to dismount. Anyway, the early hours were killing me. I left there for the last time, scurrying home past my regular greasy spoon to feed my imaginary family. Jesus, if there'd been ASBOs in my bad-boy days I would have acquired enough for a necklace, or maybe a skipping-rope, not that I'd know an ASBO if it was offered to me free down the local.

I was being bloody-minded, but I went to the care home in Humberside. This was in the spring of '05, before JP had bought out my percentage. I felt I had a right to be there, at my home. It made no sense, I know, and I was counselled not to go. I'd been barred by CSCI from my own homes purely on JP's say so. She'd gone to them and said that I was a disruptive influence. I had had no idea of this, until one day we were in an essential bank meeting and she decided to drop it into the conversation in order to discredit me. CSCI had listened to her, and on no clear evidence that I could discern, I was barred. It's funny, but if I wasn't barred I would have had no interest whatsoever in going there.

Anyway, there I was in the home when JP was alerted by one of the nurses. She and I were alone off a short corridor when she came at me, suddenly raking her nails across my open left eye. I pushed her away. Naturally she went down and started screaming. Staff came running and I got out of there.

I sat in my car outside the home for awhile, gathering my senses. Eventually, I went to the police and reported the assault. I had no choice as I knew JP would get in first to protect herself. I was right; she'd filed for assault. The following day my eye was almost closed and oozing pus. I went to Moorfields Eye Hospital in London to be examined. I'd lost seventy-percent of vision in the injured eye.

I pressed and pressed the police to charge her with GBH, but they wouldn't as there were no witnesses to the actual incident. JP meanwhile claimed that I had hit her and I had self-inflicted my wound. A DI had said to me previously that nobody, even if crazy, could inflict such a severe injury on their own eye. Injuring yourself, especially in an eye, goes against all the deepest-rooted instincts of self-preservation. He also said that it had been a natural reaction to lash out at someone who'd injured your eye, but in no way was JP's minor bruising commensurate with her having taken blows from someone as heavy as me. That a staff member had seen me sitting outside the home in my car was taken by JP to show that I could not have been so badly injured, not taking into account that such injuries take a while to come out. Anyway, I was too shaken to drive.

Without witnesses, the police said they could do nothing. But I had it on good authority that they did something. JP had been at school with the wife of one of the senior investigating police officers and she had allegedly used this connection to try to get them to drop the case. I phoned the officer concerned and confronted him. Hardly surprisingly he denied any wrongdoing. The matter was brushed aside. The case was dropped. The eye hasn't fully recovered.

Seeing the way she works, when it's done to you it's nowhere near as funny as when it's against someone else. She'd told me some years earlier how she'd faked an assault to get out of a wheel-clamping. She'd come out of Asda on a busy day and had parked in the disabled area, or somewhere unauthorised at least, and two clampers were in action on her car. She stood close to one of them and got into a loud slanging match in order to gather an audience, then suddenly threw herself to the ground, screaming that one of the men had pushed her. She lay on the ground writhing in 'agony'. The clampers got out of there fast.

I suppose one of my weakness is that I cannot accept being tossed aside. It is not even a concept that my ego can cope with, even begin to comprehend, but when I think about it, although JP had worked hard to build-up and maintain the homes, it was me who had enabled them to come about. So once they were up-and-running, it would have been expedient for her to move on. Get me banned, squeeze me out, and apply as much pressure as possible to distract me from trying to obtain top price for my shares. That would explain the constant allegations to the police. Throw as much mud as possible and hope that some would stick.

CHAPTER THIRTY-TWO

Whatever Happened to the Laughing Policeman?

To be fair, JP had devoted a huge amount of time and effort into making a success of the two homes, but she was on a very reasonable salary, had a company car, expenses, and a substantial undisputed share division. The High Court had settled the shares in my favour, which was a fair and equitable decision in accordance with UK estoppel law: it matched the financial investment each party had made. I haven't, though, dared to add up the total cost to each of us in legal fees, although I suspect JP knows to the last penny. However, the total would be a six-figure sum – a very expensive plate-throwing exercise indeed.

I was staying in a Berkshire hotel in the spring of '05 when yet again the police came a-calling. I know I'm big, but fifteen coppers in full gear? Like when DV had knock-knock-knocked, it was overkill. It was the usual dawn chorus, so Mr and Mrs Taxpayer must have stumped up a sizeable hotel bill for the Avon & Somerset to be so far from home so early.

I'd made the voluntary arrangement, an IVA, to ensure that any payments I could make on my £8-million debts were evenly distributed among my creditors. Somehow, though, someone, and we can only guess who, had convinced the police that I had sequestered the £8-million. If only. Appropriately, as my last permanent address had been in Stratford-upon-Avon, it was much ado about nothing. As I was led away so too was my Mercedes, my gold Rolex and the cash I had on me, some £3,000. These were deemed to be 'proceeds of crime'. They carried out a simultaneous raid on one of my fellow 'criminals'. They had to smash down his door because he'd already left for his £20K p.a. nine to fiver, such was the fortune he'd stashed away.

The worst was when they visited Janice. She was pinned in a corner of her hallway as every inch of her spotless home was searched. Then she was thrown, terrified and humiliated, in a cell, not then knowing when she'd be released. Having known lots of shady people, I can say that I've never met anyone more blameless than she. I'd owed her £25K and paid it back. Money laundering? That was their accusation. Get real. But it was the way that they treated her that made it so bad. If you've lived my kind of life you take what you get, but for Janice to have been subjected to such heavy treatment brought home to me that the world had changed forever from those innocent days when £25K could legitimately pass hands without everyone on the planet thinking it was their business.

The police returned to Janice's home. This time men in white forensic suits dug up her back garden looking for guns, counterfeit money, drugs, bodies. Bodies! They used to have a sense of humour. Whatever happened to the Laughing Policeman? Surely they would have laughed if they'd known I was there, hiding up a tree. Anyway, I wonder who'd told them all that – "You killed Sir James Pyke and my auntie." Now there was a clue in that telephone allegation. It appeared that JP had once again worked her charms on the boys in blue. It was a traumatic time for Janice and her husband and it didn't exactly endear me to our two children who were living at home and who held me responsible for all that had happened.

Five months later – October, 2005: on the day I was gaoled the police arrived at my rented cottage neat Stratford-upon-Avon a little later than on the previous occasions I'd been treated to their hospitality. I'd grown accustomed to their 'dawn chorus' visits, always aware that once the day was in double figures I felt safer. I'd felt safe this time. It was well after nine and the coffee was on. Anyway, although suffering from my early-morning anxiety attacks of recent years, I had nothing to fear. I was back with JP (although more on that later) and so used to being with her that I'd all but forgotten she potentially posed a threat to my freedom. We'd been together the night before and I was looking forward to seeing her again that evening.

The police arrived team-handed. Could it be that JP had alerted them to her fantasy that I was 'armed and dangerous'? She even took the trouble to ensure that Thames Valley's finest had done their job properly, coincidentally phoning just as they were in the process of kicking the door in.

The date of my trial had been set and I'd been prepared to present myself on the appointed day. I knew that a DSS overpayment, to which I had pleaded guilty and had refunded the council, carried a risk of a short custodial sentence, but I had been sent a letter in which the council had stated that refunded overpayments below a certain amount did not even merit an investigation. I felt confident that I'd get off the insurance fraud charges as they were without basis.

Sure, there was an implicit contradiction between the two allegations; if I was taking the DSS shilling then I was declaring myself as unemployed, but if I used my rightful defence to the insurance charge that I was employed but unable to work through injury, I should be cleared of any 'loss of earnings' insurance fraud because it would have been a valid claim. Clearly there was a contradiction here in that

I was guilty of one or the other, but whatever happened in court, the last thing I expected on 09th October, 2005, was to be arrested and imprisoned for the witness intimidation of JP. We had discussed marriage, unless I imagined it.

The intimidation charge was based on two statements. The first, clearly JP's, was couched in the trademark style that belied her time spent at secretarial college. That her second statement contradicted the first was ignored by the CPS. No howlers this time, though it did contain one consistent grammatical error. A friend had spotted this when reading one of DV's later letters. A cryptologist confirmed it. The second statement was likely to have been written by DV. But let's pretend he was unbiased at that time and stick with the couple's assertion that there was then nothing between them.

It's not as though the concept of prison was that much of a shock to my system or that I'd led an unblemished career with no brushes with the law. Mostly, my brief incarcerations had been the result of a 'misunderstanding', apart from the art theft. It was usually a punch or two thrown in haste which had got me a night or so in the cells. But all in all, given how close to the wind I've sailed, I'd led a charmed life. No, the problem with those three months was that while I was serving them I thought that I was in for an indefinite period. Maybe forever. I knew that I was innocent as charged, and that there was a limit to how long I could be held for the alleged witness intimidation, but it was the IVA that clinched it. Hell, maybe I had done something wrong. Even my lawyer wasn't convinced I should book a holiday in the near future.

JP had set it up nicely in that summer of '05. So simple really. Firstly she would lull me into a false sense of security and then spring the honey-trap. I had an injunction hanging over me preventing me from seeing her, so she came to me, so afraid that for the three months prior to my imprisonment she regularly drove from her farm to Stratford-upon-Avon to stay with me, even on the night before I was arrested. Naturally I had taken this as a sign we were back on track.

She stayed with me several times a week. Then, one night a neighbour heard her through an open window, speaking on her mobile outside the cottage – "I think we've done enough …" I was arrested the following morning. The question is, why did she keep up the ruse for so long and who was she calling? Her friends in the local police? DV?

I felt like a rat trapped in a system which seemed able to make its own rules. All I could see at that stage was a future which went thus – they'd keep me in prison on a trumped-up witness intimidation charge until my trial date of March 13th, 2006; I'd pleaded guilty to the DSS, and the guilty plea, according to my brief, could taint me in the eyes of a jury; as a result they'd find me guilty of the insurance charges, my defence having crumbled under a detailed testimony from the chief prosecution witness that I had never worked as a chauffeur (she can be so convincing I could even doubt it myself); I'd receive a three-year sentence and whilst still inside would be tried for the IVA, with the police putting forward a strong case based on circumstantial evidence. The jury, influenced by my current incarceration and floundering in a technical mire, would find me guilty. Influenced by the sum involved I would receive a more severe sentence on top of the one I was already serving. All this could have been made possible by JP's testimonies. I can't remember what I had for dinner last night. She can remember every financial transaction I'd made (and many I hadn't) over the past six years. Finally, under new powers, the police would seize all my assets as 'proceeds' of crime.

If the above scenario had taken place, and in my head over Christmas 2005 there was no reason for me to suppose otherwise, I was convinced I was facing five years for crimes which I knew were not crimes. Betrayed by my lover in this way, I would have drowned in a sea of bitterness. I had been looking at the end of my life. I'm not looking for sympathy, just telling it like it was. Or like it could so easily have been.

Then DV supposedly floated the idea that I had raped JP, in a technical sense, I presume. This would serve two purposes. I could be facing another serious charge and DV could choose to believe rape had occurred. Perhaps he needed that to clear his head of any idea that JP had been with me physically and emotionally. Do you drive thirty miles each way for over three months to get raped, and do you take along your 'George Foreman low-fat grill' especially for the occasion, to make sure that I ate 'healthily'? Of course, DV hadn't known about that last bit, even with his pugilistic past.

Coincidentally, a DI investigating the IVA came up with a similar idea as DV. Was this a case of 'great minds think alike' or were we looking at a concert party? Apparently, and you couldn't make it up; if a woman sleeps with a man over an extended period but can prove she only did so to obtain favourable conditions, then rape is a consideration. Has the judiciary never heard of marriage? Or prostitution? The most disturbing aspect of this latest allegation was not the threatened charge, but the suspicion that there was a conspiracy at large. Indeed, the fact that DV had taken home my case files and discussed my £1,800 DSS overpayment with his family later became a cause of disquiet among his superiors. What made my case so interesting among the myriad others which must have been simultaneously under scrutiny?

Of course, amid all the turmoil life goes on, but my under-pressure heavy drinking was taking its toll on my relationship with my children, even though they were then adults.

Here I was at an age when your grown-up children might expect a rock, a paterfamilias of senior years to whom they could turn for wisdom and advice. Maybe a drunken ex-con didn't match up to such expectations.

There's Samantha (Sammy), my first, now over thirty and mother to Sophie. It's odd that even having comfortably turned sixty, I believed I was too young to be a grandfather. Sammy has certainly inherited somebody's charm and I'd like to claim it's mine.

Poppy came next. Although she attended Redroof's theatre school just up the road from her mother Janice's house, the stage did not beckon. Poppy is academically gifted and studying psychology, so goodness knows what she makes of me. She has devoted many recent years to caring for HIV victims in South Africa's 'God's Golden Acre', with her studies running concurrently.

Then there's Tommy. He looks a lot like old photos of me but he's less wild than I was at that age, probably thanks to Janice's calming genes. Tom's in IT and a personal fitness trainer, perhaps preferring to remain looking like old photos of me.

I love them all, but there were times when they'd have been hard-pressed to know this. Then again, back in February 2006 it wasn't time for me to build bridges. I was more absorbed in wanting a piece of those who had put me in gaol. That was before I'd even found out I'd been robbed. I wrote above that I had money. It didn't take long, though, for me to discover that 'had' was the operative word. My then lawyer, ably assisted by my business advisor and erstwhile friend, had cleaned me out.

CHAPTER THIRTY-THREE

A Tinkle of Truth

Waka (pronounced wokka) came to me with good credentials. He'd been a senior associate of the Aussie billionaire, Alan Bond. In telling an anecdote, he was White Rabbit mark-two, only with Waka you felt his Walter Mitty tales had a tinkle, if not a ring, of truth. Did he have a lawyer daughter working as consiglierie to a major crime family in Vegas? Probably. Was he a qualified jet pilot? Possibly, though a later meeting with the Aussie businessman Alan Bond, revealed he had never gone anywhere near the sharp end of his planes. Had he searched for Nazi gold in Austria in he company of a businessman who'd invested A$125,000 and subsequently lost it to Waka? Oh yes.

This is a story in itself, how Hitler had earmarked a rich, historic vein to help finance his war machine, although you wonder whom he might have paid. Maybe some of the compliant US corporations that managed to get rich whilst supping with the Devil? Anyway, Waka had struck gold, but the most he got out of it was to scam Aussie businessmen and run up a sizable hotel bill for himself and an accompanying film crew. Did John Dragicevich, the big Slav from Perth, WA, known as the 'Bounty Hunter', sent to recover the money taken from the Aussie, wind up dead, face-down in a cheap Bangkok hotel room in August, 2005, and did the Thai and Aussie press speculate on the cause of death? Definitely, although no allegations were, or are, being made.

One thing is certain; while I was in the slammer Waka showed up all over: Soho, to get his hands on a house owned by the Maltese mafia; Shanghai on an immigration scam; Beijing to steal a painting – does the man have no morals?; Pinewood Studios, where he, or rather I, was 'financing' a film; the French Riviera, to buy an ocean-going yacht at a knock-down price; Aérospatiale in Toulouse in south-west France to broker an arms deal between France and North Korea; Cape Town, in an attempt to obtain gold-mining contacts to invest in North Korea; and North Korea itself, there to acquire shares in that mine. I'll have to be careful here. He certainly puts himself about, and I don't want a reader more interested in his story than mine. He's the bad guy, remember?

While I had been at a low-ebb in late 2005, Waka had repeatedly tried to get me to hand him Power of Attorney. It got pretty close at times, but thankfully I didn't sign the documents he waved under my nose on prison visits. When I first went inside, he couldn't run to a cup of coffee. Two-months later he was doing deals all over the world. Roger Pitts-Tucker had released substantial funds to him. My funds. Of course, what I didn't know then was that Roger was also enabling a British nobility-titles scam, which eventually led to a six-month suspension by the Solicitors' Disciplinary Tribunal.

CHAPTER THIRTY-FOUR

A Cannon on the Loose

I had to seek closure, as they say in modern therapy-speak. I was obsessed by JP and no matter how I tried to rationalise it I could not understand why she had, in my view, betrayed me. Family and friends told me the relationship was over and had been for a couple of years at least – "Just let it go. Move on." How many times have I heard that advice only to promptly disregard it? Most could understand why I was seeking justice, yet none could understand my apparent obsession. Janice, of course, had good reason to hate her for the malice JP had directed her way, but men too were negative. "She's trouble," seemed to be a common sentiment, the tapes having told them something I could not hear. Anyway, that aspect of JP was part of the attraction. She was a challenge. Also, none of those men were involved with her.

Six months after my release from gaol I was living in Portugal. It was July, 2006. I flew over to England for some bits and pieces, to breathe new life into my legal fight against JP and DV, to get back my missing money, and to see a prospective News of the World story put to bed. Anyway, that's what I told them over in Portugal. "Don't go to the farm. Don't go to the farm." Over and over like a bloody mantra. Why did they think I was going to the farm? I went to her farm.

I really don't know what they teach these boys at Hendon

Police College. DV came for me, eyes blazing and arms flailing. He was doing everything he could to get me down. He once boxed at Light-Heavy and now there was no sign of the 'light'. We had quite a tussle. I'd read his superior's report on his confession and knew that he had a potential heart problem, that he had clutched his chest when under stress. So during our wrestling match, when his face turned purple, I voiced my concern – "You've got a lovely colour there. Been on holiday?"

So there we stood, toe to toe like a couple of sumo wrestlers but thankfully without the obligatory costumes. I couldn't hit him and he, constrained by the same legal worries as me, probably, didn't want to hit me. Well, that's not entirely true, he would have loved to hit me and then put the boot in as if he was an old-time cozzer. Then he became one. Would you believe it, he produces these handcuffs? Or rather he screams for them. There we are wrestling away, with him trying to get me to the ground, and all the while JP is standing there, Niagara Falls flooding down her cheeks, holding a pair of cuffs. He hadn't been a proper copper for six-years. Do they get to keep them? Is it like a retirement gold watch?

She hands the cuffs to him and he tries to get them on me. No success, so he whacks me across the back with them a few times, then kneads my right kidney. "Thanks." With any luck a few bruises should show for that. "Keep it up." Next thing – "Get the Tazer."

The probably imaginary Tazer didn't show, but in readiness for it I was trying to grab a meat hook hanging from a beam. Fuck it, I thought, I'll finish the bastard here and now, just as the police arrive and take me away. So much for closure. The only closure I was facing was that of a cell door.

I had gone there that afternoon hoping that JP and I could have talked; I needed to find out what had motivated her actions. I would have talked to DV too, but it turned out he wasn't in a conversational mood. The truth is, though, I also had a feeling that he might throw a wobbly. I secretly wanted him to assault me, to put him on the back foot.

In that respect it had turned out better than expected. DV levelled a charge of common assault. At that stage I had no idea that his attack on me could amount to GBH. Then the bruises from the cuffs started to come through. A few photos of them, I thought, and we're good for ABH at least.

A post-script to this episode is that when the police released me in the early hours of the following morning I needed to collect my car from the farm. Naturally the police weren't going to let me go back there alone, so they came along. When we got there I saw that my car was blocked in by a couple of farm vehicles. The halogen lamps came on and awoke everyone as the police made DV and others move them. I think that it had probably clicked with him, or JP, that possibly he had been tricked into the assault. So, by their blocking my car in, there would inevitably have been another confrontation. There could have been no other logical reason for them to want to trap my car there. If there was no ulterior motive they would have wanted to give me no further excuse to return to the farm and cause a scene.

A couple of days after my encounter with DV I came to realize just how much he'd used his metal cuffs when he'd had his arms wrapped around me. This wasn't an act of affection. He'd been working those cuffs on my lower back, and in the adrenaline rush of our Sumo wrestling match I hadn't even felt pain at the time. I'd thought it odd when I noticed that his knuckles were bloody. It wasn't my blood, but two days later it hit me. My lower back was black and blue, as though

I'd been beaten with a club. Nice one, my son. "Where's the camera. Get these bruises while they're fresh."

I got a couple of hospitals to check me over, as you can't have too much back-up at times like these, then returned to Portugal. Effectively I'd jumped bail in that I'd failed to show up at the appointed police station, but of course, when I'd gone there it had been shut. Anyway, it was only a common assault charge I was facing; way down the criminal food chain. DV had, I thought, played right into my hands. Now he was likely facing at least ABH, maybe GBH.

Their lawyer is a clever man, so it surprised me somewhat when he took out an ex parte injunction on JP's behalf preventing me from going within one thousand metres of her farm. This meant I had a right to defend the action in open court as a 'litigant in person'. The legal eagles hate this process of law as it allows loose cannons like me to fire broadsides unfettered by years of legal training. Under the guise of ignorance I could say whatever I wanted; I could openly discuss in frank detail our relationship and dig up any other dirt that came to mind. I could involve the national press. What could I lose? The right to go within one thousand metres of the farm. What could I gain? I could see the two of them in the witness box, their reputations destroyed. I could see the care homes authority withholding her license or, at the very least, her clients' families pulling people out of the homes. I was prepared to use everything in court, including verifiable allegations of JP's mental instability; the Exorcist tapes.

Harsh? She'd put me in prison and, if she'd been allowed to get away with it, she would have loved to see them throw away the key forever. I often read of people, victims of the most outrageous crimes, saying that they forgive their enemies, that they will turn the other cheek. But I'm afraid my predilections on such matters are Old rather than New Testament.

The doctor who examined me in Portugal had himself been a victim of the state. In 1970s Lisbon, he and his fellow students had campaigned against state injustice under the dictator, Salazar. Thousands were rounded up at that time; many disappeared. So, when I told the doctor that my bruised kidneys were the result of a beating from an ex-policeman, he was only too happy to issue the appropriate medical certificates. These had a two-fold purpose. I would not have to return to the UK until I'd made a full recovery and I could delay the ex parte injunction hearing, thus prolonging the agony of JP and DV. It also meant that I would have full medical evidence to pass onto the police while I pressed for DV to be charged, with JP as an accessory.

CHAPTER THIRTY-FIVE

Finger the Gold

Half Maori/half Scot, Waka Kele had been a senior lieutenant and rumoured close mate of the Aussie billionaire, Alan Bond, before and during the latter's downfall and imprisonment. In recent years he had developed Diabetes and when I last saw him he was wearing a protective boot on his right foot and had taken on a rather avuncular appearance. Most of his hair had gone. However, rather than all this being a disadvantage in his business dealings, it has had the opposite effect, as he now looks arguably more trustworthy than he did pre-illness.

It's extraordinary how people justify their crimes. The hatred emanating from Waka when I went to his house after my release was palpable. In I went unannounced into this beautiful old rented building with a woman friend by my side and the first thing he did was take a swing at me. From what I've heard, in his rugby days he might have got away with it, but now, semi-crippled and looking past his sixty-years, he was far better off sitting down. I pushed him back onto the sofa and my friend, Janine, acted as peacemaker. We left. I'd pissed on his lamppost, so to speak.

The home he lived in was a beautiful old courthouse conversion built from Cotswold stone, an impressive abode for one so previously impecunious. However, I had no problem with that; he and his family had to live somewhere and, to tell you the truth, I had been rather impressed by

Waka's ability to come up smelling of roses. He hadn't then been living there on my money and he was putting his son through law school, somehow adroitly avoiding the fees. He had been using his charm to bend the rules and I had admired him for it. No, the problem I had was with Waka's righteous indignation. He had stolen my money while acting as my trusted business advisor while I was banged-up, yet he was angry with me for being angry with him. It was almost as though he'd convinced himself that the money really was his.

Thankfully Janine was with me to prevent things from getting out of hand. It's not that I was, or am, concerned for Waka's well-being, but, as someone pointed out, that could have been an expensive few punches. Better to go for Pitts-Tucker. He'd had duty of care over my money so he, or the Law Society, would be my best chance of retrieving it. Waka could come later.

I'd met him in Oxford in 2002. JP and I had gone there to lunch and a pre-diabetic Waka had been in the restaurant with his son, Richard Branson's son, and a few friends. I'd had no more contact after that until three years later when Pitts-Tucker re-acquainted me with his 'old friend' Waka Kele. But I was so preoccupied with JP that I didn't see it coming.

Waka had reappeared in my life in July '05. The meeting place had been a small Buckinghamshire airfield. I hadn't thought too hard about it, but Waka had chosen the location. As he produced from his otherwise empty wallet pictures of 'his' de-commissioned bright red US fighter plane, he effortlessly gave the impression of being a pilot. Just a picture of a plane and therefore he 'had' a plane. But it was allegedly in LA, so why arrange a meeting at this airfield? I later realised this was his modus operandi, the clever use of props to insinuate himself into a mark's head.

Other touches were there that day. His brother Kelly,

equally light of wallet, was with him. Kelly was reputedly fifty-one but looked late-thirties. He had a strangely handsome face with a strong Maori cast. He looked so young because in spite of heavy drinking and admitted drug use he made Charles Bronson look like a gurner. I have never seen such a still face on a living person. No chance for any lines when you have only one expression. He'd been in a pretty successful rock band in California and had, according to Waka, done time in St. Quentin for pushing coke. These last two points were his equivalent of the jet fighter. He was also said to be a talented artist with a horde of paintings stashed in Vegas.

A few days later Waka made his first stab at getting me to sign Power of Attorney over to him. I was pissed, drinking heavily at the time, what with all the pressure, and he shoved the papers under my nose in a pub. A friend was with me and he blocked it, as did Janice a couple of hours later when she was also asked to witness the document. Waka backed off, playing the long game after that first clumsy attempt to stiff me. So what did I do? I made him my business advisor, of course, the old frontal lobes yet again ensuring that I failed to link cause with effect.

CHAPTER THIRTY-SIX

I've Never Cared

For me to have been in the care home business came as a surprise to those who knew me. It was a surprise to me too. But it's a business, just like any other, and one that's needed more in our society than most. Then there's the client turnover; there's always a new intake coming along.

Of all my businesses this one has offered the least amount of laughs yet the greatest opportunities to make money. My role, though, whatever the business, has been in painting the big picture. In the case of the homes it was to raise the finance and source the properties. Let others deal with the detail.

Frankly, if I were to have got a job in any of my businesses I'd have been hard-pushed to have kept it. I've only just learned how to send an email, I've never worked nine to five; 'what a way to make a living', as the song goes. I've never wiped an old person's bum or stayed with them into the small hours as they quietly slipped away, as have so many of my nursing staff over the years. It's just the way it is.

What I'm leading up to is that by being a chancer, I've attracted chancers. It's only natural that by behaving in the way I have I should expect some flak. These people were only after the same things as me: a relatively easy ride, access to funds and a few laughs along the way.

JP is a more complex issue. She has a foot in both camps.

Unusual that. In my experience people tend towards the big picture or the small one, the majority the latter. But JP is capable of trying to royally shaft me at one level, yet can, and does, deal with the day to day minutiae of running a successful company, including driving hundreds of miles back and forth between the homes several times a week.

If this is starting to read like an example of my obsession with JP, it is instead more intended to illustrate my respect for her. Of all the people I've had dealings with over the years, and some have been extraordinarily larger than life, she has been the one who has created the most difficulties for me. This has been out of all proportion to her CV. She was fifty when I met her, and she had an interesting if not a 'let's set the world alight ' background, and I do not mean this disparagingly. Yet she has caused me more problems than anyone I've been up against. I had been used to getting my own way ever since I'd got enough experience under my belt to generally prevent others getting one over on me. It has become a habit. There are cleverer people, sure, harder ones too, but somehow I always seemed to win through. Then she came along.

I found her impossibly attractive. I now indeed think that her tenacity deepened that attraction. All the merry japes and scrapes I've been involved in hadn't equipped me to deal with JP. With the greatest respect (I distrust that expression because it's always followed by an insult), JP's background as a cruise ship entertainer, part-time farmer and flower arranger should not have equipped her to be such a formidable opponent (there, it was followed by an insult), but somehow it did. It must be something to do with milking cows at four o'clock on a January morning, or whatever you do on farms. There is fortitude there.

Maybe by introducing JP to the world of larger business,

I'd opened a Pandora's box. Maybe it's like the countless millions of people who have never been able to fully express themselves because they didn't have, or take, the chance, to do so. JP did both. Maybe I met the wrong woman. Or she the wrong man.

CHAPTER THIRTY-SEVEN

If That's the Law, it's the Law

Is there a name for someone who collects lawyers, like philately for stamp-collectors? I've certainly had a few, their numbers vying with that of wives and girlfriends. One of the better ones, Francis, was my criminal lawyer whilst I was inside. He has an identical twin brother and we pretended that we could tell them apart. Just joking, Francis. Their look was Buddy Holly, the glasses at least, although Francis nearly broke into song on my behalf on that magical day in January 2006. He phoned Janice. She phoned Pitts-Tucker. He said 'fuck', such an overused yet eloquent word. You'd think, wouldn't you, that he would have been pleased that his client, moi, was ripe for imminent release?

My getting out? That'll be the day, as Francis might have said in Buddy mode. In my wildest dreams, and I've had a few, I could never have envisaged the circumstances of my release. DV had made a tearful confession to his office superior that he was having an affair with JP – the chief prosecutor and his principal witness. Even then, he begged that the affair be kept secret until after my scheduled trial on March 13th, 2006. It's on record. In my book, he should have been done for even saying it. Now the cat was out of the bag and I was out of gaol, still yet to discover that it was now a case of rich man, poor man, beggar-man, thief. The first two were analogous to the state of my bank balance, the fourth to what had occurred. The quite unbelievable circumstances of DV's confession and the resultant euphoria at my release were quite mitigated in their effect by the dawning realisation that I had been fleeced. Still, I reasoned, justice would prevail. Little did I know that soon I would be up shit creek without a GPS.

A DS from Thames Valley (I have too much respect for his integrity to here name him; anyway, he might nick me if I did) was determined to press for a 'perverting the course of justice' charge against JP and DV if indeed there was evidence that this had occurred. He and his colleagues had put many man-hours into their investigation, but the law is the law and where was the proof? "I need the lie," said the DS, "the one lie that we can run with."

It had gone badly between the DS and me at first. He'd read JP's testimonies, carefully presented by her lawyer, and his sympathies lay with her. I was the bad man, the big bully, but the DS is a highly intelligent man and the truth will out. Once he was onside, if he voiced any criticism it was to try to encourage me to end my obsession with JP. Can you voluntarily end an obsession? One definition is:-'an unwanted feeling or emotion accompanied by acute anxiety'. The key is in the word 'unwanted'. I longed to be free of it, this all-pervading, life-dominating force, the cause of which was out of all proportion to the effect. So too were those who were trying to support me while growing weary of my endless repetitive tirades against JP and DV. Justice is justice, but how many ways are there to say it was the general tone.

The police presented their 'perverting the course of justice' case to the CPS in July '06. However, this august body decided that as all charges against me had been dropped as a result of JP and DV's relationship there was a quid pro quo situation. The fact that I had never been given the chance to defend myself in a court of law in accordance with my democratic rights did not even seem to have entered the equation. The major pending charge, the IVA one the Avon & Somerset were so keen to keep me inside for was dropped by them because it was going nowhere. There was no crime. The insurance charge I had a strong defence against: Crown Prosecution, and JP, a surrogate prosecutor, insisted that I was never a chauffeur/driver. I had proof that I was (JP had even admitted as much in one of her statements – even she can't remember everything). I'd already pleaded guilty to the DSS overpayment. This was, to repeat, £1,800. How many 'overpayments' had the government received from me through P.A.Y.E. alone on the salaries of the many hundreds of people I'd employed over the years? If I'd paid hundreds of thousands in P.A.Y.E., in law that would not have mitigated against the alleged, comparatively miniscule DSS overpayment. Fair enough. If that's the law, it's the law. So why then would JP's and DV's open dalliance, illicit in the context of what was happening, have been offset against my alleged and untried 'crimes'?

I contend that what JP and DV perpetrated was an outright perversion of the course of justice even if only by dint of the fact that they were together. Even if it were true that they were not a couple at the time of my imprisonment in October 2005, the undisputed fact is that they were whilst I was in prison awaiting trial, the chief investigator and his prosecution witness, they were planning to keep quiet about it. The conclusion is inescapable. However, for reasons already covered, I cannot legally accuse either of them of any wrongdoing against me, so their consciences must be clear. But there's more than one way to skin a cat, as I was to find out soon enough.

CHAPTER THIRTY-EIGHT

Auf Wiedersehen, Pets

After what I had been through with JP, I sometimes found it hard to remind myself that life was sometimes fun and that pets tend to be more loyal than ex-lovers, although it didn't always turn out for the best for the pets.

If a parakeet makes a good gift, are fifty that many times better, especially if they're chicks? I was asking myself this question because, trading on women's love of cute things, I thought the present I had for Joke, back in the baggage-handling days at Schipol, was guaranteed to keep her sweet forever. A consignment of fifty young parakeets came my way at Schipol. Luckily they were too young to talk, or they would have fingered me. I put the crate containing them into the boot of my old Fiat and continued on the night-shift. It was about nine p.m. When I finished, very tired, at around six a.m., I returned to my car and drove home.

I awoke Joke, who was not overly pleased to be disturbed early on an icy January morning. It was as bitingly cold as it ever gets in Holland when an easterly wind is blowing; too cold for tropical birds. I opened the boot to a now excited Joke, who was wondering what this new present might be, yet knowing from previous experience that it wasn't from an honest source.

All the birds were dead, save for one. I opened the wooden crate and tried to coax it out. It somehow managed to get up onto the lower edge of the open car boot, then promptly fell forward into the snow. Joke just stared. One moment she'd been asleep, dreaming sweet dreams no doubt, and the next she was confronted by an appalling version of Monty Python's dead parrot sketch. She was so upset. So was I. We went out that day and got pissed as parrots.

Talking of strange experiences with pets; one day I went home with a gift for the children. For once, all three were there, and I was looking forward to their reaction. "What is it? Is it a dog?" I can still see their excited faces to this day. They were all wide-eyed as I opened the back of the Transit van. I'd put wooden planks up to the floor of the van so that our new pet could walk down, it being too heavy to lift. It was a Shetland Pony. I giggled like a fool as I looked at the children's faces – Sammy, Poppy and Tommy, staring as one in awe and incredulity. I giggled a bit less when I caught Janice's expression.

I'd sold a car to some travellers. They were a bit cash light, so they threw in the pony to make up the price. Our garden, though large, was still just a suburban one, albeit well-tended. That pony chewed everything and tried to bite anybody who came near it. It was the most ill-tempered animal I've ever encountered and we'd all rather have faced a hungry tiger than dare venture into the garden to confront Sooty the pony. Our three dogs had a go, but he gave them short shrift.

That's the way it's always been with me and these kind of gestures. My intentions are invariably good, but always misunderstood. Far from endearing me to one and all, this gesture had further alienated me from the family. I took Sooty back to the travellers, and the last I saw of him he was gambolling happily around a field like a lamb in springtime. It was only when I was driving away from there that it clicked. It wasn't the first time the pony had been used in that way.

I've always liked animals, whether well-done or as a pet. One I'd especially cared for was a sweet-natured Cavalier King Charles spaniel, Suzy. I'd taken a temp job in Selfridges when totally skint one Christmas. I had to work somewhere where I could keep my head down and try to stay out of trouble for awhile. Suzy had been given to me as a gift and she was too young to leave at home while I worked, so I used to sneak her in there. I'd started off in the wine department but had soon got kicked out of there when I climbed the wine racks, feather duster in hand. Thousands of pounds worth of wine teetered precariously, so the management thought I'd be better suited to Bedding. Over that Christmas and New Year period Selfridges employed hundreds of temporary staff, and I suppose they must still do. The wages then were low, so shop-lifting was high. If you made friends across the various departments you could keep yourself clothed, fed and watered for nothing. When staff left the store at the end of the day, they had to use the basement corridors and pass through an exit security check. Most rattled and bulged with their stolen booty, but only women's bags were thoroughly examined. I only ever had the wriggling Suzy, tiny and yappy, under my coat, trying as I was to stay out of trouble. The women in my department loved her, and the supervisor of Bedding used to keep her in her small office. Sometimes she'd sneak out. One day, a salesman pulled back the covers of one of Selfridges' top-of-the-range beds to discover, to his horror, and that of his would-be clients, a great steaming 'Henry'. The security guards spotted Suzy one evening as I was leaving, alerted by her yapping. They thought I'd nicked her from the pet department, but those guys were earning even less than me and saw the funny side of it.

At least that little tale had a happy ending, which is more than can be said for the one about the pigeon that decided to impersonate Santa by coming down the chimney. It was pre-Christmas when the children were young. I was home and we were all eagerly awaiting the festivities: me, Janice, Poppy and Tommy. Sammy was with her mum. I think it was me who screamed first. There in the open fire sat a blazing pigeon. Tommy leapt up and ran into the garden, Poppy ran to her room in tears and I just sat there pointing and gibbering. The pigeon looked, if anything, depressed, but I suppose you would be if you're being burned alive. Only Janice, ever capable, had the presence of mind to do something. She plucked the bird from the fire and wrapped it in a wet towel, but was too late to save it. The family sat in silence for the rest of that evening, mourning our feathered friend. Then we got round to wondering what pigeon tastes like.

Fishermen's tales usually involve outstretched arms, but this catch was about the length of a matchbox. We're in the present day, and the staff at one of my special needs care homes had asked that I buy a fish-tank for its soothing qualities. "How's this?" "Nice, but some fish would help." "OK." I don't know whether they expected Angel Fish or maybe I'd find Nemo, but I thought a goldfish would make a fine start. Always cost-conscious, I settled for a nippy little chap who set me back £1.80. It's a lot, I know, but I was thinking of the happiness Houdini would bring. It's an odd name for a goldfish, but therein lies a tale. I'd left my dog, Minty, in the boot of my hatchback, forgetting of course that from there she had access to the entire car. I had also forgotten that although no Rin Tin Tin, even she had the nous and the fishy taste-buds to jump onto the back seat and gobble up young Houdini, who was temporarily housed in a water-filled plastic bag. I returned to the car a few minutes later and was distraught to see the fate of my £1.80 writ large in Minty's guilty eyes.

Still, it had been my fault, and Minty had only done what comes naturally. It was about fifteen minutes later, when I was walking her, that she threw up. You've guessed it, there was Houdini wriggling on the grass. As luck would have it, there was a nearby ornamental fountain, so in he went. "What you doing, mister?" This from one of a group of small boys. I told them. Their eyes said liar, but they didn't actually say it. I went to get a plastic bag while the boys guarded Houdini, who must have thought all this made a nice change from going around in circles. I read recently that the memory of a goldfish is much maligned, so when I fork out another £1.80 he'll have a few stories to tell his bowl mate. I suppose it makes sense that he would have survived Minty's sharp teeth by slipping over her tongue and then somehow swimming upstream in her larynx and thereby avoiding her digestive processes, but since neither he nor Minty can talk, I suppose we'll never know.

CHAPTER THIRTY-NINE

Don't Expect Me to Tickle Your Chin

In August '06 I'd been sitting with a friend in a bar in Portugal discussing where to move on to next and the conversation got around to Morocco. I'd never been to Marrakech, so we decided over several beers that Morocco would be next on the list. Suddenly it was like a private eye-movie. This blonde walks into the bar. A man turns to her – "How's Marrakech, Sally?"

"Fine." Not sounding fine. "Everything sorted?"

"No. They're trying to steal my fucking houses." Sally downed a large G&T like a shot and made to leave. I beckoned her over. More G&Ts. We talked. She had two ocean-front houses down near Mirleft, the old hippie haunt on the edge of the Sahara where Hendrix and Dylan used to go to avoid attention. Next day we're heading south as minders. The brief is to keep the bad guys from snatching the houses until we can help Sally sort out the legalities. We mustn't hit anyone, unless it's absolutely necessary. There's a lot of money at stake for Sally, indeed her entire future. We're just knights in shining armour in this scenario, out to rescue a damsel in distress. Pam was right. Things do happen to me, especially when I'm not looking.

If you live long enough you do of course get old, but we baby-boomers are not equipped to deal with this. Maybe that's really why people live longer these days – they're having too much fun to die. I'm over sixty now, which used to be old. I've had people in my care homes less than ten years older than my current age. But somehow life goes on, the flame undiminished, although everyone seems to think that I sail along untouched by life's problems. But the truth is that the situation with JP and DV had reached parts of me that I did not know even existed: stress – strike one. As a result I drank like a fish. I'd put Pernod on my cornflakes, if I could face a solid breakfast: alcohol – strike two. I smoked sixty a day. Of course, I'm not a smoker. I was just smoking for now – strike three.

Three strikes and you're out? Well, I was on a diet. The Hellman's Diet, I call it. I added garlic for health reasons. I was down to twenty-two stone. Exercise? The guy I've been travelling around with never stops. I burned calories just watching him. Anyway, I did sometimes wallow in a swimming-pool – I always seem to end up staying in houses with pools – and my lifestyle occasionally necessitates the odd bout of fisticuffs. Blood pressure's up, but I claim I can do that at will. It's a useful trick, as it can get you out of your prison cell for treatment.

Apart from the stress I'd recently undergone I don't know whether I've aged mentally. I mean, it's impossible to be objective about one's mental condition. I can only go on what people say to me. The general consensus appears to be that I'm half-way to gaga-land. These comments are based on people's assessment of my alleged idiosyncrasies. Women, in particular, seem to find my habits infuriating. I think they want to mother me, or is it smother me? If I pour red wine it goes on the tablecloth, if I eat food it goes on me. One woman was astonished that I weighed so much, given that so little of the food on my plate ever makes it to my mouth. I get out of the swimming-pool and walk inside the house across a newly-washed floor and don't understand the fuss. If I pick something up I drop it. I am sworn to secrecy and then blurt out that person's secret in front of them at a crowded dinner table. I only know this because I've been told it, over and over. I read that London cabbies have enlarged Hippocampi because their job gives them enhanced spatial awareness and develops their memory centres. A brain scan showed that I have reduced hippocampi. Too much grape juice I feel. I therefore reason that I should take a taxi whenever I can and let those big hippocampi boys do all the work.

It would take another to fully list my sins, although I will say quite categorically in my defence that I am not going gaga. I have always been that way.

The progress of my revenge attempt on JP and DV was getting mixed results. The press had shown interest and the News of the World had written up the story. I eagerly awaited publication. Let's face it, it wasn't exactly a 'hold the front page' scoop, but it contained the right elements of betrayal, intrigue and corruption for a scandal-hungry readership. Then The Mail on Sunday showed interest; more their type of story really. But with The Mail I ran the risk that they would present it from a woman's point of view. Occasionally you do see a man reading The Mail, but they always insist it's for the sports pages.

This hunger for press coverage was not vainglorious; it served a purpose. The care home business does not welcome those who transgress its strict code. It's well-regulated, and for good reason. So a damning newspaper article should effectively kill off an individual in the eyes of the regulators and it only needs a handful of paying clients to get wind of a scandal and they'll pull their loved ones out. You never recover from that.

Meanwhile, I was keeping the pressure up through the

injunction. Still using the angle that DV had damaged my kidney I got the good Portuguese doctor to give me another of his medical certificates. I'd already had the court hearing delayed by one month and I repeated the process. The hope was that the waiting would be intolerable for JP and DV. She had been sent my defence and knew that when the moment came in court I would say the most outrageous things about her private life, all in the presence of the press; again with her license in mind. She wanted it all to be over. I was enjoying the game of cat and mouse. If you put me in prison, don't expect me to tickle your chin.

I received a phone call from an old girlfriend while sitting at a bar in southern Morocco. Being in a Muslim nation, the bar was more like a back-alley speakeasy. She hadn't phoned in years and was, she said, just catching up. It was quite sad really, how down she'd sounded, saying that for her, then fifty-eight, her life was all but over. She's a very intelligent woman and has raised children who are successfully making their way in the world. She lives in a beautiful home and is surrounded by people who love her. Yet I sensed she missed the old days. Not just with me, but the sheer exuberance of being young.

She remembered our times together in Geneva in the early Seventies, when something always seemed to be happening around me. But it wasn't a memory of a major event that was in her head, rather a fleeting impression of a moment in time. She recalled that my hair had been long and that we had sat together eating hard-boiled eggs in a bar while listening to George Harrison's 'My Sweet Lord'. It was her hearing that song on the radio that had prompted her to call me.

What that memory was about, of course, was that we were then young and everything was before us. Now she felt that it was all behind her. Yet here I was, over thirty years after enjoying those eggs with her, still seemingly living life on the edge. To Pam, it was as though I had a similar existence to the one we'd shared all those years ago in Geneva, with me travelling the world having a series of seamless adventures. To tell the truth, I was.

Pam had followed Joke, so naturally my thoughts turned from one old flame to another. I was now toying with the idea of going to visit Joke in Geneva, where she had made her family home. I've never been very good with ages, somehow imagining that people I haven't seen for awhile have remained the same. Add to that the fact that I tend to think I last saw someone ten years ago, whereas in reality, as in the case of Joke, it was over thirty-five years.

To refer to a person being in their prime is something of a misnomer since physical and mental primes are surely two very different things. My image of Joke was of a beautiful young woman with whom I had shared some exciting times. It was suggested by friends that I leave it that way. Would I want to see her as a middle-aged, possibly overweight, hausfrau? Would she want to see me? I phoned her. "Please Paul. That was all such a long time ago." She put the phone down, clearly agreeing with my friends. I phoned again a little later. Once I have an idea, some might say an obsession, in my head, I'll see it through to the bitter end. This time she talked for longer, then ended with – "Please, leave the memories alone."

"I really would love to see you again ..."

"I have been ill. My appearance ... I have been treated for a brain tumour..."

"I'm sorry ..."

"It is OK, for now at least, but I've changed. My hair ... you will no longer see the same person."

"Joke, I'm sorry to hear of your illness, but your appearance doesn't matter to me. If I come to Geneva will you see me?"

"Perhaps." Of course, was I being truthful with myself? Would Joke have held such a special place in my memory if she had not once been beautiful? Would I have then wanted to know her in the first place?

Strangely, I think I am being honest when I say that I have never been interested in surface beauty as much as most other men. For me, personal qualities in a woman have always outweighed looks. It's perhaps an attitude that is more akin to how women see men. After all, true physical beauty is only conferred on a small minority of women. Many miss it by millimetres, others by a mile, but more possess the deeper qualities which I find far more attractive. If beauty be the wrapping of such a package, then so be it, it's your lucky day.

In southern Morocco I found myself again reflecting on life. The thoughts on Joke were prompted as much by the circumstances I found myself in as by her revelation of the tumour. I had been behaving obsessively over JP. She had occupied my thoughts and conversation almost daily for nearly two years, ever since DV had first arrested me. Initially I had been in denial, then progressively I became preoccupied with revenge, to the almost total exclusion of everything else. But bit by bit I was finding myself in situations which began to put everything in clearer perspective.

Back in Portugal there was my future son-in-law coping with his demons and an impending implosion of his life unless a very large rabbit popped out of a larger hat. Now here I was in Morocco, trying to help prevent a woman losing her life's savings. Here, €900,000 was at stake. She stood, in her mid-fifties, to lose everything she had worked for in a property deal which was going badly wrong. It all started to put my own problems into perspective. I was down financially to Pitts-Tucker and Waka Kele, but still had access to other funds. Also, I had a lawyer whose tenacity I would not wish on my worst enemy.

Briefly though, there in Morocco my resolve for revenge was weakening. In the Berber city of Tiznit I was surrounded daily by people who if asked to count their arms and legs wouldn't always reach four. Yet still they smiled. Someone said – "It makes you feel humble." It didn't make me feel humble. It just made me feel grateful that I had too much, rather than too little, flesh to feed off. Thankfully for my resolve, this brief flirtation with beneficence passed. If there was any feeling of humbleness it came from the fact that a chance meeting in an Algarve bar had involved me in the life of someone else with potentially worse problems than my own. Through this person I encountered many others who, although on the surface seemingly content, had each borne personal tragedy, the like of which eclipsed my own reversals of fortune.

I remember in particular a French woman, a successful artist, who had lost her childhood sweetheart husband to a brain tumour when he was twenty-five. They had two babies, which she carried on bringing up for another fifteen years, all the while establishing her artistic reputation. Then she remarried. Her new husband loved her and her two boys. Then he died, of 'depression', a very French subtlety, rather than suicide. He just lost the will to live. She did not say why. I did not ask. To meet her she would be taken for just another member of the French bourgeoisie, albeit an artistic and attractive one. Her circumstances did make me feel humble. I do not know what this says about me, but her seemingly perfect life torn asunder while she tried to hold it together for the sake of the children was for me far more humbling than the impoverished circumstances of the Berbers in Morocco. The latter were not smiling in the face of adversity. They were smiling because they were happy. When your culture has been for centuries to travel across the Sahara by camel for weeks on end you do not dwell in an imaginary aspirational future but live in a state of fatalistic acceptance of a very present reality. Armed with such insights I returned to Portugal. I would get everything in perspective. I would become a new person.

I looked at my phone messages. I hadn't turned the mobile on for several weeks for fear the cops would know I was in Morocco when I was meant to be in Portugal, too sick to travel. There was a voicemail from an Avon and Somerset DI saying he thought there was something odd in the way JP's approach to the IVA had been conducted from the outset. The DI was very interested. Would I get the relevant papers to him? I said goodbye, at least for now, to my new-found spirituality.

It was imperative to keep the injunction hearing, set for the first of September, at bay. If I returned to the UK I'd have to present myself to the police, and to date my lawyer's efforts to get me a written agreement that I would not be detained, nor would my passport need to be surrendered, had come to nothing.

I hastened back from Morocco to Portugal to see my doctor. It isn't usual to be so pleased when you learn that you may need surgery on your right kidney, but I was delighted. The police had the photos of the extensive bruising to my lower back. Now I had it in writing from a doctor that DV really had damaged one of my kidneys. There was a lesion. There was enough evidence to press for GBH. Two days later, Lady Luck once again smiled in my direction. I think she might also have winked at me, convinced that I was her favourite son.

Janice had been visiting the local council's offices on a routine matter. By chance, there was JP, heavier now, as Janice noted with some satisfaction. With her was DV, dapper in his Mr Saloon Bar outfit of navy blazer and cavalry twill slacks. He was carrying a stack of files under one arm and held JP's hand. Seeing Janice, they struck a pose of horror-struck insouciance. They were clearly there to attend the council's hearing into DV's conduct as the end to an eight month internal investigation. The hand-holding was clearly done to demonstrate unity. The horror-struck expressions suggested that they must have thought that Janice was there because she knew of the hearing. She phoned me. Invoking The Freedom of Information Act, I persuaded a council official to agree to give me access to a transcript of the hearing. This was subject to there being no resultant ongoing police investigation. If there wasn't, I would make damn sure there was. I mean, what if DV's story had any holes? Would he be, whilst under considerable pressure, consistent with his original statement? Would he leave himself open so that there would be a chance for the police to re-open their 'perverting the course of justice' line of inquiry?

CHAPTER FORTY

Stubborn, or What?

It's been said that I have a stubborn streak. For example, when I was told that there's a world-famous floating opera house in the Amazon city of Manaus, I refused to believe it. I've been there. I didn't see it. So there's no bloody opera house. Someone said that the founder of the Atkin's Diet had died while clinically obese. Rubbish. A high protein, low-carb diet is the only one that's ever worked for me. I can't afford to believe that maybe it's not the perfect solution after all.

For me, obstinacy has its merits. It's this contrary streak which has kept me on the trail of revenge for so long, when others might have faltered and simply got on with their lives. I can't remember whether I've always had this tendency, and the only reason I know I've got it is that others have told me so. They've also told me that I'm not so young anymore and why don't I get on with a new project while I'm still in command of my faculties? But, in life, I'll accept a few casualties and lose a battle or two, but I just won't lose a bloody war. Stubborn, or what?

How do others see me? It's a question we all ask ourselves from time to time of course. But if you feel your life's worthy of a book, then you've got to have a high opinion of yourself, haven't you? I asked around – "You're big-headed."

"Who? Moi? Anyway, that's enough from you. What about me?"

"Tight."

"So I haggle with beggars. Just trying to teach them a bit of the old self-reliance. Excuse me, waiter, how much is the water? OK, thanks. One from the tap please."

"A slob."

"I think the yellow of the egg yolk goes rather well with the blue of the shirt, don't you?"

"Fat."

"Big-boned. It's my glands (I hadn't heard that old chestnut in years)."

"Indiscreet."

"Shut up and I'll tell you a secret."

"Money-obsessed."

"I've got more money than you can shake a stick at, my son."

I was sitting on a camel, or dromedary to be precise (as in one hump or two), in my djellaba (the traditional Arab robe) and ox-blood Lobbs brogues, looking every inch a Berber chieftain. I'd been to every souk in Tiznit trying to find a djellaba to fit the larger man. I was in the company of two women who were constantly taking the piss out of my heroic proportions – 'Why not try High & Mighty on Edgware Road?', that sort of thing. So it came as a relief to be treated with respect by the locals because of my size. It was deemed I must be of good family.

After much searching my new-found friends returned with a djellaba which could have doubled as a circus big-top. It fitted, and I strutted up and down like Lawrence of Arabia in the film, in my eyes every inch 'The Eagle of the Desert'. I would ride my camel to smite mine enemies and give them their just desserts.

The enemy in this case was the Belgian ex Hells Angel, Sylvan. Adorned with an embarrassingly anachronistic pony-tail, he ran the complex, a paradise in which Sally had two houses, as though he were an Eighties Hollywood version of a Columbian coke baron. The only occupied house was Sally's ocean-front property, then containing Sally, Daisy her daughter, who was over from the UK, and my friend and I. The complex was guarded night and day, with most of the men concentrating on the house. Unlike most security men, who keep a look-out for intruders, these guys stared continuously at the house. It was a hugely intimidating situation for Sally, who usually lived there alone.

Without our presence, she'd been vulnerable to Sylvan's whims, like the time when the young Moroccan, Ali, whom she'd employed to help her look after the houses, had come to stay. For reasons best known to Sylvan, he'd taken exception to Ali working there, so one day he crashed through Sally's front-door with one of his henchman to give Ali a hiding.

Sally's predicament should serve as a salutary warning to all who consider buying property in countries where they are not totally familiar with the local laws. I tried to imagine myself in her position. Here I was, leading a peripatetic life with nowhere to call my own. I didn't especially want to live in England, yet the country still held its usual love-hate pull on me. I say 'usual', because that's the effect the country seems to have on most ex-pats. Anyway, for now I was living out of a couple of bags and did not know where I would be the next week. I had spent twenty years or so with Janice in the family home, less time off for bad behaviour, and I had hugely valued having a geographical and emotional centre to my life. In fact, in spite of my time with JP and the years which have passed since I lived there, I still think of that house as home.

To get to your mid-fifties and then someone comes along to try to snatch away all that you have worked for is arguably far worse than if the thief takes the money straight from your safe. Sally comes from a Lincolnshire farming background, and they breed them tough, but even that inbred toughness does not prepare you for a battle against unscrupulous land-grabbers, especially when you are not certain that the law is on your side, baksheesh having greased the appropriate palms. She sold her houses in the end, under pressure, so under value.

CHAPTER FORTY-ONE

A Big Place Full of Small People

Waka Kele might have thought he was in the Last Chance Saloon. When you've got to wear a boot because of incipient gangrene and you're facing all the other complications that come with late-onset diabetes you instinctively avoid box sets in case you don't reach the end. So when a chance like this comes along you jump in with both feet. Sorry, hop in with one foot. You're thinking of Paul's position in December '05: he's in the slammer; he's got health problems too, a hop, skip and a jump away from the bin himself, if he's not faking it; there's enough of his money around to take a few punts and one's sure to come good as they always have in the past; you've got Paul's ear; he's got money and you have nothing; lastly, the police could take everything under this proposed new law of 'living off the proceeds of crime'. I'd be protecting the money for him, get 'Power of Attorney' and run with it; Paul's out in what, maybe five, six years? I'll pay it back then, if I'm still alive. If he's still alive. I mean, it's dead money otherwise, isn't it?

I talked to a friend, a solicitor in London's Chinatown who's owned a Japanese strip-club in Shanghai. He had inside knowledge of the mining operation I suspected Waka had invested my money in. It soon became clear that there was a choice: go for the money, or go for the money and a 30% share of an operational gold mine. There was a lot at stake and the guys who'd stiffed me were scared. I started to crank up the pressure. The trouble is, people just hate it when you try to take away their gold mines.

The boys were getting nervous. The City of London Fraud Squad was showing interest in my missing money, but only subject to an adverse Law Society report on Pitts-Tucker's conduct, and meanwhile the gold mine investigation was coming together. A colleague recalled a company name Waka had used, so we Googled it and there he was, standing in the background of a photograph in which a group of Asian businessmen (North Koreans?) in suits stood in the foreground, champagne glasses raised. Tony Knight was in the foreground. So that's the way to get to them. They'd probably gone through China because of its contacts with North Korea. Now I had a trail to follow.

Then the boys were in China and phoning Tom, a mutual friend, almost daily, for news of my activities. I continued to play the game, always pretending that I knew more than I did. This one was about timing, my gut feeling told me that. It was when their nerves were at fever pitch that I would get the best deal. Get them while they're weak but not too weak. They had to have something to lose before they would be sufficiently afraid of losing it, but they must not be too strong for me to no longer pose a threat or I'd lose my negotiating power. If I got it wrong I'd get my money back. If I got it right, who knows?

I began another of my reveries. This one was how all the events over the past few years had culminated in a situation where I could get more money than ever before. If this, that or the other had not happened, I would not have been put into this position. It was like a financial version of the film, 'Sliding Doors'.

Meanwhile, my bêtes noires, JP and DV, the architects

of my hopefully soon to be enviable position, were on the back foot. If I had not been in the slammer this opportunity to get my hands on the goldmine would not have arisen. I was still playing my cat and mouse game with them, still using the injunction to fire off my written verbal broadsides. Then they would come back at me. It was war. My injured kidney had enabled me to get a further adjournment on the injunction. It had also enabled me to press for a GBH charge. Then I was threatening her with the press; DV's assault on me had sharpened their interest now there was violence in the mix. Apart from the News of the World, which was showing renewed interest in the story, the local papers were sniffing around. Once any one of them had bitten, it was just a question of getting the interest of the local papers in JP's home town and the towns where her two homes are situated, and it would be game, set and match. Even the previously recalcitrant care homes authority could not turn a blind eye to that, could they?

CHAPTER FORTY-TWO

Keeper of the Queen's Hawks

Waka and I had been sitting outside a pub in London's Clerkenwell district enjoying an Indian Summer lunchtime pint when he produced several sheets of official-looking, close-typed documents. What those papers contained was a thriller-writer's dream. Waka was carrying the papers as part of his brief to help an associate recover the £26-million he claimed was owed to him by the French Government. This stemmed from an arms deal involving Gazelle attack helicopter sales between France and South Africa. The deal was allegedly corrupt and this corruption seeped into the heart of the French government. In other words, it was not the sort of document to be bandied about outside a London pub.

The fact that Waka did so was, I reasoned, born of two possibilities, one being that he trusted me. After all, he was then employed as my business Mr Fix-It. I've explained elsewhere that I'm a big picture man; I always prefer to have a details man watching my back. The other possibility, given that this story was so incredible, was that he was telling the aforementioned porkies. Waka wasn't one to let the truth get in the way of a good story. But the sheer detailed complexity of the documents seemed to preclude that. I read on. The man who had commissioned Waka to help recover his sales commission from the French had worked for the South African government during Apartheid. In the document he had no name, but he was cited as having been personally responsible for the assassination of seventy-nine so-called enemies of the state. He seemed to be adept at every conceivable manner of ending a human's life; quick or slow, depending on how long the state wanted the victim alive. He was expert in the use of firearms, unarmed combat, and more arcane methods, among them being the use of poisoned clothing which, if brushed against, was lethal.

Although I am not suggesting any connection with the above paragraph, around the time of John Dragicevich's death, the Bangkok press was reporting lurid tales of 'The Bounty Hunter' having been hired to recover the gambling debts of a beautiful young American woman who owed a fortune to casinos around the Thai/Cambodian border, with senior politicians from both countries being implicated in the process. This recalled a conversation a close friend of mine had had with Waka in which the latter had discussed his partnership with just such a woman. He'd picked her up young, only eighteen, in New York City, groomed her, and taught her the tricks of his trade. For the next few years they travelled the world together having adventures. The woman's charm and beauty opened doors as they operated globally like a latter-day, white-collar Bonnie and Clyde, even spending time in a Tijuana mixed-sex lockup over a Tex/Mex border infraction. It was there that he saw her in action for the first time. Waka said that, especially when pissed, she had a distinctive party trick. She was a Thai kick-boxing expert and could, and did, deliver a high kick to the head of any man who made the mistake of thinking she was easy.

My other adversary in the quest to get my money and a share in the gold mines, Roger A Pitts-Tucker, had no less colourful a background. He's a little diamond. Somehow he

managed to run a successful maritime law company in the
City of London whilst being simultaneously accused on the
internet of all manner of malpractice involving a nobility titles
company called British Feudal Investments Ltd, although a
US private investigator insisted that it was never officially
incorporated at Companies House. You'd think a City lawyer
might have spotted that too, would you not? I came late to
computers, but even I now know that it's not difficult to run
a quick check on prospective business associates. So how did
Pitts-Tucker manage to maintain the operation of his law
firm given the plethora of online complaints against him?
Eh, Law Society?

He was conveyancing nobility titles for one Antony
Boada Cartaya, the latter estimated to have earned over
US$1-million in one year from the sale of dubious titles
based on original Manorial Lordships and Feudal Baronies
of the British Isles. According to a 1997 edition of The Miami
New Times, Boada once enjoyed the title of Baron Chafford
LL.B, Ambassador-at-Large, Republic of Liberia, and the
even more dodgy title of 'Keeper Of The Queen's Hawks'.
Even the official role of Keeper Of The Queen's Swans had
been abolished in 1993, but this did not deter Boada from
dealing titles to Americans, some of whom might well have
bought into Keeper Of The Queen's Bald Eagles. This became
the pair's favourite defence against accusations – caveat
emptor... buyer beware.

I contacted the FBI in order to have a pop at Pitts-
Tucker, thinking I could track down the mining JV, but
was met with the response that they would only deal with
other law enforcement agencies. The boys had put up every
smoke-screen and firewall they could and I had been chasing
shadows, but while I had been seeking a phantom Delaware
company and exploring the Chinese connection, the truth

lay closer to home. One of them made an inadvertent slip of the tongue and there was the information I needed. I should have been looking for a limited company registered at Companies House in Cardiff. Next step, a freezing order.

Whenever you come up against a bent solicitor, the stock reply is – "Go to The Law Society." Mmm. They'd investigated my case for many months and had come to the conclusion that Roger A Pitts-Tucker had answered all their questions satisfactorily. Of course he had. They'd given him enough time and, let's face it, he'd had plenty of practice. The Society had been inundated by complaints about this individual's malpractice yet clearly chose to look at each complaint in isolation rather than to look at the common theme in all those complaints – our Roger. Over and out then, Law Society.

They give lawyers every chance to defend themselves. They're lawyers. Of course they can bloody defend themselves. Especially the bent ones. Innocent until proven innocent seems to be the name of their game. Toothless tigers. As a lawyer put it – "Go straight to the Queen's Bench Division, freeze their assets, put a Tracing Order on your missing money, and they'll soon pop their heads above the parapet."

CHAPTER FORTY-THREE

Consigliere to the Mob

The fog was lifting. Waka and Pitts-Tucker had set up a company to exploit gold-mining assets in North Korea. OK, it could have been somewhere less fraught with difficulty, but that being the case the big boys would have already gobbled up the opportunity, licking their lips and burping with contentment. Fair play to our boys then for their enterprise and gall. When they'd incorporated their mining company in January 2006, Waka had already made a couple of visits to the Far East, to Beijing and Pyongyang in North Korea. With him had been Tony Knight, the one I'd borrowed the apartment from in Bucharest. Although he is blameless for the theft of my money, he was later aware of it and was likely also aware that the money used by Waka to set up the deal was very possibly mine. Long-haul Business Class flights, chartered helicopters and the greasing of palms do not come cheap. Once again, I found myself with unverifiable suspicions, like with JP and her fear.

Around this time, Waka was trying to turn over the five-storey house in Soho's Dean Street. I knew of this property through Tom and he'd told me it had been originally purchased in the Sixties. It dated back to the days when the Maltese ran the district's sex industry and had lain dormant ever since. The original owners had no doubt hot-footed it back to Valetta when Inspector Knacker of the Yard had come a-sniffing. Rumour had it that the police were waiting for someone, anyone, to stake a claim on it. This vulnerability was how Waka could afford to get his hands on it. I asked a friend to case the property and on the night he did so he got lucky. I'd described the building as the only empty property, half-way up the street on the western side. At the moment he arrived there a man fitting Waka's description came out the front door and went into a strip club across the street. It wasn't Waka; no dodgy foot. I phoned Knight – "The Fraud Squad are keeping a watch on Dean Street. I just want you to be aware, as my friend."

"No … how do you know?"

"They saw Waka come out last night. About ten. He went into a strip club. They said he had a red face."

"What? He was embarrassed at going into a strip club after some of the places he's knocked around?" Nervous laughter. "No, Tony. He had a red face from being in China. Was the weather warm?"

By now, Pitts-Tucker thought it had all fallen away thanks to The Law Society's report, and Waka had clearly brushed the whole affair under his existential carpet, this misdemeanor just being one of too many to remember.

I sacked my previous lawyer when I realised that months had passed while he'd sat on his hands. He returned my papers and I saw that he had less insight into the affair than had a friend who'd sussed it after reading the files over a few beers in a Portuguese bar.

I have been told by lawyers that it is very rare for two people to act in concert in a fraud case without making the odd incriminating slip and Pitts-Tucker and Waka were, despite all their practice, no exceptions to the rule.

By the summer of 2006, cracks were already appearing. Knight had gone to a lawyer in July of that year to try to recover the £25k he alleged Waka had nicked from him through dealings within the company, even though they hadn't even opened a corporate bank account. Then again, cash leaves no paper trail. Since the formation of the company in January 2006, Knight was now MD and a substantial shareholder. I went to the lawyer's offices with him, hoping to glean something, and after our joint meeting he had stayed there and spoken with another lawyer in the presence of a barrister.

My friend in Portugal spotted the record of this meeting and shook my hand. Mine shook when he told me what he'd found. In the returned papers there was a report on the meeting, probably included by accident. It seemed that Knight knew a lot, and it is a matter of legal record that he alleged Pitts-Tucker was a consigliere to the Maltese mafia, a lawyer to the mob. He talked of how our Roger had drunkenly and tearfully confessed that he'd given the money to Waka without my authority; where Waka had put it, in a bank in Liechtenstein; the account number; even the name of the man in the bank who'd handled the money on Waka's behalf. The son was beneficiary to some of it, a daughter also, he alleged.

We found an excellent lawyer up north. What had taken my former lawyer nearly six months to get his well-paid head around, our northern friend grasped within a couple of days.

My chum and I found that the mining website, previously pulled by Waka, had resurfaced. The boys smiles must have gleamed like a Colgate ring of confidence when they'd heard that the Law Society had refused to affirm any wrongdoing by Pitts-Tucker. Without their endorsement the Fraud Squad and most lawyers would not touch it. But they had reckoned without my new lawyer, a dedicated Roger-botherer.

CHAPTER FORTY-FOUR

The Ghost of Christmas Future

I was in Marrakech, two day before Santa, too late to make it a nightmare before Christmas. But there'd still be time to send the boys our season's greetings. My associate had wanted to send Waka a little gift from The Ghost of Christmas Future: a calculator (his sums hadn't added up in his joint defence with Pitts-Tucker to the Law Society; not that they had cared). Now we had a better present. My lawyer would send them a letter making them an offer they'd be mad to refuse. Hopefully it would reach them before they'd had time to gobble their cold turkey.

Marrakech, so the story goes, was founded on three tons of gold looted from Timbucktu. I had been watching the price of gold rise daily. On December 23rd 2006 it was riding high, a gleaming $622 per troy ounce, set to rise to a peak of $1,800 before a dramatic, but historically always temporary, decline. There are 132,000 ounces in a ton. Phew. Geologists estimate a fifty-year lifespan for the North Korean mine. Great. With a goldmine you can still pull women at one-hundred-and-ten.

The plan was taking shape. If Pitts-Tucker persisted with his line of defence we'd have him bang to rights. Perhaps if he and Waka had been in the same room when they'd concocted their story for the Law Society, they might have stood a chance. If convicted, Waka would be made bankrupt and possibly gaoled, but he, and maybe Pitts-Tucker, would still have a goldmine. My choices were clarifying – give me Waka's percentage of the mine and I would call off the dogs of law.

My friend pointed out that Waka would have no place to hide if his fine upstanding wife got wind of what he'd been up to. Waka likes his space, but once the lawyer's letter hit, his crime would be sitting there, staring him in the face as he looked at his wife over dinner. You can sometimes get away with living life on the edge if you're on the hoof, but when you have a home and family you either have to stay and face the music or run.

He would run, or hop it at least. He'd vowed never to go back inside, or, to use one of his phrases 'put his head above the parapet'. But that is precisely where I would put it if he did not talk turkey. He would lose everything, and I would blow the whole mining enterprise wide open.

I had been warned by my new lawyer that Pitts-Tucker and Waka Kele would, in their defence, try to go for my character defects. That could be a long trial then. To them, I'm contradictory, tight, a liar and a compulsive-obsessive. It seems I make the average Alzheimers sufferer look like the Memory Man. Does this criticism hurt? Frankly, my dears, I don't give a damn, as long as I get my money and shares in the mine. Sticks and stones may break my bones but gold will never hurt me.

A friend recently told me that he'd reached that stage in life where he cared little for what others think of him because he knows who he is, for better or for worse. I have not yet developed that rhino hide and care deeply what my children think of me. The few months leading up to Christmas past gave me the opportunity to spend a lot of time with Sammy and some time with Poppy. I would like to think this period went some way to building bridges, at least with Poppy. I suspect there was less of a healing process necessary with Sammy as she is well-versed in the weaknesses and caprices of a certain kind of man. We shall see what the Ghost of Christmas Future brings. Inshallah, as a waiter would say to me in Marrakech when in making my farewells I say – "See you tomorrow."

"Inshallah."

Even with all the Pitts-Tucker and Waka action going on, I still had time to spare a Christmas thought for JP and DV. I'd had high hopes of getting a positive reaction from the police over a leaked Waka statement that she'd been terrified when they took her hard-drive. I was urged to phone the DS who'd carried out the original investigation into them, but I put it off, day after day. Finally I took a deep breath and jumped into the icy waters of reality.

The swimming analogy is apt because that is precisely how it felt to me. I had built up the call in my mind, endlessly imagining how it would go. Finally, I had arrived at a conclusion. The DS would say 'yes', there had been a conspiracy to pervert the course of justice; he was going to pull them in for questioning. There could be no other conclusion to the affair. I rang him.

It was pointed out to me later that I had talked for five-minutes without break before the DS had had a chance to speak, so nervous was I of a negative response. "Paul, remember what I said to your friend when he came to the station? Let it go. It's over. There's nothing we can do. I told your friend that your obsession with that woman has to end. Use your intelligence to go down a new avenue in life."

"Nothing you can do? You know she was scared when her computer was taken. Surely that's a sign that ..."

"I've been onto the CPS. They say that even if she concocted the witness intimidation story with DV, there is no way anyone can prove that she was not genuinely scared of you. As long as she sticks to her story that she was scared, I'm afraid there's nothing we can do, as much as we might like to."

"Have you trawled her hard-drive?"

"No, we don't have the resources. It would cost us £3,000 of public money. We have to work to a budget ..."

"I'll pay."

"Paul, what I said stands. The fear factor is almost impossible to overcome unless we have a witness statement that she was faking it in order to get you out of the way."

"OK. What about that other thing I sent you? You know, when my criminal lawyer accidentally leaked the document that showed there was a 'dirty letter' from the CPS. One was sent to me on January 24th, explaining why I'd been released, but my lawyer's leak implies there was another letter on the same day that was effectively for his eyes only. There's a cover-up. I know there is. Everyone says that if there is a cover-up it would be to protect JP, but I think it's because if it gets out that a senior council officer was bending the rules then where would that leave the council on potential legal claims from people he's convicted over the past few years? They've got a vested interest to keep it quiet. A financial and political interest. It ..." My phone had cut off. I tried to ring back but couldn't get through.

Later, shocked as I was that the police were powerless to act, I came to rationalise their decision and decided that perhaps it was for the best. Talking to the DS had been a cathartic experience for me. It was over. I slept on it. Then came a new day. No, it was not over. There were two things I could do. I would somehow get my hands on the 'dirty letter' and I would get Waka to verify that she was not scared of me. He'd had several private meetings with her during the care homes negotiations and my intuition told me that she would have been frank with him, especially considering that both parties had been hoping that I'd be inside for years. Why would Waka help me? Gaol would be a death sentence for him, that's why.

Christmas 2006 was a frustrating time for me in Marrakech. I was with a couple of friends who were genuinely pleased to be away from the season of marital strife. I was accused of protesting too much as I continually mentioned all those aspects of Christmas which so annoyed me. In Morocco's most secular city, where Habibs are rarer than in London, every bar in the Gileez district was packed with drinkers as intent on obliterating their day-to-day existence as any temporary Christian celebrating baby Jesus's birthday. The previous Christmas I'd been in the slammer, not knowing when I'd be out, thinking it could be maybe never if the heart and spirit gave out. The one before I was with the other lost souls in the clinic. This time I was once again on the wagon as my friends enjoyed a few beers in the many bars full of friendly yet somehow desperate crowds of men and no women save for a few hookers who maybe would have enhanced their pulling power by the wearing of a Habib. Christmas Eve itself was enhanced by one of my pals taking an iron bar to the door of the whorehouse above our shared apartment because he couldn't get a Silent Night. My other mate had picked up a bootlegged copy of Tim Craig's son's first venture as 007, although there was no sound so we all tried to lip read.

It is said that Christmas is for children, yet it is for women too, as they give life to that magical dream of the bleak midwinter. The Christmas my heart really wanted was one of cosy fires and Christmas lights and feeling bloated and The Great Escape; I've seen it so many times yet still can't remember which ones finally got away. I wanted a Christmas of candlelit Midnight Mass and an early dry Sherry, a drink I'd never go near except on Christmas morn. JP? Yes, that was the last happy Christmas I remembered, there at the farm. Still, the most affecting Christmases are often the ones you have only in your imagination, and for all my protests to the contrary I felt a sense of loss. I was over sixty. Three lost Christmases and how many more to go? It's a season of reflection and loss, when the pendulum of time seems to speed up, reminding you that all your trials and sorrows will come to an end all too soon. Then a Marrakoshi told me that every day after the Winter Solstice the sun in Marrakech grows that little bit warmer on your face. It is not an end but a fresh beginning. Come Wednesday and my new lawyer would be back at work. Enough seasonal sentiment; I'd dieted off a few stone, so I bought myself a soft black leather jacket to celebrate. Someone said that in it I looked a bit like a detective from a French film noir. I hoped they meant Jean Gabin. He was the business. Time to go get me some bad guys. Sod the past. Look to the future. It's only just begun.

CHAPTER FORTY-FIVE

Stick it in Your Bread-Basket

January 2007 had barely begun when my lawyer sent me the first draft of a letter which could make me rich beyond even my wildest dreams. That letter led to others, back and forth, and meetings, phone calls, emails, Inns of Court and the High Court. The labyrinthine corridors of the latter would become all too familiar. A month or so earlier I had done my bull-in-a-china-shop routine and crashed uninvited and unloved into the mining company's lawyer's offices. I'd gone there to inspect the company documents. "They're in Birmingham," said a suit. "So's Jasper Carrott", I thought, but said nothing, unsure of my ground on that one. I went to the High Court with Tom and obtained an Order to inspect the papers in accordance with UK company law. Back to the lawyers I went, taking the Order and a camera, although I wasn't sure what I'd do with the latter. Forced to do so, the lawyers showed me the relevant documents, as a few heavy-looking characters hovered close by while I snapped away. I wasn't confident the pictures would come out and I knew I could take nothing away with me so I got my depleted hippocampi on the case and tried to remember everything. As I'd suspected, the pictures weren't clear enough, but no matter. The lawyers didn't know that, and the incriminating share stubs told a story I wanted to hear. Waka Kele and Roger Pitts-Tucker were the original shareholders, with seventy-five and twenty-five percent respectively. My suspicions were grounded. The law firm dropped its clients soon after my visit. Nothing to hide then?

We at last served a writ on Pitts-Tucker & Co on June 23rd and then went to serve Waka the following day. I knew I couldn't get close enough to him, nor could my associate, as he would recognise us and wouldn't answer the door. So we took along John, a private eye, who followed in his car as I drove ahead to point out the location. Just as we arrived outside Waka's converted courthouse home a green 4x4 reversed out of his drive and made off up the street. I jumped out of my car while my friend shouted – "Get down! If he sees us he'll go to ground!" He was right, but after so long and now seeing the quarry in my sights I panicked, a headless chicken. "Leave it to me. It's what you pay me for," said the private eye in that way they're meant to say things. We left him there. He had pictures of Waka from the Aussie press and if he turned up he'd serve him. He told us to make ourselves scarce, to meet him back at his office in two hours. Reluctantly I drove off. "No! Don't follow him! Take another route. Leave it to John," said Captain Sensible by my side. So we took another road, a lane really, that looped behind Waka's home and made off in search of a bacon sandwich. "Look!" shouted Captain Sensible. It was becoming a morning of exclamation marks. He was right, though. A hundred yards ahead the green 4x4 was pulling away from the kerb. Even my friend was catching the thrill of the chase, so we followed it, staying at a discreet distance, which meant that winding country lanes frequently caused us to lose sight of our prey. The next time we saw the car it was as before – just coming out of a driveway. "Can you see him?" I asked. "I'm sure it's him. What's left of his hair is white." This process went on for what seemed like an age. I was concerned the café would run out of bacon. The mobile rang. "It's John. I served notice on him. He just drove up in a silver Merc. He'd been to buy the papers, still in his pyjamas. He went quite white when he saw me on the doorstep."

"Thanks John. Great job." We caught up with the green 4x4 again. This time we saw the driver. His white 'hair' was his hat and he had loaves of bread in a basket. We'd been following the local baker. Still, job done, and we did eventually get two of the world's most expensive bacon sandwiches.

CHAPTER FORTY-SIX

As the Scorpion Strikes

In an age of international financial meltdown gold is arguably the hardest currency of all. The price of a barrel of crude is too politically unstable and under long-term pressure from alternative fuels, but gold remains true to its promise, yet analogous to greed.

This third of the Seven Deadly Sins has spawned countless books and films in which gold seekers are demonised before meeting a sticky end: as gold diggers; gold crazy; seekers after fools' gold. The very idea that untold wealth can be found in the ground runs counter to the rules that hold together our social structures, and a breaking of those rules has to be seen to be punished. Those deemed to be making a pact with the Devil are invariably portrayed as being in the grip of gold fever. They meet an early grave in the desert heat, seeing their dreams realised just as the scorpion strikes. Would my life imitate art?

I have dabbled in all seven of the Sins. Is it to my moral discredit or my all too human credit that I am now motivated by the fifth Sin, that of ire, wrath, revenge? I want my pound of flesh, preferably calculated at the gold spot price on the London Bullion Market. If the scorpion strikes, so be it, as long as it isn't at me.

If alchemists had succeeded in their quest to turn base metal into gold they would have killed the goose that lays the golden egg. All the gold ever mined, in whatever form it has been moulded by humankind, after some three-and-a-half-thousand years of human effort totals no more than the tonnage of a modern cruise liner. The one hundred and fifty-five-thousand tons, the total above-ground gold distributed throughout the world, whether mined by Nubians, Roman legions, in the Black Hills of Dakota in the 1860s, or by North Koreans, is transmutable, indestructible, beyond the artificial boundaries created by governments, aloof from the forces of free trade. It can be highly visible, adorning a palace or cathedral, or invisible in the shadow form of paper bonds while its reality lays under guard deep in a Swiss mountain vault. Of course, as in the sense that all banks are technically bankrupt if their account holders simultaneously called in their money, so too with gold. Paper gold exceeds true gold by a ratio of some one-thousand-to-one. But hush now on that one.

Exponential predictions of the price of gold are often overly optimistic, and were soon proven to be so. The sale of gold stocks to boost investment portfolios and the IMF's off-loading of gold reserves would temporarily deflect the gleaming arrow from its heavenly trajectory, but whatever market vagaries befall it, buoyed up by its supranational status, gold is an investor's dream in a volatile and increasingly unpredictable age. In stormy seas, gold will float the boat.

As I took stock I realised I probably had more enemies than friends. If it is true that you can judge someone by the company they keep, then it could be said that I should choose my enemies more carefully. I cannot recall an enemy ever becoming a friend, but the reverse has not been uncommon. That must say something about me, I suppose, although I do feel that enemies are sometimes more entertaining than friends, in that way the bad guy in a film is often far more interesting than the hero. Waka, for all the trouble he's caused me, at least has the decency to be good value in the entertainment stakes, albeit unwittingly.

We all complain about postal deliveries, but the mantra 'it's lost in the post', repeated often enough, ceases to be an excuse and proves to be a lie. It really does not happen very often, except, it would seem, to Waka. So there he is, holed up in Great Rollright, far from the beaten track and therefore in need of contact with the outside world, yet every time we sent him an urgent legal document it failed to arrive. Postman Pat delivers it sure enough, but blue tits or magpies or foxes always have it away with our lawyer's latest missive. So we were forced to employ more direct tactics, but after that first episode it was becoming increasingly hard to get close to him.

Waka had responded to that initial writ with what was mainly a list of denials interspersed with admissions where he thought it safe to do so. This at least enabled our lawyer to fine-tune our case, but this process was effective only if we could get evidence that Waka was in receipt of further court documents. Now, if you were trying to keep your profile as low as a lizard one would think it unwise to publicly don the garb of a general in the Maltese army. I mean, even real generals in the British Army would baulk at going down the local in full dress uniform. It's England. We take the piss. It's what we do. "How do I recognise him?" asked Peter, John the private eye's associate, who hadn't yet encountered Waka. Presumably he hadn't seen the Aussie press cuttings. "Early sixties, balding, avuncular. Got a great big black boot on one foot like he's in a chain gang. Oh, and he'll likely be dressed as a Maltese general. Can't miss him." It was his annual 'General Day' that very Saturday. According to a couple of Waka's near-neighbours, the locals awaited the great day with bated sniggers. After all, we all know of Malta's heroic resistance against the Nazis in WW11, but since Waka was one-year-old when that conflict ended his personal contribution to Malta's war effort would have been less than significant. True, the kind of Maltese Waka was likely to know have contributed significantly to the economy of Soho and provided a constant flow of customers through London's West End Central nick, but Malta has not tended to be a world-renowned military power.

Peter approached Waka, no blue-tit, magpie or crafty Reynard in sight to give him an excuse for not having received this court document. It was like a combination of two very old jokes – How do you make a Maltese cross the road? Waka had spotted Peter, years of ducking and diving having no doubt evolved his senses to a degree where he can smell a court document at fifty yards. He beat a tactical retreat, hopping across the road into the post office, one that hadn't then been closed down. Maybe he hoped his uniform would be mistaken for that of a postman. Whistling 'The British Grenadiers', Peter advanced. Caught without his troops the General meekly accepted the document Peter proffered like he was accepting unconditional surrender. The war was not yet over, nor was it the beginning of the end, but it was the end of the beginning.

CHAPTER FORTY-SEVEN

Death of the Bounty Hunter

I arrived in the fetid heat of Bangkok in March, 2007, just around the time the annual Buddhist festival of Songkran was beginning. As a man who ate the Jehovah Witnesses' biscuits and, if not brainwashed by the Scientologists, at least went through the first couple of spin cycles, who am I to denigrate any religious practice?

I spoke to a Hindu in a cafe. He said that they had a similar water-throwing festival in his religion. It went on for a few hours and that was it. He slowly shook his head in wonderment at the scene before him as squawking bar girls lined the pavement opposite, their constantly refilled water pistols and buckets soon emptied on hapless passers-by.

Even knowing the origin and meaning of the festival within Thai culture did not lessen its annoyance factor. Good nature prevails for awhile, but this was like watching children who don't know when the game is over and that the joke has worn as thin as a hooker's summer dress. "How can these people keep it up day after day?" he sighed. I have to say I agreed with him. To giggle gleefully the first few times might be forgivable, especially for those with hard lives. But to display that same enthusiasm every time you fired a water pistol or tossed a bucket of water over a passing stranger perhaps showed a certain lack of creative thought. Still, that wasn't the reason I'd come to Bangkok.

"Do you think Waka was behind the death of the Bounty Hunter?" I asked a reporter from The Nation. "No, but you could probably tell from my article that I had my suspicions that something was amiss. Put it this way, he wasn't your usual run-of-the-mill middle-aged guy meeting an early death. He was a fit fuck. Had to be, in his line of business."

We refilled our glasses, and this reporter, who ran the original story on the death of The Bounty Hunter in August '05, was keen to look into the possibility of having another look at the post-mortem results, although he stressed he was motivated by his nose for a good story rather than any specific leads. He'd linked Waka Kele to the story because it was the latter who had led a dedicated Waka-hunter, an Aussie journalist, to give the Yugoslav John Dragicevich his nickname.

Back home, I'd been reminded that we live in the electronic age. There was no need to travel halfway across the planet to get background info on Waka when the same could be done online and oh by the way phones have been around for a century or so. OK, I know, but I'm a dinosaur in that respect. I need to touch a situation. Ironically, although I was in Thailand, most of the people who had info on Waka were in Australia.

The boys had already tried to attack my reputation, hoping that allegations of my drinking, poor memory, unreliability and criminal past would somehow counter the fact that they'd nicked my money. I even learned through one of Waka's defence documents that I still had the Rubens and it's stashed somewhere in Derbyshire. And there's me thinking I'd lost it. Still, Waka my son, if it's reputations you're after, then maybe Uncle Paul can get a bit of dirt on you.

I phoned Perth. Joe Pop, a retired Aussie journalist,

had a lot of juice on Waka. He couldn't understand how he'd slipped through the net in all his years as a high-profile conman. True, the Aussie feds had raided his Sydney flat but Waka had got wind and legged it, faster on his pins in those days. When he conned the investor out of A$125,000 in the search for Nazi gold, The Bounty Hunter was hired to get it back. Waka had just passed through Customs at Heathrow when Dragicevich came up behind him and put a 'gun' to his head, The Bounty Hunter had told Joe. Waka went a whiter shade of pale as Dragicevich held his fingers hard against Waka's left temple and mentioned that his client would appreciate early sight of his money. Then he let Waka go with the Terminator-like promise that he'd be back.

Back home in Oxfordshire, wherever Waka went his very big shadow was sure to go, but although The Bounty Hunter's physical presence supplied the threat, it was his subtlety that delivered the goods. He simply left copies of one of Joe's less than flattering articles scattered around in Waka's stamping grounds. That's all.

I again met up with the reporter, asking if there was still any chance of him using his influence to reopen The Bounty Hunter case, as he had suggested might be possible. At this stage I just needed to close off any blind alleys. "Sorry mate. They don't want to go down that route. Plenty of foreigners die early here, and if it's foreigners, farang on farang ..." he trailed off, shrugging. It was late, early hours. We were sitting in the Penny Black, a bar on Soi Cowboy. Outside working girls shrieked like banshees. I've never looked up the origin of the word 'dulcet', but I bet it wasn't Thai. The source of their excitement? You've guessed it – they were firing water pistols. Inside, the girls had checked their weapons at the door. In the relative peace of a water-free zone we talked of the Land of Smiles. Like how the Thai authorities implemented their immigration policy. Unwanted guests were returned to neighbouring Burma by being tossed in the river. Not too Draconian, you might think, until you're told their hands were bound behind their backs with barbed wire. The prevailing current takes the bodies upstream, back home for all too see. It's apparently an effective deterrent. Those that come in legally don't get the hardware-store deportation treatment. They just get exploited. Ask a bar girl where she's from and it's invariably 'the north'. They say they're prettier up there. "Wha' your name? Whar you fraam?" comes the standard greeting as yet another girl offers her favours in return for money and the dream of marriage and everlasting happiness in Middlesbrough or Clacton or the similarly exotic locations the lucky ones end up in, ageing and plumping up fast as the tropical sun leaves their bones and their glow turns sallow. To them I am big, I am old, I must be rich. Then I am told of how the ever-smiling Thais dealt with their drug problem. My new friend estimated that some two-thousand-plus dealers and cross-fire victims died in a police crack-down. I made to leave. It was late and Songkran was over. With the astute use of cabs I had somehow managed to avoid a soaking during the entire four day (although it had felt much longer) festival. I don't know why, but I was proud of that. I left the building, all bows and smiles. That's when I got it. Full in the face, a bucket of cool water in the hot tropical night. The girl shrieked with laughter. So did I. At least she was happy and not chucked in a river wearing barbed-wire bracelets.

It had been a long trip to learn little more than I could have gleaned from just reading Joe Pop's articles. I had been trying to get the big picture and was forgetting that the devil is in the detail; that the key to my success was in the minds of my lawyers and my associates; in my adversaries' failures to synchronise their defence; in the Royal Courts of Justice; in my own wrath; and deep in the geological strata of North Korea.

CHAPTER FORTY-EIGHT

Jordan's Prize Assets

In the event, the News Of The World didn't run the JP/JV story. Why should they, when precious column inches were needed for some celeb's latest mammary disfigurement?

Of the nationals it was the Daily Mail that finally came good. I had been to the County Court to seek a restraining order against JP and JV or their agents, convinced as I was that there was an ongoing harassment campaign against me.

An injunction was granted. The press was there. Other than the Daily Mail, the locals got in on the act, as did regional BBC radio stations, ensuring JP's profile among her peers and neighbours was as high as Jordan's prize assets. This was Hell for a middle-aged professional woman who would probably have preferred that her bikini line were not exposed to several million Daily Mail readers.

"She lied to get me gaoled." Over and over I repeated this mantra to myself as in the small hours what was left of my conscience drove me out of bed and into the kitchen to consult a friendly bottle of red over whether I should have so publicly exposed her. I mean, her family, her employees, her clients and their families, her friends, all now knew of her behaviour, of how she looked in knickers.

Although I hadn't invited the press to attend the injunction hearing, I had not been shy in appraising them of the situation. I repeat the point about the lie, those lies, that I could get nobody in authority to believe. In particular it was the lie about the Harvey Nichols' stalker, when she'd phoned me that night just as Waka and I were driving past the Knightsbridge store, to tell me the shooting had been on the news. How she'd turned that one, making it look like it was me threatening her with a similar fate. She'd even managed to contradict herself in the two versions of the statements given to the police, the one written by her, and the other, as previously alleged, by DV. What she had done had been like a Napoleonic Code denunciation; a witch-hunt. OK, so I'd hunt the witch. A magazine writer contacted me.

Shortly after, I leafed through a copy of the magazine. So far it wasn't looking promising, the tawdry Jeremy Kyle-type storylines at odds with the smiling charms of the pretty girl-next-door cover girl. I turned the pages, nervous, savouring the moment. Yes! There it was! My story! At last someone was listening. Three pages with full-colour pics, including a semi-gloss bikini-line exposure in a multi-million readership magazine that gets left on a table in every salon and surgery throughout the land, misdeeds to be gloated over for months and sometimes years; the past much fresher than in yesterday's newspapers. Women's magazines weren't previously on my radar, but this was big: millions of readers and six shots of JP's face to match her name with what I saw as her shame.

CHAPTER FORTY-NINE

Red-Hot Poker

"Knight wants to meet." This from out lawyer in May 2008. "He wants to make an offer on Waka's behalf". We wondered why he was being so helpful. Perhaps it was to keep his name out of court, and thereby the press. He was protecting his interests too. It wouldn't do if potential investors and the guys in Pyongyang thought the seed capital for the mining joint venture came from a scam, although I stress that Knight was not involved in the appropriation of my funds. It was clear that what he was really saying was something we suspected but hadn't yet been able to confirm; that the company was potentially worth a fortune. Things were heating-up fast. I went back to my lawyer – "OK, tell him this – I want my money back plus legal fees plus Waka's shares in the mines. That's all."

We knew we wouldn't need a Max Clifford to beef up the story. This one had the lot: an international conman who was an associate of Alan Bond, with a well-connected son and a daughter with alleged links to men in shiny suits in Las Vegas; a City lawyer already being investigated over a dodgy titles scam with a 'client' who was being hunted by an assortment of US federal agencies, the lawyer allegedly also a consigliere to the Mob in Valetta; the mysterious death of The Bounty Hunter; an ex-Boss assassin; arms dealing; a plot to sink a boat in the south of France; Nazi gold; the North Korean connection, and gold in them thar (sic) hills.

This was my insurance policy. I was increasingly confident I'd get my money back, one way or the other, but no sight of the gold and I would make a small fortune from the media at the very least.

This was turning into a high-roller Poker game. Knight wasn't going for the share request at this stage but would clear Waka's debt to me and add the compensation he'd planned for him. I raised the amount and fed it through my lawyer. Two days later the latter called back – "Now he's offering even more to pay off Waka's debt." The funny thing is, I'd only thrown in the higher figure after having genuinely misinterpreted the original offer. When our team realised our error we apologised, but there was no need. It seemed that he'd pay whatever was needed. The meek may inherit the earth, but not the mineral rights. All bets were on.

A relationship was developing between me and Knight. I thought it was like the one between a man and his dog, with each of us thinking the other is the dog. He was charming, clever in the way such people can be, and could be taught to do tricks like buying lunch and fine wines in smart clubs. OK, so I'm beginning to stretch the dog analogy here; dogs don't drink fine wine or belong to clubs (Crufts?), although my late Cavie, Suzy, loved a cold beer.

Knight, based on my then limited knowledge of him, was a dog in that I felt whenever I tossed a stick he would play fetch. It wasn't hard to tweak his tail, to get a response. Then it clicked. Cats show they are master or mistress of all they survey, but dogs are more subtle. They run the show too, but they let you think you do. Knight had been tossing me sticks on an almost daily basis and I was fetching them and licking his paws. Nasty that, the taste of money, it having passed through so many hands.

When it was put to me that Knight would settle up Waka's

debt and put even more on the table I hadn't questioned why he'd accepted my earlier error so calmly. I'd been given his offer over the phone by my lawyer late one Sunday night in May, 2008. I contacted my friend and we met in a bar with overloud music. I kid you not, it was Abba's 'Money, Money, Money' on the jukebox. Naturally, we toasted the deal. Not a fortune, but enough, and there was even five percent of the mining operation on the table, not as much as I'd anticipated, but at that stage I knew I could raise him.

CHAPTER FIFTY

The Portcullis and the Fedora

In care homes they still use the old Prime Minister test to assess memory loss. We get a lot of Margaret Thatchers, even today, whereas we all know it's that nice Mr Gladstone. Everyone tells me my memory is bad: my lawyer, my brief, my friends and foes. It soon became clear that Pitts-Tucker's lawyers were going for the old Hippocampi problem – no short-term memory, purely the longer variety. Presumably that means I can't remember what I had for dinner last night but I have total recall of a meal of Cadbury's Smash back in '73 and those laughing Martians.

I'm not buying it. The old saying that if you can remember the Sixties you weren't there applies to every decade that coincides with young adulthood, if that is you have a proper misspent youth. Sure, you remember the defining moments, but you can't remember the detail, what it really felt like from day to day. If we did, the rest of life would be unbearable; all that hair in the nostrils and ears and expanding-waistlines stuff.

What I'm leading up to is that I was being urged by my own camp to stay out of court. This, rather than face hostile cross-examination by a Rottweiler QC in London's Royal Courts of Justice. It was a scenario, I was told, in which I could never prevail because of my inability to recall precise detail and my tendency to favour the emotional rather than the logical response. Nevertheless, I resolved to see it through, naively believing that because right was on my side I would win. It was a Thursday and Monday was the unexpectedly imminent date for the court hearing. I would go in there, keep it simple, stick to yes and no, and bamboozle them all with my self-perceived ice-cool clarity. "Accept their offer," was the advice. "No. I'm going through with the case."

"The offer."

"Then Pitts-Tucker walks."

"Paul, the theft's divided into three counts, given that your money was taken in three tranches. Two are as watertight as they can ever be in law, but one is not, given that their defence might try to claim it was Waka's just fee for work carried out on your behalf. That increases the risk of failure. All advice points to ninety-percent virtual certainty on two counts and less than fifty on the third. Failure on that would take you under the offer threshold. Please accept, for your own sake. At this point, money's more important than justice."

"I can handle it."

"Look, Tom said that he's seen top CEOs crack under daily cross-examination, people with a firm grasp of their case. Take the money on the table and press on by other means. Live to fight…." "I know the rest …."

"Their brief will be advised of your weak points by Pitts-Tucker. In the slammer you weren't on top of your game. You'll be asked to dot every I and cross …." "Again, I know how it goes."

"OK, Paul, but remember, at the SDT, Pitts-Tucker presented a total command of his case."

"Sure. At the Solicitor's Disciplinary Tribunal where he lost."

"He was fined and suspended, but not struck off."

"A six-month ban might as well be a life ban. As soon as

the result is in the public domain no prospective client will touch him with a barge-pole, whatever that might be."

"It's …"

"You mean what you say, that I should take their offer?"

"I do, Paul. I do. Take the money, recover your costs, then move on, go for Kele and, by association, the shares."

"I'm not happy with it, you know that. I thought you were with me. I'll have my day in Court. Press coverage, get the bastard struck-off, call witnesses, expose everyone involved. All that, gone."

"No, delayed. That's all."

"OK, I'll do it, but I'm not happy with it."

Six-months earlier, a joint legal action by the victims of the titles scam finally saw Roger the Dodger before a December 2008 Solicitor's Disciplinary Tribunal, a Star Chamber trial by peers. I'd gone along, couldn't resist it.

I still owed costs awarded against me following my legal actions against JP and DV. Pitts-Tucker spotted me. I had led everyone to believe that I was facing bankruptcy; no way was I going to fill JP's lawyer's pockets, even if I had, by keeping the case alive, contributed to the ever-increasing costs. We would do a deal, was my thinking, but in my own time. Yet although Pitts-Tucker was facing a career-defining, or hopefully a career-ending, moment, he kindly took time out to let JP's lawyer know I was there so papers could be served on me, something I had hitherto adroitly avoided. Bankrupt me and I'm out of action, thought Pitts-Tucker. He didn't succeed, though, and six months later I did that deal and left myself free to concentrate on the main beneficiary of the theft, Waka Kele.

Over several years, as Pitts-Tucker had rubber-stamped the Prince of Lusignan's (yes, that's another of Boada's aliases – I'd need another book to list them all) transactions, it was his position as a City lawyer that had lent credibility to the process. He was not a fedora-wearing Cuban with dodgy titles and his status had given the mainly foreign nationals who were duped the necessary reassurance that no way would a man with a portcullis on his letterhead ever stoop so low.

Pitts-Tucker was suspended by the Solicitors' Disciplinary Tribunal for six-months commencing March 01st 2009, and ordered to pay £80,000 costs. His behaviour was deemed by the tribunal to be 'conduct unbefitting a solicitor' and 'dishonest by the ordinary standards of reasonable and honest people'. However, the Tribunal's lengthy delay in making its findings public – almost a year – meant that the group which had made the original complaint against him had effectively run out of steam, although I read that there's no statute of limitations on the matter, so who knows?

CHAPTER FIFTY-ONE

I'd Name a Nightclub After Her

Janice took a late-night call from The Princess Margaret Hospital. I was a fan of the late princess, walking as she did on the wild side. I would name a nightclub after her, or even a bar, but a hospital? "He's been under for ten hours and we can't wake him. He may have had a stroke. Are his children contactable? It might be the time for farewells." Janice told me she was concerned. I felt cheered by this, until I realised she was terrified she might end up caring for me, dribbling there in the corner, scaring the dogs and the cat and the vicar.

Scientologists say we repeat behavioural patterns throughout our lives, but then you hardly need a PhD in psychology to know that. My Sun-In moment on my first ship could arguably be seen as an explanation of why I went under the knife. Vanity, all is vanity. You would think, would you not, that vanity in a boy of twenty would be outgrown in a man over sixty?

I'd gone in for a nip-tuck. Not one of those full face-lift jobs that could see your dick where your nose should be but just a general tidying-up of what some other dick had called my turkey-wattle. Years of feast and self-imposed famine had taken their toll, the skin under my chin stretched like a balloon about to burst, followed by the inevitable sagging as I customarily dieted off a few stone. I didn't die, nor had I had a stroke, although it was days before you could tell the difference, and some still say the matter is not fully resolved. Apart from not having a bolt through my neck, for awhile I had more than a passing resemblance to Mary Shelly's creation.

I think maybe I had had a real problem whilst under the knife, but if I did, once I was up and about and popping Viagra in readiness for a bed-bath from a pretty nurse, whatever crisis I'd faced was swiftly forgotten. I was better and no-one was talking. But Janice hadn't imagined that phone call.

If it wasn't vanity that had motivated me, what then was it? Disguise? I have so many enemies that I feel it is far safer to adopt a new persona, or something along those lines? Of course, you only have to glimpse a fraction of the back of someone's head from a hundred-metres to recognise them, so that one went out the window. No, hands up then, it was vanity. I wanted a woman, forgetting that at my age love comes through the ears rather than the eyes. "Why don't you change your personality?" said a woman who had indecorously spurned my advances. "Try being kind, generous. Try to imagine that the kind of woman you aspire to does not necessarily wish to eat in the staff canteen of a Town Hall because the Spotted Dick is subsidised. Anyway, I've seen too many spotted dicks in my time for that dish to be appetising. You're cheap. Cheap. Cheap." She was right. I am cheap. But I now have a granite jaw.

I put ads in, like the ones I used to do when dealing Austin 1100s in the Seventies, a catch-all. I reasoned that if I met enough women I would arrive at a mutually attractive compromise. Petite. That was the key-word. A friend had said that if you are too old to go young, petite was the next best thing, it being a more gravity-friendly condition. Now this may sound shallow, but if you are vain enough to have a nip-tuck you are acknowledging that beauty is only skin deep, and that's as deep as you want to go. Have you ever seen someone without their skin?

I decided to relocate to get away from all the familiar bar-propping faces. After all, I had a new face, and I wanted to point it in the direction of any petite woman who had cashmere and pearls and an Aga. Where better to find this svelte creature? I headed for the hills. The Cotswolds.

Anna didn't match up to all my specific needs – she didn't have an Aga – but she can certainly cook. The only problem is, she eats healthily, so there were adjustments to make on my part. Then again, as an ex-fashion model she met all the other requirements on my wish list. She was to stick by me through thick and thin (mostly me being thick) for six years before I popped the question. We are very happy, except when she's telling me off, but I like being told off. It's like being the garçon méchant of earlier years; at least when a woman tells you off you know she cares. I care too, this relationship being my first foray into emotional sanity since the Janice years. If Anna's patience holds out, there could be many more years to come with plenty of fine cooking and quite a few laughs along the way.

Looking back, in the Sixties, being in London was like being at the heart of a great big toffee factory. I like toffees. When I'd left the ships Bruce Wells was already on his way to being the West End boulevardier of legend, the latter a now much overused word. He was still to become a Dalek and to referee Terry McCann's comeback fight in Minder. But even Terence would have baulked at Bruce's greatest challenge, an exhibition bout with Muhammed Ali. That was in '77.

Ten years earlier, we were on the door at the Cromwell Mint, a Kensington club. A Middleweight, as Bruce then was, doesn't loom as large as today's Crombies on steroids, but I'd have backed Bruce in a ruck against the lot of them, maybe at the same time. Always watch out for the smaller bouncers; there's usually a very good reason why they got the gig. If he got stuck there was always the monkey-wrench he kept behind the pot-plant.

He got me into films. I ended up minding stars during production. I had Susannah York in the back of my car once. That is to say I was driving her to and from the set of Kaleidoscope and generally chaperoning her around town. It was not unpleasant. There were others, but it's odd, in that I didn't have a clue who they were. I now tell friends the films I was around and they say well you must have been minder to so and so, but I have no idea. The one I did recognise was John Wayne, quite a few years later than the Susannah time. I was then doing a stint at the Tower Hotel and I had to look after him. He was with Judy Geeson – 'nudie Judie' – his delightful Brannigan co-star. He had a cold and kept coughing up phlegm. And he was smaller than I'd imagined. I'd expected a giant on a horse and he looked about five-eleven max. He must have been early seventies then, so maybe he'd shrunk.

Somehow, my London mid-Sixties were always bathed in summer sunshine. The whitewashed grand terraces of South Kensington were the backdrop to my brawls and booze and birds. I try not to overuse that last expression, but alliteration is always tempting. It was a great time with a great soundtrack, interspersed with my regular forays into southern Europe and all those Pissy and Mudguts and Big Jonnie Marsden years. If Bruce Wells in Dalek mode could get me on the Tardis I'd go back there; I'd drive down the Kings Road on that summer's day when I saw my first mini-skirt being pulled along by an Afghan Hound.

As if doing battle with international conmen, bent lawyers and the rest wasn't enough, I became a latter-day knight-errant. From that day when the blonde walked into the bar in Portugal and I was a minder on the road to Morocco, I seem to have effortlessly drifted into a pattern of saving damsels in distress. First Anna P (a different Anna) slices open the top of her finger on a bottle of Clarin's Angel. This isn't product placement; just watch it with those star-shaped bottles. So I took on the insurers. Then she manages to reopen the police investigation into the death of her lover, Simon. Dead at the bottom of her garden steps and hands coming from everywhere grabbing at the inheritance. The usual did he fall or was he pushed? I get reluctantly involved in this, thinking that maybe it was the drink to which he was so partial. Then strange things happened and I began to think that maybe Anna P was on to something after all. This one is still ongoing, so no more detail for now.

Ann had a similar name, but a very different problem. Her mother had recently died, leaving £400,000, but none of it to her. She'd been fostered out just after the war. Her unmarried mother couldn't cope with the social stigma. Ann went into care, watched from afar by her mother's sadness. The years passed, Ann not knowing but of course wondering who her parents were. She had daughters of her own, born in wedlock and grown happy and successful. Then from nowhere her mother made contact. She had Alzheimer's and knew her days were numbered. She used the Salvation Army's missing persons tracing unit, and they helped to reconcile mother and daughter. It was a happy reunion, all the more so after half a century of separation, yet poignant because it could not last. They were inseparable for those final two years of Ann's mother's long life, much of it lived with a heavy heart. Then that heart stopped beating and the reunion was over.

Ann had cared for others for much of her life, a hospice nurse giving palliative care, death her constant companion.

When her own mother died, her mind slipping away from her, Ann knew that she had been blessed, that their reunion had added completeness to both their lives. Now in her sixties, Ann continues to work, someone who would always give rather than take. She knew her mother had money, but that was far from her mind, although she was aware that anything that came her way would ease her own later years. So when the will was read it came as something of a shock to realise that her mother had left the bulk of her estate to the Salvation Army and nothing to her.

She came to me, knowing that I knew my way around court, from both sides of the fence. This wasn't her world, a nice woman who would rather die than give offence. I started negotiations, but which way to go? The legal route? A lawyer advised me not to – it would be prohibitively expensive and fraught with risk. 'Greenmail', that softer version of its black cousin? Well, there were tales around of Salvation Army jollies funded out of donations. I remembered the old Panorama feature, the one that showed senior uniformed officers frolicking in the Indian Ocean off Kenya, trouser legs rolled up. I bet that didn't encourage donations for awhile. Threaten the Army's generals with media coverage of Ann's plight and maybe they'd come to the table. Or maybe they would take the moral high ground and pull up the drawbridge. Morality? Tell them the true, sad story. Appeal to their charitable instincts? That was the choice we made. I represented Anne and entered into negotiations. They made an offer – £15,000. We weren't H.A.P.P.Y., to borrow from the Sally Ann song.

I went with Ann to see them, to appeal to their better natures. There were three senior Salvation Army representatives seated at a table. They had brought along their pet Piranha, a smiling assassin of a lawyer, as if there is any other kind. I played along with our prearranged tactic, that we would stay with the moral argument, in keeping with our previous correspondence. I asked if we could come to a fairer conclusion; the Salvation Army should retain the majority of the bequest but make more reasonable provision for Ann. But their lawyer was leading them, his argument being that they would have to account for themselves to the Charity Commission; they were unable to take a unilateral decision. Ann presented well at the meeting, her patent, understated honesty more eloquent than a thousand clever letters. She shyly told her story, so quietly that we had to strain to hear her – "I married at eighteen. I remember that day so well. I was so happy yet all the time thinking how wonderful it would be if my parents had been there. Then the years went by, and I had children of my own, two lovely daughters. When the day came when I was reunited with my mother, it was even better than when I married or my children were born. We talked about everything, filling in all those missing years. I told her of my wedding day – 'I wished so much you had been there. For years I imagined what it would have been like. I used to dream about it, what we had talked about, what you wore'. 'I was there', said my mother, "I watched from a distance. I was in the crowd outside the church. I watched your whole childhood. All of it. Then I lost you. You moved away, and I lost you.'"

The eyes of the sole woman on the Salvation Army panel had filled with tears. I think that if she'd had her way she would have handed the £400,000 over to Ann right there and then in new notes. There was a stunned silence around the table. Even I was shocked. Ann had never mentioned this before. The Piranha smiled. I caught his eye. There was a glint of recognition. I knew he knew that I'd rather have gone for the jugular, that at this kind of hard dealing we were two of a kind, but I had set out my stall. I couldn't change styles at this stage of the game. Ann had done all the right things, and with her it hadn't been an act. We'd done our best. The Salvation Army had probably bought the moral argument. Not so the Piranha. It was £15,000, take it or leave it. Who says charity begins at home?

CHAPTER FIFTY-TWO

To Hear the Lamentations of Their Women

It's one thing to crush your enemies, to see them fall at your feet, and to hear the lamentations of their women, in the words of that great philosopher, Conan the Barbarian, but even my hardened heart softened at hearing those of Waka's woman. She had been bright and brisk, a Pashima-wearing, jam-making pillar of the local community at that horse show JP and I had attended together in 2006. Or, to give it her version, I had attended alone. Clearly, the camera does lie. Sadly, it wasn't digital. "Where was the photo developed? They might be able to date it. It would prove you were back together." I tried to tap the old Hippocampi, but couldn't remember where it was. Anyway, the shot shows us hand in hand in our last ever photo together, friends remarking how tired she looked, but maybe I had done my bit on that one. The woman at Waka's door made the JP in the picture look like a thirty-something. It wasn't just her appearance; something inside her had died. She had ditched her Pashima and now wore a cloak of fear and dejection. She didn't know where Waka was and so I left her to close the door on me and return to her lamentations. Her rambling home had thick walls but I'm sure I heard a cry of anguish.

Neighbours spoke to me of their shock at her apparent downfall, of how much she had changed in so short a time.

I did not revel in this, she was blameless. "No she wasn't," somebody said. "She had a large slice of Waka's shares."

"Ah, but did she know about my money?"

The local Post Office had now been closed down and the Dutch ex-Postmaster did not know where Waka was, only that he was no longer around. He hadn't liked Waka, had detested his arrogance. Then I remembered the builders, those who had mocked Waka's Maltese Generalship. They too had no idea where he was. There were rumours he was doing a three-to-six stretch, but nobody knew where or why. That I did not want, for Waka to be inside would give him an excuse before a judge for his failure to comply with Court directions. Our intended strike-out and subsequent freezing of his worldwide assets would be delayed. It was this freeze that would impact on Knight in that it would enable a legal tracing of all Waka's affairs and thus establish the still-missing link between my money and the goldmine.

I suddenly saw myself confronting Waka. There was another rumour suggesting he was keeping his head down in Freetown, Sierra Leone, scratching for diamonds on behalf of Alan Bond. I would go there and confront him. He had consistently cited being in West Africa as his excuse for serial non-attendance in Court. We let our imaginations run riot and reached the inescapable conclusion that Waka was in Africa, ergo, Waka was still with Bond. "We don't go there," came the advice. "I thought you'd enjoy a trip to Freetown."

"Yes, but I'd enjoy one that needed a return ticket."

"Look on the bright side. Think of the reduced airfare."

"If he's operating there he would have protection. Remember the Paramount Chief?"

You don't go there on that kind of business without backup. If Waka's mining diamonds there he'll have minders and we'll be as welcome as a fart in a spacesuit."

"Nonsense."

"Suit yourself, Paul. I'll get online and get you a one-way ticket." My friend was right, I regret to say. He continued – "What we do instead is speak to Alan Bond. I'll track him down, you phone him."

We went to see him at his offices behind London's Ritz Hotel. This was a man who'd once owned Van Gogh's Irises, then, in 1987, valued at US$54-million. "I was on Dennis Norton's boat one night in St Tropez Harbour in '88," said my friend. That's Dennis, he of the tickling-stick at the campsite, Tim Craig's mate. "We were on a forty-footer, moored on the outskirts of the harbour at the end of the long breakwater. Bond's boat, 'Northern Cross', was too big to take right in, so they'd moored her out there and we'd pulled in fifteen metres astern of her. She could have swallowed us through her rear doors like a whale sucking in plankton for breakfast. Bigger boats than ours were going in and out all night. It was more like James than Alan Bond. If he had a ship's cat it would have been white. He had an identical ship for the Southern Hemisphere, the 'Southern Cross'."

"What were you doing there?"

"Fishing for supper. We had lines over the side while Bond played host to the Riviera's finest suntans. There were helicopters bringing them in from offshore yachts right onto the boat's helipad and a queue of limos stretching along the harbour wall. It was as if the entire jet-set of its day was waiting to get onboard, with Puccini blaring out from speakers while the ship's searchlights criss-crossed the sky. That's the world Bond lived in then."

"Did you see him?"

"No, but I saw Johnny Halliday and Bardot, and Dennis spotted Vanessa Paradis."

"Can't be bad."

"Past her best."

"She was only, what, sixteen?

"Bardot!"

"Paradis. Jo Le Taxi?"

"I meant Bardot. Saw her naked, from a distance, funnily enough on the way to St Tropez on the Bond night. She was in her garden overlooking the bay."

"Did you go closer?"

"No, we turned the boat around. Quickly. She'd seen too many summers."

"Ah."

I didn't know what to expect when we entered Bond's St James' offices. If I said the wrong thing would a finger hover over a button while I sweated and awaited the drop into the mouths of circling sharks? There are plenty of those in Mayfair. We were apologising to Bond's PA for our lateness when the man himself approached us. Given the size of his ships and his reputation, I'd expected someone at least as large as me, but instead I was met by a septuagenarian no more than five-seven, expensively-dressed, extremely affable. He was proud of the fact that he now went to the gym. If his charm cloaked the steel that must be there to have once made him one of the world's richest tycoons, he wore the cloak well. He was now mining diamonds in Lesotho and Botswana, two of Africa's most stable countries, oil in Madagascar. Madagascar had had its recent troubles, but oil is bigger than mere politics.

We had gone to see Bond to discuss Waka Kele. Was he still in contact? No. Where was he? He hadn't seen him since the Nineties. I told him he's still running around using the name Alan Bond to open doors, most of which eventually came off their hinges. That should be discouraged. He had no idea where Kele was, but at least another blind alley was closed.

What had happened in the early Nineties still left its hurt, both for his creditors no doubt, and Bond too. History might now judge him differently, when he finally puts on carpet slippers and beyond. He'd established the Bond University in Queensland, which recently celebrated its twentieth anniversary. It is considered the top university in Australia, and its Law faculty won the World Championship at an international legal competition at the Hague in March 2009, beating Yale and Utrecht in the Final. Bond's MBAs are consistently world champions.

This meeting convinced us that Alan Bond has established a lasting legacy that may yet overshadow the dark days of his disgrace. That and winning the America's Cup for Australia in 1983. The breweries too, sport and beer being the clichéd route to an Aussie's heart, something they do give a Four XXXX about.

Our appointment had been at noon, so I was optimistic of lunch. I would have walked barefoot to the South Pole if there was a free meal waiting, but for once that was not the motive. I wanted to hear his stories and news of Waka's current activities. It was not to be. He had a busy schedule, early the next day flying to the States to see Warren Buffett, then engaged in an ongoing tussle with his Bridge companion, Bill Gates, to vie for Forbes' title of the world's richest man, so Bond was still 'connected'. Every article I'd recently read about this British-born, honorary Oz with an accent to match, had used a common banner, one that I thought was too easy, lazy journalism. But of course, they were right – Bond was back, and he had no place in his life for Waka Kele. He said.

I was in Perth, Western Australia, a couple of years after our meeting, when I raised the subject of Alan Bond with some local businessmen over lunch in a restaurant. Not only did they refuse to say another word to me when his name was brought up but they even asked the manager to ask me to leave the premises, sooner rather than later. After all, my assessment of Bond was based mostly on the impression he had wished to give me at our meeting, whereas these men no doubt had a greater insight into his dealings, and an America's Cup victory was the last thing on their minds.

He died in June, 2015, following heart operation complications.

CHAPTER FIFTY-THREE

Indiana Jones and the Nazi Gold

It was that meeting with Bond that prompted me to look more deeply into their past association –

Waka had traded on Bond's name for years. No matter that the tycoon had served a prison sentence in Australia, his national reputation as an entrepreneur remained peerless, a rags to riches to rags to new riches story that had endeared him to those he hadn't stuffed. All the better for Waka Kele, with no discernible talent other than a glib tongue and a lack of conscience, to trade off his mentor's reputation. Bond himself acknowledged another of Waka's alleged attributes; charisma, that over-and misused word that the OED defines as a person's power to attract or influence people. Friends of mine denied that he possessed this personal talisman, but we were seeing him at the tail-end of his career, and I had been taken in, damn it. After all, Waka had drawn Bond's attention to all kinds of ventures, among them the Austrian goldmines, the one that put The Bounty Hunter on his tail back in the Nineties; the aforementioned 'Nazi Gold'.

In fact it was three big Alpine leases on historic mines. Bond International Gold (BIG) briefly owned the leases at Siglitz, Rotgülden and Schellgaden, when the company was known as St Joe Mining, but eventually missed out to a Denver-based mining company. The late Sir William Gunn, then one of Australia's most famous knights, was a director of Sydney-based First Capital Ltd, along with Waka Kele.

Sir William was one of the most famous names in Australia, hugely influential in that country's wool trade and also in cattle. At nearly nineteen-stone, he was larger than life in a big country, with his Hardy Amies bespoke suits and perennial centre-parting. At times he almost single-handedly built the Australian wool trade into a world-dominant force, breaking the exclusive contract with the UK and enabling free trade of one of his country's prime assets. Just the kind of pillar of respectability that Waka Kele would prey upon. Obviously he dropped his standards when it came to me.

Sir William was blameless for what happened, and his involvement was brought about by a combination of Waka's charm and his modus operandi of getting a famous and respectable stooge to underwrite his scams.

He went to Austria with a Western Australian film crew and a trail of sweaty-palmed investors in his wake. This was heady stuff; the prospects of shares in a goldmine with the aroma of historical intrigue in the air. It smacked of an Indiana Jones adventure with a decent profit-margin and no snakes. Waka had promised investors a one-hundred percent return on an their investment within ninety-days. The money flowed in. It was one-way traffic, a classic boiler-room sting. Waka disappeared.

According to the Sydney Federal Police he gave them the slip minutes before they raided his Sydney apartment on September 27, 1994. Coincidentally, that same day the Feds raided Bondy's place. The raid was part of an investigation into Bond's affairs, the Austrian mine being purely a civil matter at this stage. Waka legged it to England, this undoubtedly saving other Perth investors. Sir William was left holding the baby, fending off creditors and trying to hold on to his reputation, a situation, his nephew contends, that hastened his death.

Investors had been forming a queue to grab a slice of a company which Waka had promised would be listed on the Australian Stock Exchange and floated on the London Exchange as 'Austrian Gold'. All he wanted was a twenty-five percent stake for Clifford Minerals, the designation of the Aussie 'float' company. Well, that seemed fair. The film company produced the video as contracted, all the better for Waka to promote the lease. Problem was, he didn't pay them. Nor did he pay the hotel that put them all up, the Kaisererhof in Salzburg. Apart from the film crew there was a group of investors, two geologists and a brace of pretty Sydney secretaries. The adjective is seen as pejorative these days. Why should their appearance matter so? Because it does, and certainly to Waka. Wherever he went, a pretty girl was sure to go. It opened doors.

Waka claimed a Polish mining team was on its way. The film crew were as yet unaware that they were not to be paid and their video was screened at Perth's Parmelia Hilton in a bid by Waka to net more investors. No-one seems to know how much eventually went missing, as soon after came the Feds' raid and Waka's disappearance, but it is likely that it was pushing US$1-million. It was just over ten years later when Waka revealed to me that he feared the crunch of car tyres on his gravel drive, and that he was always expecting something rather more lethal than the usual avalanche of writs.

He had run from Sydney to Great Rollright in Oxfordshire, but his globe-trotting was not over. He soon showed up in Zug Canton in Switzerland, Dublin, Boston and Denver, meeting, according to Jamie Fawcett, then a Sydney corporate investigator, senior legal and banking contacts of Alan Bond, cleaning up for the boss. The police were after

Waka. He was running out of countries that began with an 'A'. The Aussie businessman who hired The Bounty Hunter was the one who'd persuaded the group of Perth investors to jump on the bandwagon, on Bond's advice, he claimed, so when it all fell flat he was angrier than if he had simply lost A$125,000. Like many who come into Waka's sphere, he had been tainted by association.

A Canadian company eventually took over the exploitation of the leases, a potential fortune that Waka, in his need to con others, had denied himself. He was then hanging around with an ex-girlfriend of Bond, she now holed-up in a Kuala Lumpur hotel. It was when he'd been running with Bond ten years earlier that he'd learned of the gold leases. It's interesting then, that ten years later the Australian police were trying to interview him over Bond's affairs at a time when the pair's friendship had supposedly soured, according to Alan Bond. He was later tracked to Northern Ireland en-route from Russia, where he'd been trying to get investors interested in a water-purification plant. Presumably he had drunk from that water. Joe Pop quoted him ironically in the Perth Sunday Times – "It's really unfortunate that there is money owed to these chaps. They're all good blokes." That's all right then. Waka went on in similar style, so much so that the average reader would have thought about getting together a collection or maybe food parcels. "When you don't have money and it's Christmas and you can't buy a present or wish anyone all the best, it's kind of hard." Where's Charles Dickens when you need him? As the blessed Oscar wrote – 'You'd have to have a heart of stone not to laugh at the death of Little Nell'.

Professor Werner Paar, of Salzburg University, estimated the deposit at the mines to contain two to three-million metric tonnes, grading about 12 grams of gold per tonne. I did my sums; let's use 2009 prices to put it into perspective, using the two-million deposit figure as a basis – that's US$840,000,000, all those zeros graphically conveying what the fuss was about and why investors had dollar signs where their eyes should have been.

After the war, the mine at Siglitz became a health spa. POWs had been put to work there mining Scheelite, a Tungsten-ore once used in the manufacture of synthetic diamonds. The Nazis noticed that these prisoners were less tired after a shift than those working elsewhere and as a result the mine gained a reputation for its health-giving properties. Never mind the 840,000 ounces of gold then. As long as you've got your health.

I imagined those men in the Hilton in Perth as Waka made his presentation, maybe men who worked on a sheep farm for Sir William Gunn or in one of Bond's former breweries. Many were in syndicates, so hopefully individual losses were minimal, but all were driven by the age-old greed for gold. All business ventures seek to turn a profit, but the drive for gold appeals to the most atavistic depths of our nature. It's like that earlier analogy, where the scorpion bites as fools' gold slips through the fingers. Maybe I'm going the same way. That individual losses to Kele, on the Austrian deal at least, were maybe not too high, does not mitigate his crime. That Aussie businessman who hired the Bounty Hunter had balls. I am my own bounty hunter. I want him to pay, both financially to me and for all his past crimes and misdemeanours. As an Aussie journo said to me – 'He has spent his life betraying peoples' trust. It just amazes me that he's never been brought to task'. Those days are over, Waka. Whether you be in Sierra Leone, the Ashanti goldfields, prison or the bloody Klondike, you will be found. I will get my money back and my pound of flesh. I will not rest until it's all over, one way or another. Very soon you will not be safe in a country beginning with 'E'.

The phone rang. He was in a country beginning with 'E'. The builders he'd cheated too close to home for comfort rang me and said that they'd had their first Waka Kele sighting of the Spring. He was back in Great Rollright over Easter, no doubt trying to resurrect what was left of his life. He looked bad, they said, and I had a picture of him lamenting with his woman behind the closed doors of the Old Courthouse. It's ironic really, that a man who should live in court chooses to dwell in such a place.

CHAPTER FIFTY-FOUR

From Alpha to Omega

Where does it all go, all that anger and hatred? One moment I'm conducting a vendetta against a black-widow bunny-boiler, the next we're chatting amicably on the phone as if we'd had a tiff over whose turn it was to do the washing-up. I'd seen DV, all the swagger gone, the shirt-collar revealing an unhealthy looseness, the kind that comes from a sudden weight loss that leaves the watch hanging from the wrist. It reminded me of when I'd just come out of the slammer, my size nineteen collars creating a similar effect, so I went out and bought those smaller ones. JP would have done the same, ensuring he'd looked his best for a court appearance, so I guessed that his hospital release had been recent. She later said he'd been in hospital for two months. I guessed at heart problems, recalling his purple face during our Sumo match, but who knows? JP wasn't telling.

Still, watching them there that last time I was touched by how they were giving each other support, he not at his best but making an effort to be there when it would have been easier to have stayed at home watching reruns of The Sweeney and maybe getting up to speed on Gene Hunt for the charm quotient. If I had been told a couple of years earlier that this was how it would be I would have shouted from the rooftops, but now I felt no satisfaction, only a sense of loss.

We'd thrown it all away, she and I, throwing plates when

we could have been soul-mates. She may not agree with that last bit now, but I bet if we took the clock back to before all the madness started, then she would. I'd had little contact since the press furore. By contact I mean courtroom glimpses, like seeing DV sliding down the Greek alphabet from his alpha-male prime. Was I responsible for his condition? Maybe I'd contributed to it, but then he was only reaping what he had sown. No tears for him then. JP told me that he blamed me for his sacking; he believed I had been behind it, whereas it had been their own conduct that had brought it about. I think the truth is that neither of them acknowledged even to themselves how close they had sailed to being done for perverting the course of justice and how close each of them had come to being brought to justice themselves. Of course they would deny it to this day, and who can blame them? After all, it is my subjective opinion and that of others close to the case, of certain police officers too, but we had no proof, so if there is guilt it must be left to rest with the perpetrators' conscience and in the cobweb-dusted files of the CPS. The matter is closed.

The CPS had decided that there were no charges to be brought for DV's use of his cuffs on my kidney. The police had dragged their feet for so long that by now even I had lost interest, my anger at the CPS directed more to the issue of civil liberties than my own case. It was an open-and-shut instance of GBH according to legal advice, yet somehow the possible loss of my right kidney was seen as part of an it's-all-fair-in-love-or-war approach taken by the puppet-masters of what was once called the finest police force in the world.

When I said that I forgave JP, others counselled that she would have been as happy for me to have rotted in gaol as were Pitts-Tucker and Waka Kele, but time heals. The Daily Mail and a couple of locals had been forced into printing a retraction on their stories about the whole affair, JP's lawyer having successfully claimed that there is a difference between established fact and disputed allegations. A magazine came under similar pressure. There were rumours of substantial compensation.

I dealt with JP's lawyer to negotiate a compromise on the unpaid court fees. The plate throwing had cost JP and I dearly, financially at least and, for awhile, emotionally. She had had her reputation publicly besmirched; retractions mean little, mud sticks. We all know that. When your picture is plastered all over the media a muted retraction is all but invisible and in the sleepless small hours whispers sound like shouts. Then she'd gone though all those other sleepless nights, the early fear when my turning up in the dead of night carrying a heavy object was an all too real possibility. I was out of control then and she was right to have been afraid, but thankfully what was left of my sanity at the time had prevailed and overcame what had clearly been a nervous breakdown.

I had been through hell, came out the other side, fought a battle for my money that would, if all went to plan, give a greater return than loss, and of course, I'd wasted time. What might I have profitably done instead during those three revenge-seeking years? Financially I was ahead and prospects were good, opportunities opening up in worlds that had hitherto lain beyond my remit. But I had lost my most prized possession, if you can decently refer to a person as such. I had lost JP and will always wonder what might have been. She too, perhaps, although I suspect she already moved on long ago.

CHAPTER FIFTY-FIVE

Let's Smile Again

Things change out of nowhere. Waka had held out a hand in the spirit of reconciliation – 'let's smile again'. So I did smile as I went to court in late January 2010 to apply for a disclosure order which he had to comply with within twelve days or face an international arrest warrant. This order would finally establish the route my money had taken once it left Waka's hands. Of course, I wanted all roads to lead to a big hole in the ground in North Korea. My friend and I had gone to the court steely-eyed and firm of jaw, but from the moment my dog and I set off the security alarm things went downhill. As the afternoon progressed, it was more Carry On Judge than the vengeance of an ice-cold nemesis. I thought the moment I had been waiting for all these years would slip through my fingers as we were shuttled from one court to another. But the Judge's deceptive sleepiness masked a clear insight into the case as at the eleventh hour the Order was granted and I became the first mark to ever legally nail Waka Kele.

Like most of us in that icy January, anti-freeze was on our minds. But I was also very pro-freeze. At long last, the moment had come. The door was now open for me to freeze and squeeze the mining company. Once, I would have accepted Knight's initial offer as a payoff. Now I was looking at millions. I would once have gone for only 5% of the company. Now I wanted far more than my pound of flesh.

My erstwhile lawyer, Pitts-Tucker, and the man I'd once considered a good friend, Waka Kele, had both taken advantage of me and stolen my money, hoping that I would rot in gaol. Pitts-Tucker was down and I had Kele by the balls, but it had now gone way beyond any thoughts of revenge. Sod pride, we're talking money. I used the court order as a weapon against Waka. "Give me your sanction to go after your shares, Waka, and I'll have the order lifted. If I get them back I'll keep 70% of yours and you get the rest."

It made sense, at least to me. His shares totalled 31% of a company potentially worth billions. Even so, he played evasive games for months whilst holed-up in the southern Philippines chasing the elusive dream of Yamashita's Gold, the legendary looted treasure hidden by the retreating Japanese all over the islands in 1945. That's how I'd made contact – he'd shown up on a YouTube video. My lawyer sensed blood. "May I represent your mining interests once you have the shares?" This was really quite something coming from what had usually been the voice of professional caution. It was confirmation that this dog had been barking up the right tree, that it was not idle fancy that had kept me pressing forward. I don't know whether a Chinaman ever said it, but it sounds Confucian, apropros of Waka – 'Once you've eaten the banana, you don't need the skin'. This from my lawyer. No, I don't know what it means either, yet again, in a funny way I do. Once I had his shares, Waka would have served his purpose. Even so, I resolved to stick to my deal with him, otherwise I was morally no better than those who had stiffed me. Arcane Chinese sayings or not, what I did understand, unequivocally, was that I was near the beginning of a long, yellow-brick road that led to a place near the Chinese border where lay deposits of wealth that would satisfy even my greed. There lay the kind of money that could see me forsaking the supermarket special-offer shelves for good. Anyway, it has to end well; it's the culmination point of the whole bloody story. What's a joke without the punch-line?

Waka finally relented over the shares. As I had a High Court judgment against him they were, as his sole asset, mine. If that is I could recover them from the company. After all, they had been taken from Waka in contravention of the company's Articles of Association. If Knight didn't agree, it could get messy. All I had to do now what cut a deal with him, remembering all the while that the money, money, money previously offered by Knight, let Abba be my witness, had never materialised.

Well, hadn't I been wrong about that dog analogy? It was simply Knight who'd been playing fetch and me being a good doggie chasing a stick attached to elastic. Once the penny finally dropped I grew tired of the game and my ubiquitous friend phoned the mining engineers responsible for a survey of Knight's mine (mine too?). It seems they'd somehow surveyed it from afar, that of course an impossible task. A geological survey from six-thousand miles away does seem a stretch of the imagination. Then we laid hands on the joint venture agreement with the North Koreans. Knight had clearly ignored a major clause, and in so doing had invalidated the deal. He and his associates were to have paid US$1-million in good faith within 28-days of the signing of the JV. Their failure to so had invalidated it. The contract was void and Knight must have known that during the three-years in which he had been giving us the run-around and asking that I pay considerable expenses to his associate, a disbarred solicitor (I'm surprised there's anyone out there still practicing law). Of course, Knight was cross, very cross indeed, that we had unilaterally approached his mining engineers. He wasn't playing any more. So that's OK then?

Like it's OK to waste my time and money for three years, Tony, and allow Kele to go scot free without me ever having had a chance to get him into a court of law, thanks to your generous dealing of something you no longer have?

So, thanks to Knight's prevarication, the opportunity to nail Waka Kele had slipped through my fingers, other than using the platform of print. To summarise: by doing the shares deal I had called off the law. Now it was too late to retract that action. After all that had happened, the dream of the big pay-day had evaporated at a stroke. Knight had prevaricated for his amusement and my discomfort and at great legal expense to me as I had endeavoured to manoeuvre Kele into relinquishing his share of the deal in return for leniency.

Then again, it wasn't all bad news. Although Knight had enabled Kele to walk scot free and had left Pitts-Tucker to take the flak, he had inadvertently opened another door for me. It was Tom who suggested it. He reasoned that if Pitts-Tucker, Kele and Knight could set-up a joint venture with North Korea, so too could we.

CHAPTER FIFTY-SIX

Bilbo Babbitt?

Waka Kele, for someone who doesn't like to put his head above the parapet, certainly did so when he posted the YouTube video on which he was asking for investors for a documentary on the legendary Golden Buddha, part of Yamashita's Gold. Soon afterwards he was looking for more investors to help recover a vast hoard of nickel babbitts on the Philippine island of Mindanao. No, they're not creatures from The Lord of the Rings, but are instead chocolate-sized bars of nickel with 'American Smelting and Refining Company' and 'XXXX' embossed on them. Invented in the 1860s, they were used as bearing-linings during the US colonisation of the Philippines. Not as valuable or sexy as gold, but in volume they carry considerable earning power. They have been the origin of many a Pinoy scam over the years, so when Waka contacted me during our brief 'Let's Smile Again' phase, I wasn't tempted to invest. A web blog eulogising Waka's charm, charisma, and containing a subtext that he should be firmly ensconced on a golden throne on Mount Olympus, was shot down in flames like Icarus en-route to the Sun as the comments below the blog revealed the dark underbelly of someone who should be canonised as the patron saint of Walter Mittys. One read: 'I've been trying to find him since 1991!! I wonder who he is hiding from just now'. (Me?) 'Woe betide that S.O.B. if I ever catch up with him'. This relates to alleged real estate frauds in Utah.

So it went, underscoring earlier sections in this book, such as Waka's pilot's licence being a fraud, although doubting that he was ever in cahoots with Alan Bond. Oh yes he was, that much is true amid all the smokescreens Waka lays down.

If one comment is accurate, and of course we have to beware of the veracity of internet entries, it would seem that Waka at last came good, transporting thousands of tons of nickel babbits to a port for loading onto Chinese ships. Given that this allegedly happened (and may still be happening) in a hotbed of Muslim armed insurgency, Waka and his team of 'Russian friends' are said to travel in a convoy of four 4X4s protected by M16 carbines and a helicopter with foreign markings hovering overhead. For those who fancy a trip to the Philippines to pay him a visit, his last-known location was Surigao City, where he holds court at The Tavern Hotel, although 'held' is possibly more accurate as this location was posted in 2011, so he's likely hopped it by now, but it's always worth a try since it seems he's built a life there.

Anyone with his rep who's daft enough to pop up in a YouTube video whilst surely knowing that he's still subject to a plethora of worldwide private man-hunts, could be said to be losing their touch. Will I hunt him down? No, I'll leave him to rot there, or wherever he shows up. The best weapon against him is publicity, whether in a book or online. Look up the video, then remember his face. It doesn't matter whether he is called Waka or Whaka Kele, Innes Wallace Kelly or even Vincent Sullivan, reputedly one of his later aliases; you'll now know what he looks like. Throughout this book I've spelled Waka without the 'h', as this has been his style in recent years, perhaps to try to throw internet searchers off the scent, but most have known him as Whaka. Anyway, it's the same man.

Hopefully you won't be taken in by a con artist who's plied his trade for over forty years. I have to say, though, he looks well in the video, far better than when I last saw him as I'd pushed him down onto his sofa in the Old Courthouse. I previously described him as looking far older than his years; now he looks younger. Life on the road estranged from his family must agree with him. Oh yes, his face – Google 'Waka Kele and the Golden Buddha', but watch it; even knowing what I know, he tells his tale with such verve that every time I view it I'm almost taken in once again. Good hunting.

CHAPTER FIFTY-SEVEN

Ping Pong to Slam Dunk

We had already been to the North Korean Embassy, the UK
lair of a key member of Dubya's 'Axis of Evil'. Well, they were
evil, having an embassy in the middle of nowhere on the
North Circular Road close to Acton, in an urban, featureless
landscape, the Pyongyang of London. It was 2007, and we
had been after info on the mining company. My friend did
his keep schtum bit as we approached the front-door of what
is effectively a large suburban house. "There are cameras and
microphones everywhere around here," he whispered. "So?"

"MI6, the CIA, the FIS, the CSIS."

"Who?"

"Those last two? The Russian Foreign Intelligence Service
and the Chinese equivalent."

"What, no SMERSH? You're paranoid."

"Difficult childhood. Ring the bell."

We were welcomed by a charming, if slightly bemused
attaché. He was the only person we would see during our
ninety-minute visit. "It's all done with mirrors," said my
friend later, as I imagined small men in oversized hats
peering at us from behind mirrored walls as a Korean Rosa
Klebb brought us tea.

The discussion had progressed well as we broached the
subject of the JV. I had previously spoken to a banker friend
in Mayfair who'd said he would consider bankrolling such a

project, but mainly that he was interested in the possibility of raising sunken shipwrecks, especially those containing treasure. The DPRK's closed-door policy since the Fifties meant that these possibilities hadn't been explored in the age of modern underwater technology. There were rumours of wrecks of the great Fifteenth-Century Treasure Ships of the Chinese Admiral Zheng He, and of a gold-laden Russian warship that had gone down in the Russo-Japanese war of 1904-05. The latter was a war fought by the Japanese to exert dominance over the Korean peninsula, still a sore point for Koreans.

Then we got to the point – "Do you know Tony Lombard-Knight?" I kept it as casual as I could. "He is a good man. A good friend."

"Is XXXX (discretion here) Mining Ltd successful?"

"I have never heard of this, but Mr Knight, he is a good friend of our country. I spoke to him on the phone only thirty-minutes before you arrived."

We concluded business, the attaché making it clear that if we put money on the table the DPRK would facilitate any arrangements which might be mutually beneficial. In other words, they were looking to do business and step into the modern world. We'd taken flowers, the first time I can recall giving them to a man. He'd looked pleased. I had the idea from the HSBC ad where they recommend researching local customs. The attaché put ours on a table with the others. I counted six prior offerings, fresh-looking, so that was today's visitor-count. My bunch fell to the floor. The attaché replaced it. It fell again. The Dear Leader, Kim Jong-Il, looked down from his framed position above the table. Once more it fell. "This is good omen in Korea," said the attaché. I don't know if there's a Korean expression for 'dodgy table'.

We said our farewells. My friend said that if they played

their cards right they could get an embassy in Kensington. We got in the car. Then I saw, over the garden wall, a basketball net when you might have expected a Ping Pong table. Maybe they are not so different from us after all. Fast forward then to 2011 and another meeting at the embassy, we there to rekindle the JV dream, or, as Tom had put it, to make the fairy-tale come true.

This led to a meeting with the ambassador, Mr Bong, and we shook hands on a deal that we thought was in the bag. Little did we know that Kim Jong-Il's picture would soon be replaced by that of his son, Kim Jong-Un, nor did we know that our dream ticket would be sullied by association with Sven Goran-Eriksson, although Sven, Sven, Sven (as the song went) was blameless and unaware of the repercussions of the actions of the fraudster, Russell King. You may recall the Notts County football club purchase fiasco, the funds for which would have come from Sven's relationship with King and his claimed involvement through Swiss Commodity Holdings in a North Korean gold-mining JV worth US$2-trillion. Yes, that's trillion.

A reader might question the morals of someone seeking to make money out of a supposedly pariah state, but that Ping Pong to slam dunk analogy is hopefully a pointer to the future. Whatever privations the populace may now suffer would surely dissipate with wealth flooding in, as history teaches us with the collapse of the USSR and the opening up of China. To assuage any guilt we offered to finance schools and clinics for the miners and their dependents. In fact, even as we did so, the North Koreans told us that this would be a prior requirement.

We held a meeting in plush offices opposite Claridges Hotel in Mayfair with a board table's worth of the great and the good, also attended by a senior North Korean diplomat, who in turn was dogged by an elite corps of traffic wardens, forcing him to seek sanctuary for his car at the Argentine embassy, North Korea's budget not running to a fleet of cars with D-plates. The meeting went well and that was it, or so we thought. It was only as the weeks dragged by while we awaited an invitation to send a delegation to Pyongyang that the truth finally came out. The Russell King affair had hurt the North Koreans and they felt humiliated that someone had traded so blatantly on their offer of a JV and that they had, by association, received a bad press. Not surprisingly, this had led to a distrust of foreign businessmen. Now the only way in for us was to come up with cast iron investment offers from major international financiers, who in turn would only become involved if they had prior access to the deal, such as senior-level visits to Pyongyang and a chance for prior geological exploration of the mines. North Korea effectively said money on the table or no dice. The financiers said, a deal first or no money. Speculative ventures à la Knight and the boys were off the menu. It had all gone to the dogs.

Down but not out I travelled to Beijing in late 2012 to visit a consortium of Chinese investors, whom I met in the company of someone trusted by Pyongyang. At last, it was working. Two gold mines were identified and we prepared for an exploratory visit in the company of a senior ex-Rio Tinto Zinc mining engineer. That was before the UN Security Council Resolution 2094 sanctions, in the wake of North Korea's latest nuclear test, which effectively precluded the interest of potential investors. What's a chap to do to get his own goldmine? Get lucky?

CHAPTER FIFTY-EIGHT

Life is on the Up

Still, life goes on. Last year I was sitting in my car in the parking space of one of my special needs care homes, Minty by my side. It was Spring and the sun was shining as another inevitably disappointing English summer lay ahead. Whatever could go wrong?

Enter The Angry Mob, that's what. These were not, though, the Kaiser Chiefs' mildly-irritated mob. No, this was a mob and it was *angry*. There were about twenty of them, but given their size it looked more like forty.

I was simultaneously on the phone and making notes, but soon added a third string to my multi-tasking as I watched them waddle towards me. They were all women of, no fat-shaming intended, plus size. Curvy, *real* women, as the Daily Mail likes to refer to them. Put it this way, the local Greggs must have been stripped bare by ten every morning. They all wore that aggrieved look that the Mail also likes in its photos – you know the kind of thing: Mr and Mrs X finds a dead Amazonian frog in their brand name crisps and are seeking X-Million quid in compensation, or free crisps for life likely being the preferred option. OK, so their weight prevented any sudden moves, but they were getting closer by the second, and they were all looking at me. As the first hands grabbed the underside of my car it dawned upon me that all they wanted was to overturn the vehicle and tear me limb from limb. Presumably Minty would get off scot-free on account of her furry cuteness. The car rocked and I was getting seasick in a way that never occurred when I was sailing the seven seas. Somehow though, and I never fail to give myself credit where credit is due, I managed to outwardly pretend that none of this was happening. I perused my notes and pretended to make a phone call while questioning in my head what had led to this ignominious end. The Mail would no doubt speculate that food additives and Jeremy Corbyn were to blame and that there was also likely a terrorist link, whilst mentioning the value of my properties. The things you think about when Death taps you on the shoulder and beckons you to follow him. So, who was to really blame for this sorry state of affairs? I knew that Corbyn was in the clear; never met the bloke. OK, then, hands up… it was me, as usual.

My business was now offering care to the special needs residents of my two homes, many of them being on the autism spectrum, which of course necessitated the employment of highly-qualified carers, but alongside the professionals I had somehow acquired the services of staff who were on a virtually free ride on a rich gravy train. Now I had ensured that said train had gone off the rails. For the sake of the business, the professional staff, and most importantly, the residents, cuts had to be made. I'd recently been spending more time with my bank manager than my wife. Now it seemed that certain staff members didn't agree with my business methods. Oh well, you can't win 'em all. My problem is that sometimes I haven't been able to win *any* of them.

Unknown to me, my administration manager had been handing out jobs to friends and family like confetti, with no regard to the balance sheet, and ignoring the simple fact that I'd rather not pay wages to people who didn't have a role on the firm other than to turn up for tea and biscuits.

Back at the car, Minty wore the same expression she wears in every situation, so it was no good looking to her for help. I have to hand it to VW though, emission issues aside, their chassis are robust, but my Golf could have easily been flipped as each of the angry mob was, after all, only attempting to lift their own bodyweight.

"You bastard!" I heard those soothingly familiar although not technically correct words, but this wasn't the time to discuss my family tree. At least being called a bastard was one of the milder epithets. I could try to make a run for it, I supposed, but these days I didn't even run from the law. Perhaps I was morally wrong and deserved my fate. I mean, how *dare* I have a purge of staff who were probably doing no more than trying to top-up their benefits. Iain Duncan-Smith would no doubt speak at my memorial service. This thought didn't necessarily cheer me up.

It was the first time in my life that I was pleased to hear police sirens. Not the full blues and twos, but that whoop they do when they're cross and attention-seeking. It was, though, a full-on fishtail into the car-park. Minty seemed to cheer up at this, not that she'd ever cheered-down. A young WPC about a third of the size of the mob's ringleader calmed the situation with surprising ease as the mob dispersed with the speed of chefs in a Chinese restaurant when Immigration comes a-calling. Maybe my IDS reference wasn't too wide of the mark.

It does go to show, though, that once you've established a behavior pattern in life that pattern does tend to continue. Remember that earlier analogy about people being either music boxes or pianos? Perhaps I'm a music box after all, but for me it's been a great tune and I still enjoy humming it.

I can't recall too much of what the police officers had to say but I do remember driving off and waving to them and they waved back as though we'd just had a nice weekend together. I sold my remaining two homes soon afterwards and like a good music box went back to the scene of a former success.

Harley Street had changed since I'd been one of the red-tops' 'fat cats'. The whole area, like most of central London, had a distinctly new feel to it. Now, speaking English made me feel like a foreigner. Not that I mind. The whole point of living in London, for me at least, is that it always was quite alien in relation to the rest of the country. Nearby Marylebone High Street is now booming with bars and eateries and everything looks glossier. Of course, all the old faces from the Eighties were gone. Many dead or retired, I suppose, given that I was far younger than most of my then contemporaries. Looking at the cars in W1 showed me that no matter how well you think you are doing there's always someone doing better. Still a lot of Arab money, but that was true even back in my day. "Always remember, Paul, your day is today." That was my ubiquitous friend speaking, But he was right. If you retain your energy levels, your experience will always give the young Turks a run for their money. Not that this was an issue, as for now there was relatively little competition for our new concept.

Extracorporeal shockwave therapy treats a range of disorders by delivering impulses of energy targeted to specific damaged tissues, increasing blood-flow to the affected areas. This treatment can be applied to damaged tendons which have resulted in chronic tennis or golfer's elbow, or to knee or foot tendon damage. But it is this increase of direct blood-flow that has the most impact on a condition which affects some 40% of men over age 40 – erectile dysfunction, given that this is primarily a symptom of impaired blood-flow. A short course of 20-minute, anaesthetic-free sessions in my

Harley Street clinic by qualified doctors can work wonders, leaving bemused office colleagues to ask what you've had for lunch to put such a smile on your face. Life is, as they say, once again on the up.

CHAPTER FIFTY-NINE

Mr Eagles Regrets?

When the carefree early days had turned to the dark times which open this book it had seemed to me that I had reached the end of the road. My health was ruined, both physically and mentally, and I had been betrayed by the woman I loved. The wild, roaring-boy of my twenties could never have dreamed that his older self could be almost destroyed by what happened with JP, but when Joke had seemingly betrayed me over the Rubens we were but kids, and recovery comes along then as soon as the next pretty face shows up. So there came all the happy days with Pam, then my too-brief marriage to Nessie; the crazy years of the camping business and Battle of the Bands, being a fat cat of Harley Street.

Then the stability of Janice and the children gave a centre to my life, if not theirs'. Lots of money flowed from the care homes. All in all it could not have been better, although perhaps I could have been so to others. Once again, though, the old days seem to be coming back and opportunity isn't just knocking but hammering at the door, all a world away from where this book started, a life successfully turned around. Of course he would say that wouldn't he? To tell your own tale can preclude objectivity. Yes, there have been times of which I have been ashamed and there have been times when others have been hurt.

As we live our lives, few of us can be totally aware of our effect upon others, and I am no exception. I am sure that I have left a trail of people who wish they had never set eyes on me, but hopefully there are others whose lives may have been enhanced in some small way, whether through my having given them a job or having given them life or having simply brought some laughter to the table. I have often been a bad man by the standards of many, yet I've met worse. I have questioned the financial greed which has so often motivated me and also my implacable need for revenge against those who have done me harm, yet I have also questioned their motives. Are they worse than me or are we all as bad as each other? Or have I simply met the people I deserve? There are my long-suffering wives and partners and children, who as yet barely know me. I do not know whether the contents of this book will come as much of a surprise to them, but hopefully the fact that I am capable of remorse will go some way to building bridges. Then there is that person whose love turned to hate. Was it a fault in her, or was I the architect of my own misfortune? Her for sure, but as I've said before, I'm no angel.

Could life have been better if I had chosen another path? We all ask ourselves that. Yet for all my regrets I also know that I have been party to more memories than I can dredge up from the recesses of my brain, and in that sense I still bear the traces of that bubble-car smash. A chance comment here, a moment of déjà vu there, and this book could have been twice as long. My motive for wanting a book written? The advice of friends telling me that I had a tale to tell. Yes, I still have some friends, despite my behaviour, much of it probably far worse than the self-censorship a first-person narrative allows. What this book has reminded me of is that

I have at least lived a life, one in which the years didn't drift past.

If the above sounds like closure, forget it. This eagle hasn't even thought about landing.

The End (for now)